宁夏大学优秀学术著作基金资助
宁夏回族自治区外国语言文学重点学科建设项目资助

基于项目合作的
外语培训国际化模式
策略研究

周震◎著

Project-based Foreign Language Training Programme for Chinese Companies and Organisations:

Towards Effective International Communication Strategy

中国社会科学出版社

图书在版编目(CIP)数据

基于项目合作的外语培训国际化模式策略研究 = Project-based Foreign Language Training Programme for Chinese Companies and Organisations：Towards Effective International Communication Strategy/周震著. —北京：中国社会科学出版社，2017. 8
ISBN 978-7-5203-0733-8

Ⅰ. ①基… Ⅱ. ①周… Ⅲ. ①外语教学—国际化—教育模式—研究
Ⅳ. ①H09

中国版本图书馆 CIP 数据核字(2017)第 169226 号

出 版 人 赵剑英
选题策划 郭晓鸿
责任编辑 慈明亮
责任校对 李海莹
责任印制 戴 宽

出 版 中国社会科学出版社
社 址 北京鼓楼西大街甲 158 号
邮 编 100720
网 址 http://www.csspw.cn
发 行 部 010-84083685
门 市 部 010-84029450
经 销 新华书店及其他书店

印 刷 北京明恒达印务有限公司
装 订 廊坊市广阳区广增装订厂
版 次 2017 年 8 月第 1 版
印 次 2017 年 8 月第 1 次印刷

开 本 710×1000 1/16
印 张 19.75
插 页 2
字 数 305 千字
定 价 88.00 元

凡购买中国社会科学出版社图书，如有质量问题请与本社营销中心联系调换
电话：010-84083683

This book is dedicated to my beloved parents

Mr Zhou Zhaoliang and Mrs Zhu Youyun

As well as my dear wife Windy Ding Wenying and daughter Sabrina Zhou Zihan.

Contents

Preface

When they develop training strategies for Chinese professionals, providers and managers should be prepared to assign a significant role to project-based foreign-language training; this is a key inference to be drawn from Prof. Zhou's investigation into the modalities through which professional training programmes in the People's Republic of China can foster effective business-related language skills.

In testing and then endorsing the underlying rationale for this recommendation, his investigation embraces wider implications beyond the demands of language training pure and simple; it takes account of the need to develop language skills in tandem with a subtle range of business and personal skills that must now be considered vital for professionals in Chinese enterprises and organisations whose operational performance demands an effective international interface, or stands to gain from one.

Importantly, the approach that emerges from Prof. Zhou's study represents a significant step towards reconciling enhanced cultural sensitivity with procedural pragmatism. Interplay between cross-cultural legitimacy and intercultural praxis has rightly come to attract considerable attention from researchers in recent years, and informs core components in standard business education programmes at undergraduate and postgraduate level. This developing interest has accrued from a more refined understanding of the challenges encountered by those who participate professionally in the proliferating intercultural relationships that characterise today's globalised business community.

Establishing challenges is one thing; striving to import due acknowledgment of them into a mutually accepted modus operandi for organisations, trainers and learners is another. While coherence between these two realms may at times appear an unachievable ideal given the complexity of individual and organisational interactions across the globe, Professor Zhou's work will leave readers with a sense that valuable further progress has been made.

Indeed, the research and conclusion she presents provide a signpost towards improved efficacy in the design of future language training, and in so doing question the currency of approaches that are frequently adopted in the training of professional clients in full-time employment. A persuasive plea to rethink the provision they receive emerges.

Quite how radical a departure this is from features of contemporary language training that are widely accepted as familiar and conventional may come as a surprise. Classroom-based use of authentic or quasi-authentic stimulus material from the world of business and commerce and the exploitation there of in a guided interactive manner that simulates workplace discourse and praxis no doubt seem robust techniques, commonly employed in foreign language acquisition for vocational purposes, and underpinned by the credentials and expertise that training providers have established.

They may, however, yield to different precepts as Professor Zhou's research seeks to recast such models in order to accommodate greater scope for the customisation of work-based training, the empowerment of learners, and the diversification of the skills they develop. It is a route towards the optimisation of learners' progress that calls for imaginative innovation in programme design.

With its enlightening evocation of the cultural, educational and vocational traditions that influence the Chinese workplace, its demonstration of the need for training programmes consistent with these traditions, the statistical rigour with which the accompanying data is presented, and the resulting authority with which it constructs its rationale for change, Professor Zhou's account will furnish both training managers and providers with insights that influence their practice in years to come.

Colin Beaven

Formerly Principal Lecturer (Portfolio Responsibility Languages)
Southampton Solent University, UK

Abstract

The rapid development of China's economy has seen increasing demand for foreign language training in Chinese companies and organizations. Nevertheless educational institutions across the world have struggled to design appropriate foreign language training programmes for Chinese companies and organisations. Many models have been proposed and put into practice. However, little work has focussed attention on the actual needs of Chinese staff and the real demands of Chinese organizations and companies, so there is a continuing dilemma in terms of satisfying expectations of both training providers and trainees.

In this book, we account for the development and test of a project-based foreign language training model for Chinese employees. The model aims to develop the ability of foreign language training suppliers to establish a management strategy for project-based training involving international educational communication. A series of propositions have been generated based on the two-tier levels of project-based training model designed in this research, which is based on the literature review of Chinese foreign language education, Chinese learning styles, organisational learning objectives, project-based foreign language learning theories and existing programme models. The book also includes an initial research which was conducted to identify where training and development needs and deficits lie within China's organisations and companies. Chinese staff and managers are chosen to investigate their attitudes. A mixed method of combining quantitative and qualitative analysis was employed in the study in order to validate these propositions.

The book also has offered a number of successful outcomes relating to its aim and objectives.

- Firstly, individual project creation by Chinese trainees is a creative approach to meet learning objectives.
- Secondly, foreign language programmes need to aim to develop work-related or professional skills alongside language skills rather than learning the foreign language only.
- Thirdly, the divergence of perceptions in terms of training needs analysis and on-going assessment among Chinese staff and managers is discovered.
- Fourthly, pedagogic design needs to blend formal instruction and independent learning.
- Fifthly, joint evaluation by bringing trainees, training providers and partners together customises evaluation.
- Sixthly, decision-making within Chinese organisations and companies involves top-down and bottom-up orientation.
- Additionally, understanding the operational structure of a training partner is important to the success of implementing a training programme through international educational management.

These contributions will add updated knowledge to education management and also enable further value to international educational institutions and practitioners.

Acknowledgements

This book is a part of my PhD thesis. To complete it, I wish to acknowledge the professional and personal support offered by the following individuals and organisations.

Prof. David Watkins, my Director of Studies, for his expertise, experience, guidance and knowledge that have proved invaluable to me at all stages of the research process and helped the thesis come to completion.

Mr. Colin Beaven, a committed supervisor and one of the most important people in my life, for his dedication to giving me valuable comments throughout the research. He is a clear example in the West who embodies the spirit of the Chinese Confucian model supervisor – '*Liang shiyi you*' – to be both a good knowledgeable teacher and a helpful friend.

Prof. Tom Thomas, another one of the most important persons in my life, for his generous help and candour enabling me to start my research journey.

Dr Barbara Lee and Dr Stewart Bruce-Low, my second supervisors, for making time to give me feedback in the beginning and final stages of some parts of my PhD study. Without them I would never have come this far.

Prof. Jenny Anderson, Prof. Ashok Ranchhod, Dr Steven Jackson, Dr Graham Benmore, Dr Whysnianti Basuki, Mark Cranshaw, John Holder, Velichko Ganchev, Mike Howell, Robert Kirby, Karen Chen, Shi Leiqing, Peter Gordon, Rosemary Bock, Nigel Bradley, James Steele, Jasem Almansoori, Dina Nziku, Nasiru Taura and Dr Shahina Pervin, colleagues and friends at Southampton Solent University, for their invaluable advice and generous support in various ways.

Prof. He Jianguo, Prof. Chen Yuning, Prof. Wang Yanchang, Prof. Xie Yingzhong, Prof. Ji Bin, Prof. Li Bin, Prof. Zhou Yuzhong and Prof. Guo Hongyan, leaders and colleagues at Ningxia University, for their forbearance, patience and words of encouragement over the journey of editing.

Prof. Sun Jiwen, a colleague from Ningxia University, for his kind concerns over publication of the book.

And for all companies and organisations that allowed me full access to their staff and managers to complete the survey. This includes many people employed by the companies and organisations, who gave me time, support and copious information.

I am thankful and indebted to my dear wife Mrs Windy Ding Wenying and my lovely daughter Sabrina Zhou Zihan, to my beloved parents and sisters, for their significant support, sensible understanding and encouragement during my whole long PhD research process.

Chapter 1 Introduction

1.1 Introduction

Foreign language training is becoming big business in China, particularly in English, as the language of global commerce (Dean, 2005; Gross, 1998; Jin, 2003; Liu, 2006; Nunan 2002). The Economist (2006) commented that the rapid development of Chinese business is fuelling a market that comprises everything from foreign language materials and textbooks to language training programmes. Increased demand for foreign languages comes from a broad spectrum of society including companies and organizations. Foreign or domestic investors are moving into China in a cluster to serve the growing group of Chinese who believe they have both the interest and the means to learn a foreign language, and who see it as vital for improving their future (Chee, 2000/2003; Taylor, 2006). Foreign language training is compulsory in many organisations (Hu, 2002a; Ireland, 1991) and people of different professionals are learning the foreign language and taking it as a tool or a path to build a better career in future (Jin, 2003; Kealey, 2009). Chinese companies and organizations are pushing their employees to learn English (Chen, 2001; Dean 2005).

The demand for personnel with foreign language competences has resulted in increasing demand for a professional layer of personnel with the competences relevant to operating in an international market economy. These include high foreign language proficiency and the knowledge of operating international businesses. In particular, among those competences, the knowledge of foreign languages is among those with greatest potential to help the Chinese to develop successful businesses because they enable one to obtain better information about the business environment and new ideas about production, raw materials, marketing and trade channels (Hagen, 2007). As part of China's preparations for increased participation in the global economy, it has been reported that there is an explosion of Chinese overseas students and training participants from a wide range of job occupations in English-speaking countries who are attending various kinds of training programmes; according to a recent report (Xinhua, 2010), the Chinese government has decided, for example, to send 300 officers to the Harvard Kennedy School over the next five years, and many local enterprises such as Bank of China, People's Insurance Company of China (PICC) and some large companies such as the China Petroleum Company (China-Pre.) ceaselessly encouraging foreign language training programmes for their staff development (ChinaGate, 2011; Xinhua, 2011).

However, have these endeavours brought immediate benefits to Chinese companies and organisations? Or have Chinese managers and staff been slow to develop as planned and taken time to review the programmes run in the past? Have they ever considered the effectiveness of these programmes, and have they ever thought how to improve them? All these questions have been challenging Chinese companies and organisations (Jiang, 2008; Liu, 2006; Wozniak, 2003).

Specifically, two types of research initiative have helped to formulate the research rationale for this project.

Firstly, from a personal perspective, the author has been in charge of foreign language training programmes as a manager in a locally organised Chinese university in the north-west part of China for six years, and has managed ten English programmes for local companies and organisations, such as Qin Tong Xia Aluminium Manufacturer of Ningxia, Ningxia Orient Tantalum Industry, Ningxia Northwest Bearing Industry, and Pin Luo Middle School. Apart from this, the author has been involved in other programmes such as Southampton

Solent University's summer language training programme for young lecturers from China and a cadre training programme run by an American University. In addition, there are regular contacts with an on-going programme at Reading University, UK, a China's national programme sponsored by China's Ministry of Education.

From the experience of managing these programmes, it became clear that many problems such as how to assess the learning outcomes, how to access the gaps in previous programmes, how to define the effectiveness of a programme, how to explore an effective pedagogic model for Chinese adults' teaching and learning, and how to generate a creative model that can be followed effectively by trainees and training providers, still remain to be further investigated.

Secondly, from a macro-perspective, as part of its modernisation process, China has embarked on a programme of management education on an unprecedented scale. Indeed, since education was traditionally seen as a source of power (Ogden, 1993), the primary goal of education not only taking place on campus or off campus has been to lay the groundwork for modernisation (Hu, 2005b). Since 1990, the Chinese have been taking technology transfer and training much more seriously than most emerging economies, e.g. asking foreign universities or companies to agree to a massive programme of "human technology" transfer involving the creation of comprehensive business education and training programmes in which English language training has been hugely involved as a gateway to access to other fields of collaboration

With the on-going shift toward a freer socialist market system, Chinese management educators also see the need for more open communication, more independence and decision-making power for managers in terms of developing the intellectual resources through a variety of approaches (Kealey, 2009; Li, 2003). To pursue recruiting strategies and promote retention of key individuals, companies in China are becoming more aware of the value of training as a staff retention tool, amongst other things, making the employees feel more like part of a team (Kealey, 2009). Nevertheless, with over 80,000 foreign joint ventures currently registered in China, and non-Chinese individuals regularly doing management teaching and training in China, there is a vital need to understand the immediate needs of Chinese partners and trainees (*ibid.*).

Along with the increased demand for foreign languages training for staff from various organisations and companies, the Chinese government has been aware of the inevitable need for reform of administrative management to ensure its human resources are deployed effectively (Liu, 2006; Lu 2000; Zhai, 2000). In recent years, the Chinese government has been focusing on establishing a "Ministry of Human Resources and Social Security of the People's Republic of China", a newly created ministry which is responsible for national labour policy, standards and regulations. This includes labour force management and legal procedures for construction of a labour force which aim to improve labour contribution to deal with the dramatic impact of China as a manufacturing nation on world markets (2009, online).

As such, two perspectives fundamentally shed light on this research looking at issues relating to effective management of language training programmes. Many questions arise in the process, such as what foreign language education went on in the past, what challenges Chinese foreign language education has faced, and whether foreign languages skills are the Chinese companies' or organisations' only training needs. To address those questions, it is hoped that the book attempts to contribute a significant development in the field of education management for Chinese working adults from companies and organisations, which appear to have increasing need for effective strategic management of foreign language training.

1.2 Objectives of the research

The aim of this research is to develop a novel model for training Chinese staff and managers in foreign languages through international collaboration in the era of China's economic transition. The following related aspects will be evaluated: needs, shortcomings in current practices and the justification for an enhanced training model.

The objectives of this thesis are summarised as follows:

Objective one: To define training and development needs and deficits within China's organisations and companies.

Objective two: To identify existing shortcomings in current practices implemented by programme providers.

Objective three: To evaluate the significance of the implications of two-tier level project-based second and foreign language training programme for Chinese employees.

Objective four: To develop the ability of foreign language training suppliers to establish a management strategy for project-based training involving international communication.

1.3 Research methodology

In order to achieve the objectives, five procedures comprising inductively analysing the literature, evaluating initial research, identifying themes and synthesising propositions as well as mixed-methods of justification were designed (see Figure 1–1 and details in Chapter 6).

A mixed method of combining quantitative and qualitative analysis was employed in the research, using questionnaires and interviews. Two hundred and fifty questionnaires for (non-managerial) staff were sent to eight companies and organisations and 136 responses were received, a return rate of 54.4%. Of the eight questionnaires for managers, eight came back, with a 100% rate of response. A high return rate was caused by unusual 'informant' approach (Bruce *et al.* 2009; Harzing, 1996), commonly used among business organisations, that the research used to ensure the high response. Based on the results of the questionnaire survey, eight interviews with eight managers from surveyed companies and organisations were conducted to clarify their opinions of the language training programmes they have encountered. The follow-up interviews were also arranged to explore the questions in depth (see details in Chapter 7).

For the quantitative research, the questionnaire was designed to investigate issues linked to all proposed propositions. To analyse the results, a range of statistical tests were adopted. As most of the observed data are not normally distributed, a range of non-parametric statistical methods was adopted. To ensure the reliability and confidence of the quantitative analysis in this research, the exact test of PASW (Predictive Analysis Software for Social Science) and relevant effect size were used.

Although the quantitative analysis helps to verify the observed data, it cannot explain the reasons behind the statistical figures. Qualitative analysis has to be used to explore the areas where the propositions are rejected or in order to add additional detail where significantly different results emerge from comparison of attitudes between managers and staff. Propositions that are disconfirmed were examined to establish the underlying dynamics. Coding of the qualitative data was conducted to code the interview content with NVivo 8 (a computer-assisted qualitative data analysis software programme) after transcription.

1.4 Contributions to knowledge

The research at a more conceptual level develops a novel model with two-tier levels to train Chinese companies and organisations using updated knowledge of targeted learning content, customised evaluation added to project-based foreign language training, and international educational management.In addition, the main findings and perceived contribution of the research can be summarised as follows:

- Individual project creation by Chinese trainees is a creative approach to

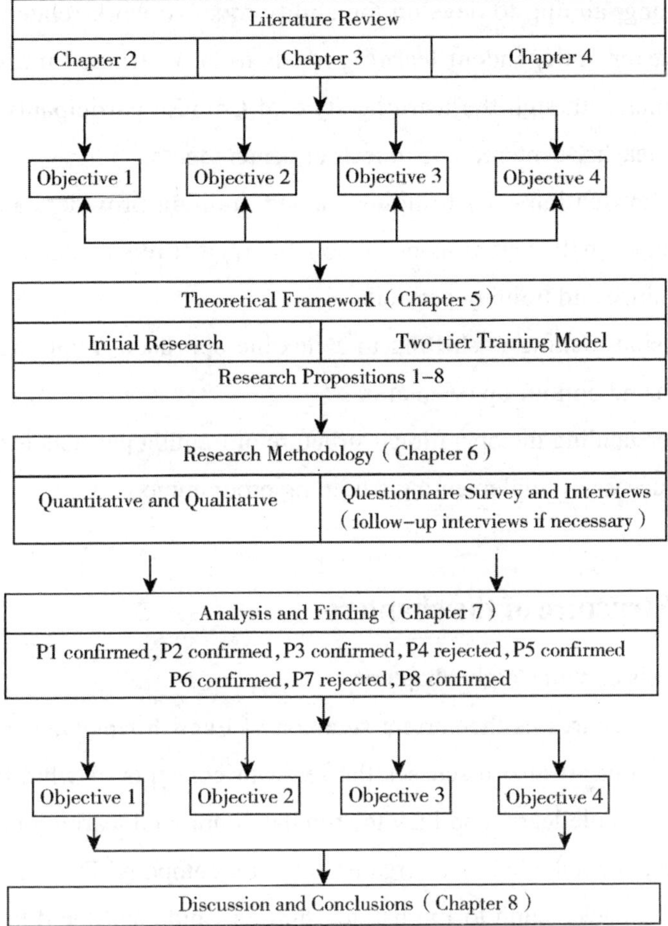

Figure 1-1 Framework of the research design

the challenge of meeting learning objectives.

- Foreign language programmes should aim to develop work-related or professional skills alongside language skills rather than learning the foreign language only.
- Learning content needs to be carefully designed in terms of foreign language skills, communicative ability and cultural awareness because of the divergence of perceptions among Chinese participants.
- Pedagogic design needs to blend formal instruction and independent

learning, aiming to develop the ability to solve work-related problems. However, independent learning needs to be instructed throughout the training, although the learning style of Chinese participants is shifting from teacher-centeredness to learner-centeredness.

- Joint evaluation – by bringing trainee, training providers and partners together – will customise evaluation, but regular reports need to be agreed by trainee and training partners.
- Decision-making is shifting to a flexible approach involving both top-down and bottom-up orientation.
- Understanding the operational structure of training partners is essential to the success of implementing a training programme.

1.5 Structure of the chapters

The thesis contains eight chapters:

Chapter 2 addresses the current situation of English language teaching and learning in China. It also discusses the relevant concepts of what learning is, how Chinese people learn, and how to stimulate improved learning performance when training is conducted in an organisation or a company. These attempts aim to identify the background to English teaching in China and the dilemma faced how Chinese people manage their learning under the influence of Confucianism, and what their demands are when learning English language.

Chapter 3 initially introduces the concepts of 'project' and 'project management', and reviews project-based foreign language teaching and learning (Beckett, 2006). Furthermore, it carefully explores the theoretical foundation and benefits of project-based learning. Finally the research identifies through looking into the implication of project-based learning in China that it is not being utilised to its fullest potential, and therefore proposes that blending project-based foreign language learning into a training project would offer a better and innovative platform for training Chinese people in foreign languages.

Chapter 4 based on the literature affecting English language teaching, Chinese learning style as described in chapter 2, and project-based foreign language theory in chapter 3, analyses how foreign language training providers from the UK and non-UK operate their programmes, and explores the advantages and disadvantages that lie ahead if conducting a foreign language programme for China's companies and organisations. In addition, it also carefully reviews two existing representative programmes and identifies their deficiencies.

Chapter 5 firstly synthesises the interrelated ideas and identifies the focus of the research needed. It then explores the gaps that exist in reality through conducting and analysing the initial research. Thirdly, it proposes a novel model with two-tier levels and addresses the propositions to validate the strategic theoretical framework implemented to train Chinese companies and organisations. In addition, it also presents the aim of the proposed project model as a balance between East and West in the area of management education through cross-cultural communication strategy.

Chapter 6 shows how pragmatism methodology – a mix of quantitative and qualitative methods – was used in the research. It explains *ontology* – how the researcher sees the reality of research, and also discusses *epistemology* – what counts to the researcher as knowledge. The questionnaire designed is presented and the statistical analysis methods adopted are carefully selected. The research procedures are designed. Procedures for data collection and sampling are described. The reliability and validation factors of the research are considered.

Chapter 7 presents both quantitative and qualitative analysis and findings. The key statistical findings of each proposition and main interview findings are set out. Furthermore, each proposition is evaluated from the results of the survey.

Chapter 8 further discusses the findings of the research. It presents the validation results of the proposed model and slightly modifies it based on the results of the analysis. It also expounds the contribution to knowledge made, points out the limitations, and makes recommendations for further related research. In addition, it discusses the practical application of the results of the research.

Chapter 2 Literature Review

2.1 Introduction

This chapter aims to review the situation of English language teaching and learning in China and background to English language education in China. It also discusses the relevant concepts of what learning is, how people learn, how to manage effective training in an organisation as well as how to motivate people to undertake effective learning within an organisation. At the same time, this chapter will also focus on a discussion of Confucianism and how it affects Chinese learning styles and managerial behaviours. In addition, the purpose of this chapter is to evidence the rationale for the research.

2.2 Background

The rapid growth of international businesses in China has resulted in a severe shortage in the supply of advanced technology, human resources and training management to keep pace with this development (Chen *et al.*, 2000; Gross, 1998; Kong *et al.*, 1989). As a result of these shortages, many of China's companies and organisations face the challenge of how to train individuals who could easily put their efforts to the development of their companies and organisations. Other challenges facing companies and organisations include acknowledging and addressing cultural issues, such as local employers' inability to communicate in English and lack of familiarity with Western business practices.

Kealey (2009) reported in *China-Britain Business Review* that after graduating from Cambridge University, Dominic Richards founded the English Teddy Bear Company. He expressed his concerns in terms of the situation of using English language in China:

> *"I was struck by two things on my many visits to China before I made the decision to operate here. The first is the energy of the place and its people. The Chinese are working hard to transform their lives and this inspired me. There is little in life more important than effective communication and I knew that we could make a difference in companies' operations and individuals' lives through excellent communication training. Secondly, the United Kingdom has long punched above its weight in the world and this is because we have been innovative, outward-looking and trade-focused for centuries. In order to continue to flourish we need to be of service to the East. The English language is our language, and this is a major cultural asset which we can work with." (ibid.,* p.22*)*

However, while working in China, James Hudson, the company's co-founder, discovered a need for targeted foreign language training:

> *"I saw a huge need for corporate training while I was working with the Bank of China and China Post. There was clearly a lack of tailored and comprehensive training packages that truly met the needs of both employees and companies."(ibid.,* p.23*)*

As the reports carries on, Chinese companies, internationally active companies in particular, in China were reporting a distinct lack of satisfaction with the training services provided there (Dalton, 2008). The major problem was the use of local human resources, specifically Chinese or other non-native English speakers, to train in English. As a result, companies were worried that they simply weren't seeing results from their investment, and they saw an immediate need for something that could help companies develop effective employees (Kealey, 2009, p.23).

So what are the issues facing businesses in China today in terms of training? One of the key problems is how to train effectively and have appropriate pedagogic methods available to Chinese companies. Whilst most Western companies know the value of training, China is still striving to catch up, struggling to balance cost and effectiveness. Although there is a wealth of English language training available in big cities in China, corporate skills training through an international communication strategy is a relatively new concept for many Chinese companies, for those companies in northwest China in particular.

The Chinese government attempts to resolve the issue by importing training resources abroad (Zhang, 2003). According to Xinhua the official press agency of the government of the People's Republic of China, there have been short-term training courses abroad for about 8000 leaders from different levels of Chinese government since 1992; many other such programmes are still underway through collaborative strategies with the USA, the UK, Australia, Japan, New Zealand and other countries (Xinhua, 2010). Chinese people have been aware of the benefits and believe training staff in English is making for a more talent-focused workforce (Dalton, 2008).

Meanwhile, the result of recent research carried out by Universal Ideas, a management training consultants has clearly demonstrated and quantified these sentiments. It showed that there were just three per cent of companies reporting that current providers were fully able to meet their training needs. The areas of greatest perceived weakness were training model, leadership and strategic management (Anon, 2006, p.70). Following on from this research, some 81 per cent of companies stated that they would like to take foreign language training as the priority for their organisation's development as language skill training also featured as one of the top wishes. This is perhaps not surprising in that it relates to senior management where these skills might be expected to exist in the long run for those companies which might be expected to struggle to achieve improvement (Kealey, 2009).

2.3 English language education in China

2.3.1 Background

To comprehensively understand the demand, we need to track back the changes that have taken place in language training in China over the last two decades.

In 1978, Deng Xiaoping, launched national modernisation reforms, with the "open door" and "Four Modernisations" policies as their main pillars (Hu, 2005a). Foreign language education figured prominently in the drive for modernisation (Adamson & Morris, 1997). Deng was convinced after observing the global situation of economic development at the time that China would need to access scientific and technological advances worldwide to develop the scientific knowledge base which was increasingly demanded for national revitalisation (People's Education Press, 1986). It was recognised that access to international know-how, knowledge and strategy needed to be a target for the Chinese economic drive, which would trigger a large pool of personnel to achieve proficiencies in foreign languages. To revive foreign language education after the damage caused by the Cultural Revolution and expand foreign language education to all levels of schooling, primary, secondary and higher education, became an integral part of the modernization drive as it was believed that foreign languages would play an active role to accelerate steps towards entering globalisation (Hu, 2005a).

Meanwhile, this change has affected the development of Chinese companies' and organisations' management systems. Decentralisation of companies and organisations was introduced soon afterwards in the mid 1980s. The economy gradually changed from one based on central planning to one on market socialism. Over the same period of time, Chinese companies and organisations were transformed in line with this guideline. With trend towards the economic 'global village', economists and traders in Chinese companies and organisations are slowly but impressively turning to the world market (Dalton, 2008). Foreign language education since this point has been playing an increasingly important role in China with English as a *lingua franca* particularly for such areas as business, information accessibility, the Internet and cultural exchange. All of these have brought great changes to every aspect of Chinese life. According to Held & Thompson (1999), "globalisation can be thought of as the widening, intensifying, speeding up and growing impact of worldwide interconnectedness". According to Wallraff (2000), "the conventional wisdom holds that English is destined to be the world's *lingua franca* – if it isn't already". Zhu (2003) also supported this by pointing out that foreign language speakers, particularly English language speakers, are regarded as linguistically privileged because they have relatively easy access to information or knowledge relevant to the future development of a company or organisation compared with those with less developed English language skills, such as Chinese people. However, to achieve a high level of foreign language proficiency for Chinese learners, particularly for current managers who received their education during the 70's, and 80's, turns out to be not easy for historic reasons that have curbed learners developing their English ability (Hu, 2002a; Ogden, 1993; Oxford, 1995).

2.3.2 History of English language education in China

Although English language education was re-introduced in schools in the early 1970s because of the change of political relationship with the USA after the official visit to China paid by former president Richard Nixon, English teaching and learning were not making practical progress and existed in name only. As a result, an acute shortage of both English–proficient personnel and of facilities for English language education appeared when China embarked on the modernisation drive (Hu, 2002b).

2.3.2.1 Dilemma currently facing China's foreign language education

China had been short of educational infrastructure over much of the last decade of the 20th century, although it had enjoyed phenomenal economic development and social stability (Hu, 2005b; Zhu, 2003). However, with its increasing integration into the global economy, China was faced with unprecedented challenges of globalisation, technological advances, knowledge-driven economies and pressure for innovation. The Chinese government recognised many educational deficits would undermine national competitiveness and therefore staged a new wave of educational reforms at the beginning of the new century (Hu, 2002b; 2005a). The new reforms consisted of changing the existing educational structure, updating teaching content in response to international globalisation, absorbing progressive thinking from abroad and encouraging innovation in pedagogy so as to deliver quality education. There was an emerging progressive ideology that stressed both individual development as well as development in the higher education organisations. What is more, China has embarked upon another wave of education policy reform by implementing the policy of expanding student recruitment in an attempt to react to the needs of the more talented in society (Hu, 2005a).

The development boom caused by the reform on the one hand provided more Chinese young people with opportunities to receive higher education, but on the other hand also strained resources and challenged the facilities within higher education, which many universities and colleges failed to develop at the same pace as the increase in enrolment. Upon this point, the quality of foreign language learning and teaching is certainly a concern here, as well-equipped facilities are considered necessary preconditions for healthy foreign language development, for instance, creating an effective language learning environment and enhancing investments on improving learner's language skills. As Chen (2004) stated, obviously the increase in enrolment negatively affected the quality of teaching and learning for Chinese students and also inevitably made higher education institutions unable to provide better service in response to demand for foreign language training from companies and organisations that have been hurriedly prepared for entry onto the stage of international business competition.

Secondly, along with this wave of education reform, China has additionally been faced with a shortage of personnel with English skills. On the one hand, it is accepted that the change of policy to recruit more college students is based on the perception of producing more talents who will receive training to improve their foreign language abilities at university to meet demands from Chinese companies and organisations. This has been widely believed to be the best strategy to catch up with developed countries and also get better profit in the field of international business (Hu, 2002b, 2005a). However, on the other hand, much more serious problems such as the inadequate infrastructure for quality English language teaching caused by the expanding recruitment have become the obstacle to investment by universities and colleges in order to expand English provision. This has become even more severe and obvious since increased recruitment has been implemented from the year 2000. In addition, as a result, the enlarged number of students worsens the already severe teacher shortages in English language teachers (Chen, 2004; Toloken, 2007; Wu, 2001).

Given the evident overstretching of available resources in the eager expansion of English language education, it is not surprising that the quality of ELT has been a subject to widespread criticism. Over the past 25 years universities in China have produced a large number of graduates with low English proficiency or only some proficiency in English, but these graduates are the main source of recruitment for companies and organisations (Chee, 2002/2003; Hu, 2005b; Lin, 2002; Wu, 2001). Retraining them in terms of English language to meet their companies' and organisations' needs is undoubtedly one of the biggest challenges in the process of staff development.

Thirdly, there are a growing number of managers from various companies and organisations engaged in multicultural communication who are no longer satisfied with more general skills of personnel produced by universities (Graddol, 2002; Hu, 2005). Graduates recruited for international purposes but generally unable to meet the real need of their employers because they are produced by universities through a certain kind of curriculum which actually emphasises formal instruction in the classroom and assessments in examinations. There is no sense of practical use in terms of the knowledge learnt at universities, and a huge gap between the expectations from the real world and the outcomes that university education can actually provide, because many companies and organisations expect talented personnel with knowledge of cultural awareness, proper communication strategy, international business knowledge and foreign language proficiency (Bandevelde, 2001; Hagen, 2005).

On top of this, in terms of foreign language proficiency in particular, Chinese universities have faced many more challenges in terms of how to improve so that they can match society's demands (Hu, 2002b). He (2011) argued that due to a weak grounding in pedagogy within Chinese higher education, which focuses on teaching and learning language knowledge, such as language rules, sentence patterns and grammar rules, a view which basically predominates in English classes in China, English language proficiency is poor. A large-scale survey conducted under the auspices of the State Education Commission between 1996 and 2000, revealed that the English proficiency and quality of the students in higher education surveyed was disappointingly low, although they had studied English for as much as 10 years or even more (Lin, 2002). The study showed that the great majority of surveyed students had only a fragmentary knowledge of English, a surprisingly low level of communicative competence in the language, and very limited abilities of using work-related English language. There may have been many reasons behind all these deficiencies, but the vital one is that English teachers at universities lack knowledge of effective teaching and learning, lack professional knowledge which could be used in actual work, and know little about recent developments in pedagogical orientation (*ibid.*). To get these issues resolved, the research by Lin (2002) suggested that improving the quality of English language teaching and learning and creating an innovative pedagogy for Chinese adults are the key points to make positive changes in training for Chinese personnel. In addition, it is also essential to promote collaboration with international society in order to make full use of the well-established advanced facilities abroad to make good the shortage in Chinese higher education and to ensure professional training strategy is upgraded.

2.3.2.2 Major changes to foreign language learning and teaching in China

Until the 1980s, the central government has gradually become aware that the problems that existed of out-dated foreign language education had obviously challenged and hampered progress in building communication with the outside world (Lin, 2002). To improve this situation, the government therefore began to lay emphasis on the strategic role of English and give it top priority on the national agenda for educational development in the modernisation process: the projected demand for human resources in all companies and organisations to hire employees with good English qualifications was recognised (Zhu, 2003). Moreover, one of the biggest reforms is that in September 2001 the Ministry of Education in China instructed all colleges and universities to use English as the main teaching language in technology, economics and business related courses (Guo, 2002).

It is important to understand the relationship between the current socio-economic situation and foreign language learning and its impact on social development. Chinese education needs to make changes to face these challenges in order to ensure that English language teaching and learning orientation meets the demands from Chinese companies and organisations in terms of language skills requirements, or properly manage this necessity to meet the needs of globalised competition. In view of this, Chinese education has made three changes.

Firstly, it is crucial to improve the level of English language education to make sure that it enables people to train their language abilities so that they are able to access updated information technology. English language continues to be the *lingua franca* used for communication between Eastern and Western countries, and has been widely learned, but focusing on language knowledge itself. However, technology such as the Internet has a prime role which is now beginning to be acknowledged in the popular media. People who try to keep themselves informed and up-to-date must have a solid command of English. This has already had a great impact on the acknowledgment of foreign language teaching and learning (David, 2002). The decision to make this change to up-to-date targeted based foreign language learning has also highlighted the role of the foreign language as a tool to access international businesses and make communication with them possible. Thus, it has raised awareness among industrial and business companies and other organisations that foreign language training needs to be increasingly prominent if they are to gain advanced and up-to-date technology (David, 2002; Hagen, 2005).

Secondly, it is believed that teaching and learning English at any institution in China should place great emphasis on mastering the English language as an international language used for international business purposes (Zhu, 2003). This major change is based on the acknowledgement that the English language has been widely used in information exchange, the application of science and technology and the emergence of transnational corporations (Crystal, 2006). Warschauer (2000) points out that the past three decades, with the impact of the world economy, have seen a growth in the role of the English language both around the world and in China as the *lingua franca* for economic and scientific exchange. Many joint ventures in China adopt English as a *lingua franca*, and many companies are beginning to employ staff with an English qualification as a basic requirement, a development which creates a national need for training in English in parallel.

Thirdly, promoting the level of English teaching and learning in China is aiming to train English language learners in the skills used for information processing and analysis. Zhu (2003) states that many jobs that existed in the business and industrial areas are being replaced by new types of work which are based on a shift from brute force towards jobs that require advanced information processing and analytic skills (Hu, 2002b). As a result, new forms of business in China are emerging which essentially depend on the application of science and technology and a high level of national and international communication management (Carnoy, 1993; Wang, 2006). Besides, technological changes also facilitate international operation and more competition across international borders. All of these will make a great impact on both the understanding of the concept of English teaching and learning and associated policy making in China. Therefore, the training for employees or managers in foreign languages for international communication requires the development of their functional skills incorporating an international consciousness as well as foreign language skills development. It is also vital to develop their understanding of globalisation. This is to say that companies and organisations in China need foreign language education: not facts about company's or organisation's location and internal cultures, but, given the increasingly global nature of trade, they need to learn about and relate their managerial tasks to the outside world.

2.4 What is learning and learning style?

Atkinson *et al.* (1993) gave the answer to the question as "a relatively permanent change in behaviour that results from practice". Biggs (1999; 2007) defines it more comprehensively:

- Learning is created by the learner's learning activities.
- Learning depends on their motives and intentions.
- Learning is a way to produce the motivation which is regarded as the product of good teaching, not a prerequisite of teaching.
- Learning comes from good interactive activity.

Weightman (2004) further specifies the distinction of defining learning in organisations by pointing out that an important aspect of learning in organisations is the form of accumulated learning called experience. Learning in organisations is seen in the gradual learning of better ways of getting things done. Even more important is a more formal sort of learning in organisations where people systematically set out to learn a different way of doing something by taking part in a course or a programme. All this kind of learning involves a change in knowledge, skills or even attitude (Whiddett, 2002).

On top of this, learning styles account for individual differences in the manner in which the learners process information from their environment (Claxton *et al*, 1978). Learning styles also suggest that groups or cultures exhibit particular learning preferences. For Keefe (1979) and Coffield *et al.* (2004), learning styles are the "characteristic, cognitive, affective and psychological behaviours that serve as relatively stable indicators of how learners perceive, interact with, and respond to the learning environment".

Clenton (2010) states that if learning styles can be measured reliably, the implications are obvious for language training, and there is an exciting prospect that styles awareness may help attain the objectives of teaching and learning.

2.4.1 How do adult people learn?

It is essential to know *how* people learn before we start learning systematically or helping someone else to learn because it might enable us to reduce the time it takes us to learn something. When difficulties arise, we can start analysing where the problem lies and remedy it.

Wang (2008) states that the outstanding learning characteristic of adult learners is that they have work responsibility. Because of this, adult learners often aim to develop their understanding with their obtained knowledge that supports them to acquire new knowledge in a new academic discipline. Wang (2009) continues that it is essential to account for what valid knowledge for adult learners is and stresses that valid knowledge in adult education consists of not only instructional strategies, but also content of the field. He also adds that adult learners are actually objectivists who believe that a course must present a core body of knowledge to be learned. The effective transmission of this core body of knowledge becomes of central importance. They usually prefer sitting in lectures and using standardised learning materials to discussions, and like their courses to be well organised and clear, and their instructors to be authoritative figures in the field (Bash, 2003; Brookfield, 2006; Elias, 2005).

With these common general principles of adult learning, there are several different models of how adult people learn which apply to training adults (Weightman, 2004).

2.4.1.1 Experimental psychology model

A model that has been very influential in education and adult training is that of Gagne (1975). This summarises the findings of various experimental psychologists who have studied the individual's behaviour in an experimental context in an effort to understand how the learning processes operates (Whiddett, 2002). Gagne (1975) identified a chain of eight events that occur. He puts forward the view that whatever sort of learning is taking place, it happens in a common order (Weightman, 2004).

- Motivation. The learner has to have a will to learn, and to want to learn a particular thing or the final product of this type of learning.
- Perception. This involves identifying a clear objective. Learning would be difficult if one hasn't understood the different categories in the area.
- Acquisition. What has to be learned is related to the familiar, so that it makes sense. For example, learners can help themselves by recalling their own experiences to help to make sense of a new area of learning.
- Retention. People are consequently processing the two-stage process of learning which comprises a short-term memory where basic concepts are stored first, and a long-term memory to which they are eventually transferred to be gained as an ability.

- Generalisation. This is the ability to apply the learning in situations. People may generalise what they learn about motivation in the workplace to thinking about motivation at other places they have experienced previously (Whiddett, 2002; Weightman, 2004).
- Performance. This is putting into practice what has been learned. It is the test of learning.
- Feedback on performance. This is where the learner finds out whether the performance was satisfactory or not. Feedback can help to analyse what went wrong, how it could be avoided, what needs more practice, what to do next and so on.

These eight events are useful as a practice checklist when helping learners to prepare for learning and it is also a useful model for analysing more informal methods of learning (Weightman, 2004).

2.4.1.2 Experiential learning model

Another useful model of how people learn is that of Kolb, Rubin and Mclntyre(Kolb, 1974). Figure 2–1 shows their experiential learning model. In their view, all the stages are necessary if learning is to take place.

The model suggests that learning is a cycle of the following stages:

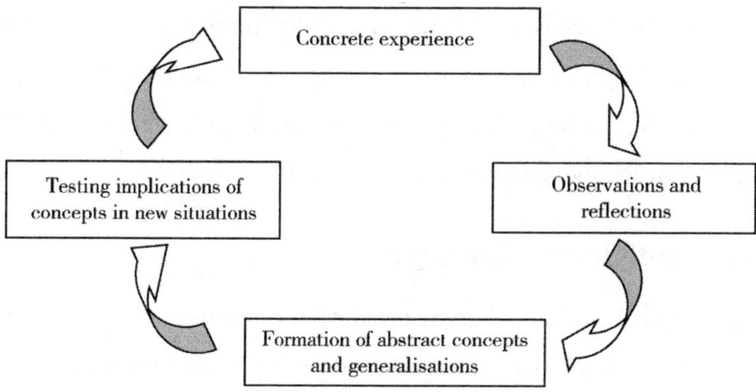

Figure 2–1 Kolb's learning model (Weightman, 2004)

- Concrete experience or experience that involves performance. For example, making a presentation of learning objectives.
- Observation and reflective analysis of the experience. This is most useful if done from many perspectives – discussing the learning objectives.
- Generalisation on the basis of experience, or doing some thinking. Such generalisations use abstract concepts to integrate the observations into the theories we have about the world.
- Experimentation in future action based on the generalisation, or doing something similar. The application of ideas requires active experimentation.
- New experience derived from this experimentation – getting the learner to present what s/he has learned.
- Initiation of a new learning cycle.

If imagining a spiral of these experiential learning cycles we can see how a model of continual improvement and learning could be developed, with the learner becoming increasingly confident and ambitious in his or her performance and analysis.

Additionally, Kolb, Rubin and Osland (1991) developed the model of a learning cycle as in Figure 2–1 to suggest that since the learning process is driven by individual needs and objectives, so learning styles for the experiential learning become highly individualised during the process. Each of the stages of the learning cycle can be a strength or a weakness in learning. Individuals will find some part of the cycle easier than others (Biggs, 2007).

2.4.2 Individual differences

Everyone will prefer different parts of the learning cycle and will attach more efforts to some parts of the cycle than others (Nicholson, 2003). The fact is that learning has to respect individual differences (Kolb *et al.*, 1991). The British writers Honey and Mumford (1992) used Kolb's model in a different way, emphasising the particular stages of the cycle that favour particular types of individuals. Such types are: as Weightman's (2004) summary puts it: activists, reflector, theorists and pragamtists.

Whichever model of learning styles is used, it is essential to establish that there are individual differences in how people learn from experience. People are learning relying on their own learning styles. Those responsible for learning, training and development of people must ensure that there is sufficient variety of learning experiences and learning resources available to suit different learning individuals.

2.4.3 Effective learning in different situations

Having understood how people learn, we should further investigate to determine whether different sorts of learning material require different learning methods to optimise learning. Traditionally, a distinction is drawn between cognitive learning, learning skills, and developing attitudes. Each of these is thought not only to be a different learning objective but also to require a different learning process. Weightman (2004) categorises learning as *comprehension, reflex learning, attitude development, memory training* and *procedural learning.* He also draws attention to the fact that most learning situations require more than one of these types of learning and each categorisation is a helpful means of sorting out which would be the most appropriate means of learning something, based on different needs from various situations (*ibid.*).

2.4.4 The learning organisation

How to deal with learning in organisations has attracted considerable attention from researchers on management, and they tend to describe organisations that cope with learning well as "learning organisations" (Bee, 1994; Kay, 1993; Morgan, 1997). The idea of a learning organisation was first articulated by Argyris and Schon (1978) and developed by Morgan (1986) and Pedlar, Burgoyne and Boydell (1991).

According to Marguand and Reynolds (1994), managers wishing to build their organisation's capacity to learn should attempt to create knowledge-based partnerships with people within and without the organisation in order to share ideas and information so that a real understanding develops; should change the role of managers in order to faciliate the learning; should create systems and patterns to allow staff time to extract learning; and should develop a powerful vision of organisational excellence and individual fulfilment.

In many ways, a learning organisation is one that manages knowledge well (Weightman, 2004). This is inceasingly seen as a crucial competence for organisations competing in a global market. In view of this, Pedlar, Burgoyne and Boydell (1991) added to the features of a learning organisation, for which they prefer the term 'learning company', in which a learning approach to strategy needs to be established and policy-making is implemented.

2.4.5 Stimulating improved performance in the learning organisation

2.4.5.1 Why an organisation needs training?

Training is not a new concept in the organisational environment. It has been used for many centuries for ensuring successful strategic development in the organisation (Yelon and Berge, 1988). The key point for training is how to sustain its bond with organisational needs and to ensure that the objectives of the training are met in the process of training implementation (Goldstein and Ford, 2002).

The development of an organisation has to depend on the contribution by individuals. An individual will therefore develop her/his human effort investment, that is, her/his skills and knowledge by investing in training, which will allow her/him to make a better contribution to the organisation. Investment in training and developing employees' skills therefore emerged as a key component of human capital deployment (Mincer, 1974). An individual's human capital can best be defined as knowledge and skills built up throughout schooling, vocational training and work experiences (De la Fuente and Ciccone,

2002). Within an organisation, one individual's human capital is linked and contributes to developing organisational capital – collective competence, organisational routines and company culture (Edvinsson and Malone, 1997). Overall, an individual's human capital starts with personal professional development and ends with contribution to the development of either organisation or individual.

Generally speaking, the definition of training is to teach a person a specific skill, especially through practice (Nordhaug, 2003). Bartel (1994) defines training as teaching, developing, or modifying the behaviours of an employee in such a way that the employee can help to attain the goals of the organisation. According to Bartel (1989), well-trained and dedicated staff have an enhanced working experience and contribute significantly to an organisation's reputation. At the same time, inexperienced new employees and low morale among members of professional staff can harm an organisation's performance. Bartel also argued that an investment in training increases productivity (*ibid.*).

Gibbon and Waldman (2004) identified task-specific human capital as crucial to organisational development as it is mostly built up by vocational training and embedded in working experience, which is actually the basis of a body of knowledge specific to an organisation. Meanwhile, Au (2007) revealed that a training programme is the most important attribute to develop staff qualifications and also indicated that the higher a memebr of staff's position is, the higher the perceived need for training.

In the context of Chinese organisations, the specific perceived need by Chinese staff and managers is to enhance their managerial capabilities and embrace international business practices (Jiang, 2008). A feeling of wanting to be a part of the international business community and to possess equivalent business acumen to that of Western management counterparts has provided the motivation for Chinese organisations to immerse themselves in English and its culture, to learn what is perceived to be a universal business, and to study Western management practices with a view to adopting them in developing their ability to handle Chinese businesses and improving the skills required for their workplace. Implementing a training programme has become standard practice in developing their international competitiveness within Chinese organisations (Littrell, 2005).

Tang Jie and Ward (2005) argue that the speed of change for Chinese organistions in the high-technology realm meant that innovation was essential. To achieve this, organisations have to prove themselves capable of learning, thus acquiring new capabilities quickly and thoroughly. In spite of this, learning also rests on the free flow of information, on being able to tap the experience of thers. To this point, the need to keep abreast of world trends in their field has developed a willingness to learn from abroad, an openness of mind that puts them at an advantage when it comes to forming international alliances. They not only have a keen sense of their capabilities, but also are equally aware of where their development is lacking in comparison to others. This greatly encourages the desire to learn new knowledge and renew skills required for the future. In this situation, there must be a keen sense of what could be learned, what could be digested and what could not, given the stage of development the company or organisation has reached. However, sometimes companies and organisations with the desire to learn high technology or up-to-date knowledge are groping in the dark and wishing to see the relevance to *their* needs of information gleaned from every corner (Lu, 2000).

2.4.5.2 Deciding what skills to train and develop

To carry out training systematically in a company or an organisation, it is increasingly vital to identify and describe the skills and competencies required, measuring the skills and competencies of the postholders, seeing if there a gap between the two, identifying training needs, and then developing those skills and competencies that are less well developed (Pedlar, 1991). Weightman (2004) has suggested the following ways to identify training needs:

- At appraisal sessions when the manager and the individual discuss what training would be appropriate over a period of time to help improve and develop the individual's contribution and career prospects.

- As a result of changes that the company is taking on that may involve a training and development programme for the whole company.
- As stimulation of the individual who wants to improve and develop his ability, either for current work or for career purposes.
- As part of a recovery programme after the identification of poor performance of an individual and bad influence on the future of company.

All of these can be for training in various skills that the company needs for development. Meanwhile, it is clear that these behaviours can be analysed into smaller steps for success in the future (Morgan, 1997; Nicholson, 2003). It is also obvious that deciding what skills to train and develop for the individual is equally important as a way of directing the performance of people in an organisation or company, and this has been traditionally regarded as management by objectives. It actually involves (Morgan, 1997; Drucker, 1989):

- Setting targets and objectives.
- Getting individuals to agree these objectives and the criteria for measuring performance.
- Evaluating and reviewing the outcomes.

2.4.5.3 Deciding how to train and develop

Having decided what needs training and developing, the next question is how to go about it. Like most management decisions (Bee and Bee, 1994; Reid and Barrington, 1999), training and development have to be made on the basis of resources and opportunities available. There is no point in planning a perfect but impracticable programme. This pragmatism also needs to be applied to what makes sense. There is also a cultural aspect to this. In more centralised organisations such as those in China, staff are told what they need to learn and are given training experience to deliver this; whereas more self-managing organisations such as those in Western countries will expect staff to identify their own learning priorities and find the resources available to achieve them. This may result in a difficulty to identifying trainee's learning needs and also will cause mismatching to their learning objectives.

The next section looks at common training methods which help us find a training and development opportunity for people from different cultures (Weightman, 2004; Kealey, 2009).

- Action learning – this actually involves the linking of a real, structured task and action within the learning process using action learning sets. Action learning sets are groups of people who discuss the problems associated with the task using an identified facilitator. It can be difficult to keep the group on the task as individuals develop, but it is a technique found particularly useful by senior staff who enjoy being part of a group, as they can feel very isolated in normal day-to-day operations.
- Project – a project allows greater freedom to display participant's initiative and creativity. The participants need the full commitment and co-coperation of the trainer.
- Role play – people are asked to act the role they would play at work or in training. It is particularly used for training for face-to-face situations and is suitable for near-real-life situations where criticism would be useful. The difficulities are that people can be embarrassed and the usefulness of the exercise is very dependent on the nature of the feedback given.

2.4.5.4 Deciding how to manage individual performance

It is essential to have a way of evaluating an individual's performance in a programme (Gross, 1998). Weightman (2004) agrees with this by stating that the one certain thing is that we are unable to neglect the association of participant's performance in training when conducting evaluation. Some would argue for the autonomy of individuals to offer their work in whatever way they feel is appropriate. Others would argue that there is a need for outside authorities to ensure standards that individuals apply in their work, while still allowing the individual to offer this work as and when he or she wishes. Others, usually managers, want things much more tightly controlled by the employers or managers. Questions about what work should be done, how it should be done, the quality expected, and the rewards for work and companies, are all associated with individual performance management (Gross, 1998; Weightman, 2004; Marquand, 1994). Who should take the decision about these is inevitably an element in the politics of the debate (Weightman, 2004).

At the same time, measuring employees' performance inevitably means judging them in some way. There is always a point at which someone is judging another, so subjective of the judgement is inevitable (Gross, 1998), in spite of efforts made to try to reduce it. So, one should be aware of that very careful consideration of the assessment process is necessary (Weightman, 2004).

Weigthman (2004) and Whiddett (2002) discussed the issue and pointed out that organisations are constantly trying out different forms of assessment. This is partly because of a perceived imbalance with whichever method is being practised, and partly because there is always a desire to make it even better. Different types of assessment that have been tried and which could be included in any particular scheme are:

- Self-assessment – where individuals decide whether they are having difficulty or not with some required behaviour, and this can be the basis of discussion.
- Peer assessment – not usually done formally unless in examining how effective the team is.
- Line manager assessment – This may include observation and collecting evidence. Sometimes it is much more informal, and does not involve such systematic measures.

- Assessment by others who come into contact with job holder – this is sometimes used to give a certain objectivity, for example in assessment agencies. It should be used carefully because it can be costly.

No matter what methods of assessment an organisation uses, managing the individual performance in training is at the heart of managing people (Drucker, 1989; Whiddett, 2002; Weightman, 2004). The more we can learn about people and how they see the work we are asking them to undertake, the more likely we are to be able to discuss the task in terms that make sense to them. The more we understand about them, the more likely we are to find the rewards that will motivate them to offer exceptional work. In another words, the evaluation is also based on how much related culture is embedded in the individual participant that we need to take account of (Marchington, 1996; Weightman, 2004).

2.5 How do Chinese people learn?

Chinese people possess a unique learning style (Li, 2010; Levinsohn, 2007). One could not achieve success in terms of training Chinese people without understanding how Chinese people learn and what learning styles they possess. As Littrell (2005) identifies, it will, of course, lead to problems when the training provider and trainee are generally unfamiliar with the culture of the other, and are unaware of the cultural accommodations they must make. Indeed, Chinese people are likely to possess a unique learning (and even teaching style) which is inherited from its traditions (Littrell, 2005; Warner, 2004).

2.5.1 Confucianism

Confucianism is a philosophy of life that provides a value system based on the teachings of Kong Fu Zi (Confucius), a Chinese educator born in 551 B.C (Child *et al.*, 2003). Confucianism emphasises a society based on social harmony, duty, and benevolence. In principle, Confucius believes in people by trusting them with the sense of self-awareness of doing what they are required to do because the foundation of this philosophy is that Man essentially places emphasis on a preference for government by virtue. Self-control is the basis of the industrious virtues for the Chinese people to achieve success in the aspects they are working at (Littrell, 2005). Thus Confucius encourages people to be responsible for what they are doing through promoting a sense of self-control (Littrell, 1999; 2005; Lu & Alon, 2003).

Confucius has had strong influence for more than two thousand years on Chinese in all aspects. In the context of this research, Chinese learning styles and Chinese corporate management are specifically discussed.

2.5.1.1 Chinese learning styles

Confucius emphasises respect for education (Fung, 1966; Tang, 1991; Yang, 1957). However, this respect for education is linked with a tradition of unquestioning obedience to superiors, teachers, and a respect the privilege of education itself (Littrell, 2005; Keller and Kronstedt, 2005). Various theorists have defined schemes of classifying learning styles (Peacock, 2001; Littrell, 2005), but Littrell (2005) summarises the identified learning styles for Chinese learners with the characteristics of synthesising and comprehensive understanding abilities. These include:

- Instructed learning – Chinese learners believe that knowledge is something to be transmitted by the teachers and educators, and the learners or trainees receive learning from the teacher rather than discovered by themselves (Harshbarger, 1986). The students influenced by this learning style often dislike learning without the guidance of the teachers, prefering listening to teacher and relying on teacher's instruction (Liu, 1997; Sato, 1982). Formal instruction might be the best pedagogical approach for those students with such learning styles because they are reluctant to manage their learning by themselves (Song, 1995).

- Self-managed and Analytic learning – interestingly, Littrell (2005) finds that Chinese learners prefer conducting a field study independently. They will like to focus on sequential details rather than the overall structures, and they are often going from the big picture to precision, from general to specific (Oxford, 1995). To conduct this, analysis and independent field study are involved in order to find cause-effect relationships (Honey, 1992).
- Thinking-oriented and reflective styles (Littrell, 2005) – Nelson (1995) argued that Chinese people typically formulate judgement based on logic and analysis, favouring thought over emotion. Anderson (1993) also supported this view by detailing that Chinese learners show great reflection rather than awareness of feelings of others. Independent study might be a suitable approach for those learners with this kind of learning style because they like to take time to pursue what they want before arriving at the correct answer (Nelson, 1995).

A native Western-educated and experienced lecturer engaged in teaching Chinese students is likely to confront a teaching-learning style conflict (Littrell, 2005). A mismatch in teaching and learning styles might inevitably cause learning failure, frustration and demotivation (Peacock, 2001; Reid, 1999). Worthey (1987) noted that while diversity within any culture is the norm, research shows that individuals within a culture tend to have a common pattern of learning and perception when compared to members of another culture. However, understanding and accommodating the difference should be a goal of an effective education. Accommodating difference is also the reponsibility of the educational experience so as to face the reality of internationalisation (Peacock, 2001).

This research has drawn attention to the neccessity of reconsiling of these learning styles, and reaching consensus. It suggests that an improved teaching and learning approach is to design training programmes by blending self-managed study and instructor's guidance.

2.5.1.2 Confucianism and Chinese corporate management

Confucianism encourges *Ren*, a capacity of companssion, *Yi*, a sense of moral rightness and *Li*, a norm for protocols (Chan, 1963; Chan, 2001). Ip (1996, 2002) defines *ren-li-yi* as the core principles for Confucian Chinese companies and organisations. He states that most Chinese companies and organisations display the following major features: paternalism, harmony and authoritarianism (Farth and Cheng, 1998; Smith and Wang, 1996; Westwood, 1997). These three features have been conspicuous and have embedded themselves into managerial behaviours of a firm (Child & Warner, 2003; Ip, 2002;Warner, 2004).

Paternalism is a practice that is originally based on the mindset that parents or aged people know best (Ip, 2000). This practice is often executed by ignoring the views from staff and employees who are in lower positions. Reflecting on descision-making in a company or organisation, obviously senior managers are usually the most qualified persons to make a decision and others should obediently oblige (Chan, 2001; Ip, 2000). Thus, 'top-down' decision-making has been the norm. To some extent, this act has been critised as a bad practice for a company's development. It is also being viewed as breeding arrogance among those in power, and hampering the communication between company's decision makers and employees regarding company's needs (Chen, 2001; Ip, 1996).

Entering a new era in modern development of companies, Chinese managerial culture, on one hand, strives to minimise the bad influence of the Confucian; on the other hand, it does not neglect the idea how to make use of the Confucian notion to make profit from business interactions. This notion originates from the Confucian belief that "harmony can make profits" for business (Warner, 2004).

Chinese companies and organisations cherish belief that harmony is the central theme guiding a company or organisation to achieve balance when challenged with disputes about business profits, as Ip (2008) concluded. In order to sustain organisational stability and hamony, a culture of respect for the person, for business partners is being introduced into the modern management in Chinese companies. Respect has been seen as the best way to avoid conflict and then maintain harmony (Lockett, 1988; Westwood, 1997). A particular example of this is to maintain a regular dialogue between different levels of hierarchy as well as different parties involved within management (Trompenaars, 1993). The obvious evidence is that managers working for a multinational corporation's joint venture or companies coodinating with international business is highly complimentary about Chinese managers because they maintain the same strong commitment to Confucianism of organisational and societal harmony and personal and interpersonal harmony when confronted with an assessment, evaluation or decision-making dilemma (Child & Warner, 2003; Tse, 1999; Wang, 2002).

2.6 Discussion and conclusion

This chapter reviews the literature relating to the background to English language education in China, discussing the relevant concepts of what learning is and how people learn, as well as how to enhance learning effectiveness when training is conducted in an organisation or a company. In particular, it discusses how Chinese people undertake their learning under the historic influence of Confucianism. These attempts aim to highlight the background knowledge of the problems that challenge Chinese English language learners, what their demands when learning English are, and what kind of learning styles they possess.

A review of Chinese Confucianism and discussion of its impacts on organisational management are also essential to understand the characteristics of management within Chinese companies and organistions. Certainly there are some negative sides that a Confucian company may possess, but as Ip (2009) said, it is not unreasonable to find that paternalism and harmony entailed by Confucianism co-exist with its postitive sides. This point clearly shows that paternalism has been deeply embedded into Chinese culture of management, 'top-down' decision-making for instance, and can be seen at different levels of management, but it is not surprising to discover that the orientation of corporate management is in favour of harmony and particularism when facing the opportunity of making international business. It would be advisable for any cooperation proposals to be based on the principle of how to make use of the spirit of Confucianism to ensure that the success of a bilateral win can be achieved. Therefore, how to respect partners and by what means can one extend '*Li*', respect, to both training providers and clients in the context of foreign language training management becomes vital to success.

However, the influence of Confucianism may be losing its strong influence in the era of modern China, as Egri and Ralston (2004), in a study of Chinese managers with three age cohorts of "less than 41 years", "41-51", and "older than 51 years", reported. They consider younger managers to be higher in individualism values, lower in collectivism values, and lower in the values of Confucianism, with the differences significant to $p<0.05$ or better (Egri *et al*, 2004; Littrell, 2005). This finding has indicated a shift from the influence of Confucianism to modern global value is under way along with Chinese economic development (Keller and Kronstedt, 2005). This more recent development also has to be taken into consideration when a programme is managed through international channels to ensure the balance of the different cultures is engaged.

This implies that managing a collaborative programme with a Chinese partner should possess certain major capacities: to adapt and respond to both the Chinese developmental context and the global economy, to create wealth and profit but also to contribute to the common good of a viable and operational model and to take adavantage of the positive sides of Confucianism such as harmony and paternalism (Ip, 2009). As Gundling (2003) discusses, a training institute's global strategic-planning process should involve obtaining specific local market knowledge and an understanding of the specific culture's values and history they are serving (Wong, 2007). Wilkinson and Young (2002) added to this view by pointing out that Chinese people also believe that utilization of both cultures into a cooperation programme in harmony brings prosperity to two sides, and will not succeed if it otherwise fails to do so. A company and organisation would seldom survive and prosper if only through their individual efforts. Each company and organisation depends upon the activities and performance of others and hence upon the nature and quality of the direct and indirect relationship a company and organisation develops with its counterparts (Gundling, 2003).

In terms of an appropriate training programme for Chinese staff through international collaboration, it is also crucial to identify their learning styles. The result is that a native Western educated and experienced lecturer engaged in teaching Chinese language learners is likely to confront a teaching-learning style conflict. Such style differences embedded in different cultures from two sides, Chinese learners and educational institutions from different countries, consistently and negatively affect Chinese learners' performance (Wallace and Oxford, 1992), which inevitably determines the outcomes of the training programme. So designing a suitable foreign language training programme and matching appropriate teaching approaches with Chinese adult learning styles, along with embracing as inclusively as possible the value systems within its management approach, can enhance effectiveness and facilitate achievement (Brown, 1994).

Chapter 3 Project-based Foreign and Second Language Learning

3.1 Introduction

In the new environment of globalisation, all managers – either by themselves, or through teams of people working for them – are looking to managing change through different approaches. Since the 1990s, project-based management has become a new popular mangement approach through which companies and organisations respond to change to develop ahead of their competitors (Gareis, 2005; Shared, 1986; Turner, 1993), and hence project management is a skill that all managers need in their portfolio.

This chapter provides the definition of projects and general knowledge about project management. It also draws on Beckett and Miller's research on project-based foreign language learning theory. It starts from the definition of project-based learning (PBL) and further introduces what project-based foreign language learning is, how it works and its effects in terms of managing a training programme for foreign language learners. It aims to give a broad review of the main strands of foreign language learning theories in order to enable the research to contextualise the design approach for the purpose of practicality.

3.2 What is a project?

The simplest definition of a project is "something which has a beginning and an end" (Andersen, 1987). This definition is a useful start, but needs qualification. First, many projects do not have a measurable beginning; they develop over a period. Secondly, the daily production in a baked bean factory can be said to meet this definition. However, when repeated day after day, it is not a project (Turner, 1993). In fact, several other definitions have been attempted, including: a human practice which aims to create change with mixed objectives (Andersen, 1987); an effort to achieve a specific objective within a schedule (Cleland, 1983); and a one-time creative effort by people to do something that is unique and not repetitive within the organisation (Smith, 1985).

The above definitions have several common threads. They mention (Turner, 1993):

- Complex endeavours to do work which creates change
- Mixed objectives, especially constraints of quality, cost and time
- The involvement of people, often from throughout the organisation
- Uniqueness

To be complete, the definiton of a project should therefore reflect this successful achievement of the purpose. The approach to the management of projects derived in the research is based upon the following definition of a project.

The above Figure 3–1 shows that the project is an endeavour in which a project with specific objectives is designed in a novel way, to undertake a work of unique scope, of given specification, to ensure the achievement of the beneficial change defined by objectives.

There is an important point implied in the above discussion: that is, the difference between a project, the facility it delivers, and the product produced by

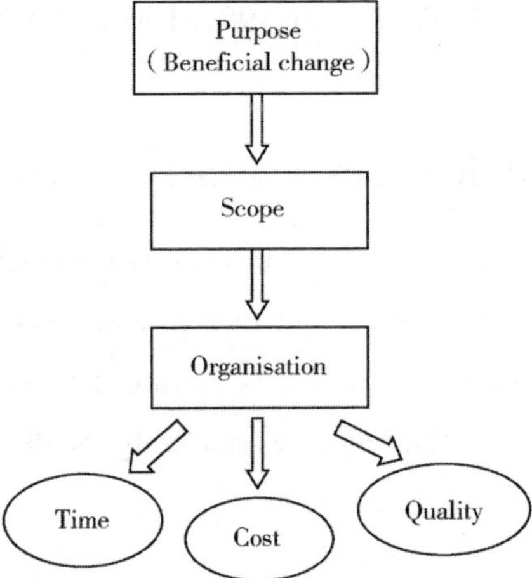

Figure 3–1 The five objectives of projects (Source: Turner, 1993)

the facility (see Figure 3–2).

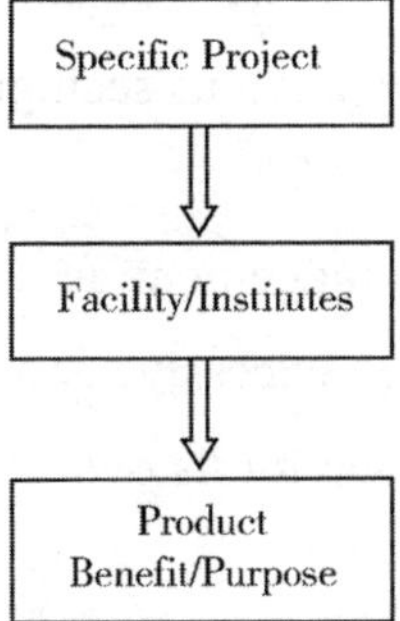

Figure 3–2 Projects, facilities and products (Source: Turner, 1993)

In the sense of this reseach, products are what the organisation or company has successfully achieved – the goal that a specific project aims to. And a project also determines where the product is produced and therefore delivers the purpose or benefit of the training participants. At the same time, facilities are required to think about where to produce the products, and these can include product designs and management processes. A project should be defined by specific objectives, and its completion marks the end of the project. Projects are undertaken by organisations in order to deliver, construct and implement a training programme for their staff (Andersen, 1987; Shared, 1986; Turner, 1993).

3.3 What is project management?

Turner (1993) answers this question from two aspects. The first answer to this question is that it is the process by which a project is completed successfully. The second is to consider whether this can be developed into a structured management approach. He continues by answering the direct question. There are two views:

- The traditional view defines project management in terms of a body of knowledge of tools and techniques.
- The alternative view, also proposed by Turner (*ibid.*), defines project management in terms of the management processes required to undertake a project as defined in the previous section.

As for defining project management as a body of knowledge, it can be argued that this view produces an excessive and unnecessary focus on the work itself, i.e. that work should be done for its own sake (Shared, 1986; Smith, 1985; Turner, 1993).

Turner (1993) also states the alternative view which defines project management as the process by which a project is completed successfully; that is, it achieves its learning purpose, whatever the learning is. There are three dimensions to this process:

- The project objectives
- The management processes to achieve the objectives
- The levels at which the processes are applied

In fact, the first dimension addresses the word 'project', the second the word 'management', and the third links project and management together, and links the project to the outside world.

Looking back at the definition of a project, it is understood that it requires the management of five project objectives. They are managing scope, managing organisations, managing quality, managing cost and managing time. So to achieve each objective requires the use of management processes that address the unique and on-going nature of projects. There are two views on management processes:

- *The problem-solving cycle* addresses the uncertainty, viewing the project's purpose as a problem, and applies standard management processes for problem solving. There are various ways of expressing this. A classic approach uses four basic steps: plan; organise; implement; control (Morris, 1979).
- *The project management life cycle* directly addresses the problem of the transient phenomenon that usually happens to a project. Having a beginning and an end, projects need to go through several stages of development.

In addition, Turner (1993) views project management as management which requires three fundamental levels. They are the intergrative level, the strategic level and tactical level. He concludes by pointing out that the issue in creating a project is to see how these three levels can be used to create a structured approach to the management of projects as a modern management discipline.

3.4 What is project-based foreign language learning?

Project-based learning (PBL) was first conceived by the efficiency expert David Snedden to teach science in American vocational agriculture classes in the early 20th century (Beckett, 2006). It was later developed and popularised for education by William Heard Kilpatrick, mainly through his pamphlet '*The*

Project Method' (Allen, 2004; Beckett, 1999; Holt, 1994). PBL was introduced into the field of second language education about two decades ago as a way to reflect the principle of learner-centred teaching and learning (Hedge, 1993). PBL is a comprehensive approach designed to engage learning participants in the investigation of real life problems (Barron, 1998; Blumenfeld *et al.*, 2001). Its defining characteristics include the use of authentic materials and a focus on learner-centred learning.

Eyring (1989), in his early second language acquisition literature, shows that the major goal for applying project-based learning and instruction is to provide opportunities for language learners who are taking English as foreign or second language to obtain comprehensive input and produce comprehensive output. Haines (1989) further examines this and identifies that the objective of project-based foreign language learning is to provide learners with opportunities to 'recycle known language and skills' in natural contexts. Many researchers show educators that apply the theory of project-based foreign language learning achieving goals such as:

- Developing analytical skills (Gardner, 1995)
- Time management skills (Coleman, 1992)
- Responsibility (Fried-Booth, 1986; Hilton-Jones, 1988)

Furthermore, it is also claimed (Beckett, 2005) that learning through a project is beneficial in terms of:

- Getting- to- know-each-other multicultures
- Learning about other cultures

At a general level, it has been referred to as a language education approach that reflects student-centred learning, which originates from the context of Western learning culture (Fried-Booth, 2002; Hedge, 1993) within the framework of experiential learning or 'learning by doing' (Eyring, 2001; Fragoulis, 2009; Kohonen, 2001; Legutke & Thomas 1991). It has also been discussed within the theoretical framework of learner autonomy (Fried-Booth, 2002; Van Lier, 2005), cooperative learning and critical thinking, which are believed to be features of the Western fashion of learning style (Nelson, 1995; Harshbarger, 1986). By organising a direct link between language learning and its application as well as through creating opportunities to study a foreign language, PBL gives those learners a channel or an opportunity to develop their abilities in the target language by interacting and communicating with native English speakers (e.g. Fried-Booth, 2002). At a more specific level, it has been described as an approach (as indicated previously) that promotes comprehensible input and output (Eyring, 1989) with the emphasis on practising listening and speaking skills and as a content-based approach (Stoller, 1997), with emphasis on teaching language and content (Stoller, 2004).

In addition, PBL has been promoted as an appropriate approach to content-based second language education (Stoller, 1997), English for specific purposes (Fried-Booth, 2002) and other foreign language-related education (Fang & Warschauer, 2004). This is largely based on the reflection that PBL ensures that the goal is reached and enables constant motivation to be maintained from the beginning to the end of the learning process through an attempt to create the learning content before the learning actions. For these reasons, there has recently been growing global interest in project-based language learning (Fang &Warschauer, 2004).

3.5 Theoretical foundation for project-based foreign languge learning

3.5.1 Constructivist theory

The characteristics of project-based learning mentioned in above section are all based on principles derived from constructivist learning theory. It is a complex combination of learning theory contributed by Jean Piaget, Lev Vigotsky and John Dewey (Matthew, 2003). Constructivist theory holds that learners play an active role in the construction of their own knowledge (Goldbery, 2003). Motivation and strategy used have a large impact on the effective learning (Levis, 2003). In the sense of learning styles, the learning of PBL needs to be learner-centred, and individual learners should be given confidence to making their own meaningful generalisations.

Piaget believes that when learners come across new knowledge in a foreign language, it causes uncertainty because learners find this new knowledge does not fit within their prexisting knowledge and ability framework (Beckett, 1999; Fosnot, 1996). This results in a deeper learning, where the learners aim to expand their preexisting schema. Uncertainty has a key role to play when learners are confronting new knowledge because it becomes a motivation to the learners (Regan, 1999; Piaget, 2000).

It is essential that PBL has to be contextualised within real world situations (Beckett, 2006; Prefume, 2007). According to Constructivist theory, learning can be facilitated when knowledge to be learned contains familiar prior learned knowledge. Therefore, learners can make meaningful connections by linking the new information to their established knowledge (Prefume, 2007). Furthermore, this is to imply that the knowledge learners obtain is more likely to transfer to new areas if they are able to see a relationship between the instructional context and that of its authentic applications (Larkin, 1989; Prefume, 2007; Oxford, 1990). When new knowledge and new skills are taught in real world contexts where learners are helped to link up their prior knowledge and related skills, learners then will be better able to apply those newly learned knowledge and skills in future settings and situations (Svinicki, 1998).

3.5.2 Benefit orientation

Although project-based learning has existed for nearly a century, it has been advocated as an effective means for promoting purposeful language learning for only 20 years or so (e.g. Fried-Booth, 1982, 1986, 2002; Haines, 1989; Ho, 2003; Legutke & Thomas, 1991; Papaunreou, 1994; Stoller, 1997). During these two decades, most support for project-based learning has stemmed from teachers' anecdotal reports of the successful incorporation of project work into language classrooms with young, adolescent and adult learners, as well as classrooms with general, vocational, academic and specific language aims (Allen, 2004; Carter & Thomas, 1986; Coleman, 1992; Ferragatti & Carminati, 1984; Gardner, 1995; Gu, 2002 and 2004; Hilton-Jones, 1988). Many reports from participants who have completed second language and foreign language projects with improved foreign language skills, content learning, real-life skill, sustained motivation and positive self-concepts have attributed this to project-based foreign language learning (Beckett & Slater, 2005).

Despite anecdotal reports with interesting insights into project work, Beckett (2006) argues that research in good conscience should build a defensible theoretical framework for project work by consulting research in the broader fields of second langauge and foreign language teaching and learning. He continues by pointing out that by exploring research on motivation and self-esteem, we might gain an understanding into why project-based learning or selected aspects of project-based learning lead to positive outcomes. By doing this, we can possibly ascertain the roots of the benefits often associated with project work and then use that information to build a strong case for project-based foreign language learning as well as inform our instructional practices in principled ways.

3.5.3 Configurations of project-based foreign language learning

The scope of project-based foreign language learning is captured by the many labels given to the process of learning that incorporates projects (Beckett, 2006):

- Experiential and negotiated language learning (Eyring, 2001; Legutke &

Thomas, 1991; Padgett, 1994)

- Investigative research (Kenny, 1993)
- Problem-based learning (Savoie & Hughes, 1994; Wood & Head, 2004)
- Project approach or project-based approach (Ho, 2003; Levis & Levis, 2003; Papandreou, 1994)
- Project work (Fried-Booth, 1986; 2002; Haines, 1989; Henry, 1994; Lee *et al.*, 1999; Phillips *et al.*, 1999)

Obviously, these labels reveal many of the features commonly attributed to PBL: experiential learning, negotiated meaning and experience, research and inquiry, problem solving and , of course, project work. Meanwhile, project-based learning is able to bring in other features as well. According to Beckett (2006), these include:

- In- class group work
- Out-of-class activities
- Cooperative learning
- Task-based instruction
- A vehicle for fully integrated language
- Content learning
- Mechanisms for cross-curricular work

Conducting a project-based foreign langugae learning programme entails elaborate sets of sequenced tasks during which students are actively engaged in information gathering, processing and reporting, with the ultimate goal of increased content knowledge and language mastery. It will have a wide range of flexible measures in managing a project based on various objectives and purposes. The foundation of building up a project is set as a functional reality because it is built upon a set of problems that require a solution. That means, as Beckett (2006) comments, that project-based learning has been translated into practice in many different ways. This may be due to the particularities and peculiarities of different instructional settings which are largely defined by the diversity of participants, instructional objectives, institutional constraints and available resources. The various configurations mentioned above also reveal the flexibility of the approach, which is a priority when choosing it to meet the diversity of demands from individual learners. The principal characteristics of project-based foreign language learning can be captured from and underpinned by the following examples given by researchers working in this field. Haines (1989) points out that project-based learning focusing on topics or themes as well as reaching an agreed goal provides participants with opportunites to recycle known language and skills in a relatively natural context. Skehan (1998) adds that project-based learning enables learners the gradual development of autonomy with progressively greater self-responsibility. It is no doubt a structure for preparing learners to undertake learning in their own way, suitable to their own ability and style (Beckett, 2005). Additionally, Hedge (2000) finds that project work can develop genuine communication needs for learners who are able to use foreign languages to negotiate, analyse and discuss information and ideas. All of these can provide the foundation for attempting to employ a project for foreign language adult learners.

What is even more essential to understand project-based learning is that it will motivate learners and maintain the efforts needed to complete the learning.

> *"Project work is participant-centred and driven by the need to create an end product. However, it is the route to achieveing this end-product that makes project work so worthwhile. The route to the end-product brings opportunities for learners to develop their confidence and independence and to work together in a real-world environment by collaborating on a task."* (Fried-Booth, 2002, p.6)

In the meantime, the research confesses that a wide variety of potential applications of project-based learning makes it difficult to conclude one single definition that takes into account the various approaches and covers everything in which the concept can be translated into practical use (Beckett, 2006). However, a definiton can be presented for the purpose of effective project-based foreign language learning to take place. Beckett continues to underpin this by pointing out that project-based learning is to possess the following properties in accordance with the three fundamental levels of project management (Levy, 1997; Turner, 1993) discussed previously.

- Have a process and product orientation
- Be defined, at least in part, by participants, to encourage their ownership in the project
- Extend over a period of time
- Encourage the natural integration of skills
- Make a dual commitment to language and content learning
- Require participants to take some responsibility for their own learning through the gathering, processing and reporting of information from target language resources
- Require tutors or programme providers and participants to assume new roles and responsibilites
- Result in a tangible final product
- Conclude with participants' reflection on both the process and the product

3.5.4 Benefits of project-based learning in EFL contexts

Although project-based learning has been advocated as an effective means for promoting language and content learning in English as a foreign language (EFL) classrooms (Beckett & Slater, 2005; Fried-Booth, 1986; 2002; Ho, 2003; Mohan & Beckett, 2001; Sheppard & Stoller, 1995; Stoller, 1997), little research has been done to explore the significance of applying project-based learning theory into project management of an organisation or a company. Most of the available literature consists of anecdotal reports of how language teachers organised project work for the purpose of English learning in a general respect. This leads to the possiblity that using a project-based learning strategy will benefit Chinese adult learners from different companies and organisations, given a project-based foreign language learning programme managed through collaborative channels with training programme providers. The immediate rationale is based on Gu's reports (2002) of a successful 12-week project that teachers organised at Suzhou University in China. This is the only literature so far available using project-based foreign language theory in language education in China. Gu finds that project-based learning enhanced Chinese EFL learners' motivation, improved their performance in writing and communication and initiated their active roles in learning. In a related report, Gu (2001) cites a Chinese learner's comment to show that project-based learning offered an opportunity for learners to communicate meaningfully.

Furthermore, Sheppard and Stoller (1995) suggest that this approach to learning theory could give insight into using similar programmes when needed. Soon after Stoller (1997) also proposed procedures to be followed to ensure that learners involved a project-based learning programme largely benefit from the learning process. These include:

- Theme agreement, learning objectives and outcomes by the participants and programme providers.
- The participants and providers structure the project.
- The participants participate in the programme and gather information.
- The participants compile and analyse information by themselves.
- The providers prepare the participants for the language demands of the culminating activity.
- The participants present the final product.

- The participants evaluate the project.

Apart from following these steps, what is vitally important is that learners will experience the authenticity that the programme can provide and the language that the learners are exposed will be learned and practised. While engaged in project work, paritcipants will take part in authentic tasks for anthentic purposes. Many practitioners report a host of benefits resulting from participants' engagement with project-based learning (Allen, 2004; Carter and Thomas, 1986; Coleman, 1992; Ferragatti and Carminati, 1984; Gardner, 1995; Gu, 2002; 2004; Stoller, 1997). Moreover, another commonly reported benefit of project-based learning is the intensity of participants' motivation, involvement, engagement, participation and enjoyment. These positive outcomes can be synthesised in the following Table 3–1.

Meanwhile, Alan (2005) stresses that project-based learning theory also inspires creativity as particpants move away from mechanistic learning and toward endeavours that allow for and benefit from creativity. This is because the participants from different areas are given a voice in defining both the process and the product of the project and are also given an opportunity to engage themselves in project planning. Besides, this type of learning also encourages an open mind and stimulates creativity, which either meets the demands from Chinese companies and organisations or serves to fill the gap in learning requirements for Chinese adults.

Table 3–1 Most common benefits attributed to project-based learning in foreign language settings

Rank	Common Benefits
1	Authenticity of experience and language
2	Intensity of motivation, involvement, engagement, participation
3	Enhanced language skills; repeated opportunities for output. Modified input and negotiated meaning; purposeful opportunities for an integrated focus on form and other aspects of language

Continued Table

Rank	Common Benefits
4	Improved abilities to function in a group (including social, cooperative and collaborative skills)
5	Increased content knowledge
6	Improved confidence, sense of self, self-esteem, attitude toward learning, comfort using language, satisfaction with achievement
7	Increased autonomy, independence, self-initiation and willingness to take responsibility for own learning
8	Improved abilities to make decisions, be analytical, think critically, solve problems

Source: Beckett (2006)

Moreover, another benefit widely reported is participants' enhanced language skills. Practitioners have reported improved reading, writing, speaking, listening, vocabulary and grammar abilities, possibly due to the fact that project work facilitates repeated opportunities for interaction or output, modified input and negotiated meaning. Apart from this, project work also lends itself to opportunities for an explicit focus on form and other aspects of language, most easily accommodated and appreciated during three aspects in the development of a project, namely just before the information-gathering, processing and reporting phases of the project (see Alan & Stoller, 2005; Sheppard & Stoller, 1995; Stoller, 1997).

The next widely reported benefit of project-based foreign language learning is participants' improved social, cooperative and collaborative skills. These skills are developed over time as participants work with peers to gather, process, synthesise and report information related to their projects to ensure that participants arrive at a successful project outcome (Alan & Stoller, 2005). In the meantime, due to the gathering, processing and reporting of "real" information related to the project theme being planned and covered, practitioners report that participants complete their projects with increased content knowledge. In fact, project work is compatible with content-based instruction and its dual commitment to content and language teaching (Stoller, 2004).

It is also reported that participants have improved self-confidence, enhanced self-esteem and positive attitudes toward learning, are more comfortable using the language and show satisfaction with personal achievements. The final outcome of the project gives participants a chance to view and assess the results of their hard work. Moreover, the tangible outcome serves "as a sort of public record of the project" (Skehan, 1998). What is more, participants will demonstrate increased autonomy, independence, self-initiation and a willingness to take responsibility for their own learning as a result of project work. Although contributing less to the projects, participants still develop a sense of ownership and pride in the projects by becoming more autonomous and independent (see Skehan, 1998).

Interestingly, it is also reported that project work results in improved decision-making abilities, analytical and critical thinking skills and problem solving. Conditions for optimal learning, in general, are said to require challenge and opportunities for decision-making, critical thinking and problem-solving (see Csikszentmihalyi, 1990, 1993, 1988; Egbert, 2003).

3.6 Project-based foreign language learning in China

Beckett (2006) produced an overview of project-based foreign language education in China. Guo (2007) further summarizes perspectives and issues in relation to project-based English as a foreign language education strategy in China, arguing that although the Ministry of Education in China in September 2001 instructed all universities to use foreign language, English in particular, as the main teaching language in the following areas: information technology, biotechnology, new-material technology, finance, foreign trade, economics and law, it is an enormous undertaking that calls for an integrated approach to language and content teaching since the English language has traditionally been taught separately from subject matter content in China (Gu, 2002; Hu, 2002a). This has resulted in that China has produced many graduates and professional talents working in a variety of occupations but has not acknowledged content and project-based foreign language learning education. Another major matter is that many Chinese education institutions have not been equipped to teach integrated English and content, concentrating on English language learning only. This obviously results in shortage of talents with blended foreign language and professional skills in Chinese companies and organisations.

Evidently as discussed previously (see Chapter 2), due to obstacles such as culture, tradition, education background and shortage of facilities, there are a number of constraints that challenge the implementation of project-based learning. Gu (2002) points out that project-based foreign language learning seems to be a great challenge for Chinese educators, who are used to teacher-centred classrooms. Both tutors and trainees need to make adjustments in transitioning from a tutor-centred structure to one that encourages student autonomy (see Levy, 1997, for a similar discussion). Fang and Warschauer (2004) report that a number of Chinese language trainees expressed discomfort with the emphasis on learner control and responsibility. For example, as one participant commented, "if all the students were asked to teach themselves, what do we need teachers for?" (Ip, 2009).

However, after attending a seminar to show some Chinese professors how to teach language and content simultaneously in 2004, Guo (2007) changed her mind and concluded, based on a questionnaire distributed to the professors after the seminar, that the professors were enthusiastic about employing project-based foreign language learning because they recognised its value. In order to make better use of it, at the same time, they also discussed a variety of constraints that might inhabit the adoption of project-based learning in China. Professors' concerns with regards to implementing project-based learning could be highlighted as following:

- Challenging tutors and training participants' traditional perspectives and notions of teaching and learning

- Desiring knowledge of how to manage these steps first before they would be able to help their trainees
- Unable to provide appropriate guidance for students due to little knowledge about this
- Unable to find sufficient resources available to effect learning because of inaccuracy and out-datedness of many resources available
- Difficult for participants to access authentic materials in English
- Difficult to manage participants to present their learning outcomes
- Unable to efficiently evaluate the programme

3.7 Summary and discussion

This chapter has discussed several concepts in relation to projects and a project-based foreign language learning theory. It explains that a project is a unique scope of work and is usually undertaken using a novel approach aiming to achieve beneficial change. It has also examined project management and indicated that project management is the process by which a project is brought to a successful conclusion. Meanwhile, this chapter continues to discuss project-based foreign language learning which has earned the endorsement of many second language and foreign language practitioners over the past 20 years as many researchers believe and report there are positive effects on language learners' motivation, language skills, ability to function in groups, content learning, self-confidence, autonomy and decision-making abilities. Although not having fully been acknowledged by Chinese educators, it has increasingly drawn many researchers' attention, as many researchers' and teachers' assertions are supported by studies in areas related to motivation, the development of expertise, the role of input and output in language learning and the value of learner-centeredness in learning instruction. Research in these areas suggests that the following conditions contribute to the positive outcomes so often associated with project-based learning:

- The project should be content-driven.
- Participants need be engaged in a complex set of manageable yet challenging tasks. The tasks should be structured so that participants have the opportunity to reinvest knowledge in progressively more complex problem-solving activites.
- Participants must be given real choices, possibly through the negotiation of selected aspects of the project (including goals, themes, procedures, outcomes).
- Projects must be defined and orchestrated to stimulate participants' curiosity and interest.
- Participants should be held accountable for their work.
- Participants should be given the opportunity to engage in the deliberate practice of the skills and language required for the successful completion of each stage of the project.
- Particpants must be given on-going feedback so that they can evaluate their own learning, progress and attainment of process- and product-oriented goals.

A vital point needs to be made regarding the goals for project-based instruction in second language acquistion. Clearly, as it is presented in the literature, project-based foreign language learning instruction has great potential for teaching foreign languages to Chinese adults in accordance with their educational background and language qualification obtained. It is also a viable approach to tackle the dilemmar challenging Chinese foreign language education. Moreover, it is worthy of research incorporating the theory into the practice of training Chinese adult through muticultural collaboration. This is based on the fact that it has been noted that project-based foreign language education is not being utilised to its fullest potential. As Beckett (2006) suggests, researchers need to re-examine the general literature as well as practise further to find out if and how general education goals may be imported into the field of foreign language teaching and learning. Skills such as problem-solving, critical thinking, decision-making, independent and cooperative working, and in-depth learning of subject matter should be developed across the entire learning strategy.

From all of the above it follows that project-based foreign language learning can potentially be incorporated into training programmes for Chinese employees. It seems to be the most suitable learning theory which can be used for training programmes for Chinese staff as far as practicality is concerned and if its relevant components are involved. In other words, project-based foreign language learning theory offers a platform to establish an innovative channel through which a foreign language training programme for Chinese adults learning a foreign language in an international background could possibly be carried out. However, to justify this proposal there are still a number of questions that need to be addressed in terms of how to incorporate Chinese adults' learning styles, how to embrace the real demands from Chinese companies and organisations, and how to fill the gap between the provider's offer and Chinese adults' needs. To answer these questions, an innovative model needs to be created which will be welcomed by both partners and can be successfully and strategically managed through multicultural management.

Chapter 4 A Historical Review of the Approaches Used in Training Programmes

4.1 Introduction

In this chapter, the research aims at analysing how foreign language training providers operate their programmes and the elements that determine sucess. A detailed explanation of UK and non-UK perspectives on foreign language training strategy and its management will exhibit the advantages and disadvantages that lie ahead if conducting a foreign language programme for China's companies and organisations. Moreover, a review is also conducted of two prevalent and representative programmes run by various foreign language training suppliers across the world, and the language learning theories underpinning the implementation of two existing programmes. This information is required in order to make sense of the operation and performance of foreign language programmes which will feed into analysis that seeks to identify deficiencies in the current programmes.

4.2 Guidelines for training providers

Smith and Arkless (1993) outlined guildelines on good practice in foreign language training and they highlighted the practice by The Association of

Language Excellence Centres (ALEC) as an example for other providers. ALEC is a representive professional body and information source committed to developing the profile and analysing the quality of business and professional foreign language training. In 1993, ALEC released an agreed document with the collective views of some 50 Language Excellence Centres, written for the benefit of organisations and educational institutions that intend to provide language services that assist the business community in responding to the opportunities of the intercultural market (ALEC, 2002; Smith & Arkless, 1993). The document gives a broad outline of the quality of service to be expected from a Language Excellence Centre, as agreed by ALEC members at the Brasshouse Centre meeting on 4th Nov., 1992. The Guidelines explain in more detail what they believe constitutes good practice which can inspire training providers to effectively undertake foreign language training for organisations engaged in intercultural business. These are summarised in section 4.2.1 to 4.2.3.

4.2.1 Professionalism

Smith and Arkless (1993) state that being a provider of foreign language training should have an underlying commitment to quality. This will depend most directly on those responsible for the operational management of the supply. Being a qualified provider one should be professional in one's attitude with appropriate business skills and experience, in particular the ability to organise. The quality of any language centre should be well-defined with clear objectives and responsibilites. Besides, service providers should also be expected to cover all competencies involved in management: aspects such as customer service, total quality management and competent manner in negotiation, etc. Smith and Arkless (*ibid.*) emphasise that professional delivery has to be matched by professional management. Foreign langauge teaching not only has to be applied to meet the needs of business but also has to be complemented by other skills such as professional work-related skills required by the customer.

4.2.2 Training needs analysis and a language evaluation

The factors that impact most on the effectiveness of foreign language training are largely determined by a needs analysis before the programme and a language evaluation after it (Canagarajah 2002; Snow *et al.*, 1989). This requires language training providers to conduct a training needs analysis for each individual to be trained as part of any corporate programme. This encompasses details of the individual, their position, a brief job description and general language background, present level of language skills, expected relevant skills to be trained and learned and specific reasons or goals for training. In addition to this, more specific information should then be identified about their likely use of the role of the language in different working backgrounds. In these respects, guidelines for foreign language providers point out the important role of needs analysis and thus advocate that these should be undertaken by giving different values for each, e.g. on a Likert scale.

Furthermore, Smith and Arkless (1993) suggest that organisations and companies need to conduct a language audit in an attempt to assess the effectiveness of both the programme management itself and the development of the language ability of trainees. The assessment will rely on a thorough assessment managed by the training providers, and the outcome or feedback from the assessment will be then presented to the companies or organisations. Companies and organisations will take the outcome as an evidence to evaluate whether the needs both of individuals and organisations have been met in line with the companies' or organisation's objectives.

In addition, Smith and Arkless (*ibid.*) continue their arguments in support of the importance of feedback by commenting that client feedback from companies and organisations is equally important to either assuring the quality of present programmes or improving training management for the future. However, they also mention that clients are not necessarily in a position to comment on the finer points of language teaching and learning, since their ideas of good and bad may be heavily coloured by their work experiences and other misleading influences. For this reason, there have been attempts to rule out feedback from companies and organisations expecially in the context of intercultural collaborative learning has also frequently taken place (Svinicki, 1998).

4.2.3 Pedagogy

As for ALEC's Guidelines on Good Practice in the Management and Delivery of Foreign Language, it concludes that there is no panacea for learning a foreign language (Larkin, 1989; Smith & Arkless 1993). It also identifies a general consensus on an eclectic approach which lays emphasis on the following (*ibid.*):

- Training sessions should be in or through the target language as far as possible rather than about it. The ambience of learning should be predominantly that of the target language.
- Emphasis on use of the language as much as possible for real communication is vital and infinitely more effective than concentration on learning the form of the language as endless repetition in which no message is involved.
- Actual work where the foreign language is widely used is much more helpful for learners in order to have a deep understanding of the meaning of a language they have been learning.
- Teaching should never go beyond content-based language.

Although cautioning not to go beyond content-based language learning and teaching, the guidelines, still remains to foucs on target foreign language acquisition. They have not clearly defined the aspects of *what* content and *what* work experience to involve.

4.3 Practice of foreign language training in the UK

The training institutes in the UK have largely been in line with the guidelines mentioned above. Language training has been a prominent element of government policy aimed at increasing educational competitiveness in the UK (CILT, 2003; Clarke, 1999; Hagen, 1999; Morgan, 1997: Wright and Wright, 1994). This results in the traditional belief that Language skills contribute to international success and an improved understanding of intercultural collaborative business partners' culture (Clarke, 1999).

Brumfit (2004) highlights the characteristics of foreign language training providers designing programmes for trainees, and draws attention to the following points a training institute is required to meet if intending to deliver a language course:

- Improve language-related abilities such as speaking, listening, reading and writing, which focus on developing communicative ability.
- Identify and disseminate successful collaboration models which are directed towards the promotion of language skills only.
- Develop programmes to raise awareness of the importance of language skills and of the availability of a support system.
- Improve the articulation required to the needs of business.

Knowles (2006) takes the view that the dominant view on literature of foreign language training running in the UK emerges from a macro-level analysis that success is primarily dependent on developing trainees' communicative competence, namely foreign language skills including speaking, listening, reading and writing, only within individual markets. This has resulted in a significant amount of expenditure and energy going into this predominant aspect of foreign language training in companies and organisations as the prime means of helping them avoid losing business in overseas markets. Unsurprisingly this perception has been exported into language training programme within international markets (*ibid.*).

4.4 UK perspective of training foreign language

Manolova and Manev (2004) differentiate between internally "controllable" factors which consist of the psychological management attitude depending on people's perceptions of language proficiency, and externally "uncontrollable" factors which include the demographic management characteristics, such as time and effort consumed and approaches employed. Their review concluded that overall it is the externally uncontrollable factors which have greater effect on success than the internally controllable ones (Krowles, 2006; Mughan, 1993).

This perception underpins the UK perspective on developing language skills in a training programme and also leads to the rationale for running foreign language programmes. From the perspective of a large number of UK foreign language providers, according to Manolova and Manev (2004), language proficiency is a non-deciding element that is studied by a group of decision-makers in relation to the internationalisation of business purpose. This conclusion is mainly based on various factors. Firstly, it is believed that training foreign language is only undertaken for sake of developing language skills themselves and has nothing to do with the ultimate goal of the individual trainee (Oxford, 1990). Secondly, to master a foreign language is often seen as a therapy for lack of success in internationalisation in a way that other solutions have not attained. The obvious evidence is shown by the survey conducted by Footitt (2005) who aims to discover the specific strategy to avoid the pitfall of lack of foreign language skills. The specific strategy includes claiming to offer language training to their staff, appointing native speakers, recruiting staff with language skills and using translators and interpreters. These strategies are defined as "the take-for-granted adoption of a range of techniques to facilitate effective communication with clients and suppliers abroad" (*ibid.*, p.2), which apparently are short term measures rather than an attempt to achieve strategic sustainability. Thirdly, the categorisation of language proficiency among staff in terms of increasing the value of business is usually problematic and likely to arouse controversy. Previous research places language proficiency in the category of "controllable" (Manolova and Manev, 2004), and this should keep trainers highly alert when designing a training programme. What is more, developing foreign language skills is usually achieved following a great deal of hard work which includes time, energy and effort that is precisely tailored to meet particular training demands (Harris, 2005).

However, developing a foreign language skill depends on the trainee's attitude and perceptions and might be changed to belong to the demographic traits and "uncontrollable" and "subjective" (Morgan, 1997). Foreign language trainees need to demonstrate a conscientious, well-motivated commitment to enhancing communication with foreigners and understanding of foreign cultures to ensure mutual development (Manolova and Manev, 2004; Knowles, 2006).

4.5 Foreign language training programmes managed by non-UK organisations

A growing assumption is that foreign language capability is a prerequisite for entry to the global economy (Chen *et al.*, 2006). This certainly incentivises many developed countries such as the USA, UK, France, and Germany and other European countries as well as Japan and Korea to make efforts to develop more effective and appropriate foreign language training programmes. This study will look at two representative programmes, task-based and content-based learning programme and online Chinese project, which have so far been generated and widely implemented into real international collaboration programmes at USA universities such as the University of Pennsylvania Lander

Institute.

4.5.1 Task-based and content-based learning programme

The task-based learning and content-based learning are well-known as the 'Bangalore Project' (Beretta, 1985; Brumfit, 1984b) initiated in 1979 and completed in 1984. The word 'task' is often used to refer to the special kind of activities carried out in learning settings. Such activities are usually depicted by the emphasis placed on meaning and the involved skills assigned to the process of how to do things, and the prevailing role given to content in the teaching and learning practice (Sanchez, 2004).

Conceptually, a task-based and content-based learning programme is based on the theory of constructivism (Goldberg, 2002). It is a philosophical approach viewing reality as socially constructed (Robson, 1993). It is considered that the task of the construction, either abstractly or concretely, is to understand the multiple social constructions of meaning and knowledge. The proposed task and content are intended to gain knowledge which allows the acquisition of multiple perspectives. A constructivist-based training programme to improve work performance will, therefore, emphasise the role of the individual learner in constructing knowledge about tasks. It encourages learners to actively collect the information, ideas, and tasks to be learned, and instructs them in developing language abilities (Chong & Duance, 2003).

Babanoury (2006), a researcher at the University of Pennsylvania, presents the unique feature of offering a task-based and content-based learning programme to students with a business background according to the Lander Institute of Management and International Studies at the University of Pennsylvania. He comments that:

> *"(t)he core mission of the Lauder Institute is aimed to bring up business students for their roles in their future career by improving their language skills, teaching them how to bridge cultures with ease and become*

truly assimilated to the surrounding cultures on which they will later rely in making a global professional business." (p.17)

The programme has three separate but interrelated objectives corresponding to three different levels in its implementation: Content, language acquisition and culture (Babanoury, 2006).

This programme has stressed the individual needs analysis according to Babanoury's (2006) investigation. Babanoury (2006) continued to explain in this research that the teaching of language for business purposes is highly ranked in the needs analysis before a training programme starts and puts forward the claim that the main appropriate features characterising the programme are inclusive of:

- Language for special use purposes, business in context
- Content-based instruction
- Task-based teaching
- Communicative language teaching
- Technology
- Adult language proficiency

The objectives and designs of this project were also in line with the US National Standards for Foreign Language Learning and organised into five goal areas known as the "Five C's" (Karen, 2000). They are:

- Communication
- Culture
- Connections
- Comparison
- Communities

Stryke and Leaver (1997) examine content-based instruction and write that the 'new goal' is to empower learners to become autonomous learners and that abilities in English language skills, communicative competence and other skills are acquired during the process of learning about a specific task. The role of the individual learner has been placed on the top, which is in accordance to the theme of constructivism. The aim of the programme is also based on the essence which is "the engagement of learners in communication to allow them to develop their 'Five C's' and which also "doesn't exclude a focus on other aspects such as linguistic awareness or knowledge of rules of syntax, discourse and appropriateness" (Savignon, 2003). However, he continues to argue that it might be one of the best choices for a programme model aiming at language skills only. This proposal is contentious.

According to Vygotsky, learning always involves some types of external experience being transformed into internal processes through the use of language (Newman, 1997; Snow, 1989). Vygotsky also advocates promoting the development of higher level thinking and problem solving in language training, and expresses that if learning situations are designed to have learners utilise critical thinking skills in connection to their experiences or learned knowledge, their thought processes are being activated and new knowledge gained (Littlewood, 2006). Vygotsky's concept of "Zone of Proximal Development" is of relevance here, that is: the distance between the actual development level as determined by independent problem solving and the level of potential development as determined through problem solving under adult guidance, or in collaboration with more capable peers (Norton & Toohey, 2001). He also argues that rather than examining how to determine learner's intelligence, it is better to examine their ability to solve problems independently (Berk & Winsler, 1995). In this respect, the task-based and content-based project programme were designed as the implementation and testing of a learner-centred educational model aimed at enhancing business language use (Babanoury, 2006).

In spite of the goal of improving language proficiency and level of cultural awareness, business-related tasks for each member were also included in the programme encompassing the following topics: i) the study of French legislation on franchises; ii) strategies against competition; iii) the localisation of an American product for the French market and the financial cost of opening a franchise. The business tasks of the marketing teams looked at the typical consumer profile and U.S. versus French consumer habits as well as the advertising strategy used in the U.S. in the business field both teams focused on.

Prior to the beginning of implementation of the project programme, work on expectations either in terms of language and business and analysis had to be done in the language classroom in preparation for ensuring the success of the project programme. Regarding the language, specific language tasks were practised with learners and the relevant necessary vocabulary was introduced, such as the vocabulary to present and defend opinions, to challenge other people's points of views, to hypothesise or to guess at meaning and to summarise, etc. (Babanoury, 2005).

The programme was planned collaboratively with four different sessions (Figure 4–1).

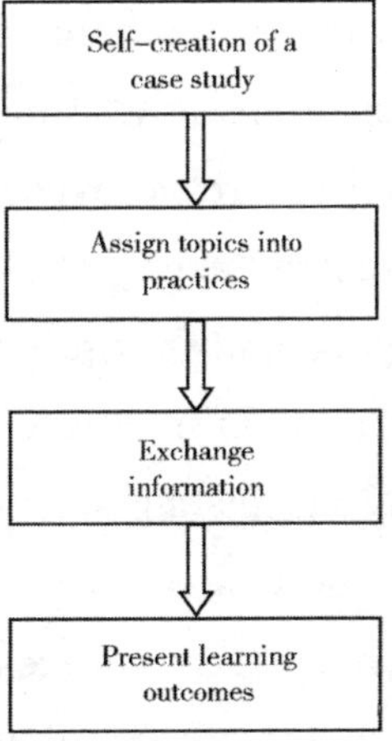

Figure 4–1 Four sessions of task-based and content-based (Babanoury, 2005).

The first session was to set up the project details requiring self-creation of a case study based on each participant's work background: this was conducted between faculty, technology specialties and administrative staff of the two partner institutions in an attempt to clear up the barriers in terms of technology. The second was to introduce themselves to each other and to discuss the role of franchiser/franchisee, and assign topics of research for the next two sessions. The third was to exchange in-depth information about the region which both groups were located and interested in. Both structured and unstructured discussions were held. The last session was to organise studio audience to determine the capability of managing and developing related business with three segments of strategy, marketing and logistics. Each segment would be run with presentation and debate. The further discussion on this programme will come in section 4.6.

4.5.2 Online Chinese project

The Online Chinese project is another currently widely used programme model. The Online Chinese project is an initiative with an adaptive core curriculum constructed and designed by the Penn Lander CIBER faculty and staff. It is a joint degree programme combining an MBA from the Wharton School with an MA in International Studies from Penn's School of Arts and Sciences. Apart from designing solid training in language and culture competency at a superior level in accordance with the guidelines of the American Council for the Teaching of Foreign Languages, the institution has also initiated a series of business language programmes at survival level. This capability aims to further effective communication in international business situations where English or other languages play a mediating role (Kuo, 2005).

The theoretical basis of the Online Chinese Project is Schank's Goal-based Scenario (1992) which seeks to address the mismatch between the participants' interests and the design of the learning objectives. In pointing out that the learning goal directs one's desire or interest to change ones knowledge base, Schank put forward a curriculum design based on workable Goal-based Scenarios that motivate participants to learn and to develop the skills to serve their learning goals. The curriculum includes:

- The need to have clear target skills to be learned throughout the training
- Specific cases that illustrate skills during the training
- Identification of facts that are generalised from case studies
- Definition of subjects that together classify the specific skills and cases across the duration of the training programme
- Design of domains that show specialised areas of interest used as a learning background for skills and cases
- Design of processes that learners will go through as they acquire knowledge and skills

Anchored instruction theory also provides a basis for running the Online Chinese programme. The anchored instruction approach is a way to set up "an anchor" to help learners become more actively engaged in learning by attaching it to real situational instruction around an interesting topic. The learning environments are designed using rich instructional materials to bring out participants' engagement that assists learners to develop effective thinking skills and attitudes that contribute to effective problem solving and critical thinking (Oliver & Omari, 1999; Oliver, 2010).

The rationale for anchored instruction is to emphasise the need to provide learners with opportunities to think about and work on problems, which is an emphasis of cognitive constructivists. Anchored instruction also emphasises group or collaborative problem solving (Cognitions and technology group at Vanderbilt, 1990, pp 5-6). It suggests that learners' knowledge often remains "inert" and cannot be activated if not responding to changing problems. It situates learning in realistic problems, allowing learners to experience professional dilemmas in a given field (*ibid.*).

Inevitably the goal behind the Online Chinese project's design of the online curriculum is to overcome the "inert knowledge problem", a feature similar to Chinese learners' "introverted learning style" as discussed in Chapter 2: a quiet, shy and reticent approach in the process of learning (Liu, 2009; Chen, 2003), in which people perceive knowledge as facts rather than as tools and thus fail to apply relevant knowledge to solve problems in their real lives (Kuo, 2005; Dinmore, 1997). Anchored instruction is a key teaching approach for overcoming the inert knowledge problem with situated and problem solving learning environments which help learners to transform facts into tools (Kuo, 2005).

Apart from determining the basic structure of the series of scenarios by the theories of Goal-based Scenarios and Anchored Instruction, the next problem for the Online Chinese project to solve is that of how participants explore and uncover problems they might encounter when they are engaged themselves in goal-based scenarios. The very question needed to be examined for the Online Chinese project is that of how the target linguistic features can be presented properly across the entire learning process (Kuo, 2005; p.6). In other words, without a proper pace of guidance learners could be too overwhelmed to encode the message intended to be conveyed by the sounds, the linguistic forms and the meanings in the target language in the designed scenarios. In view of this, therefore, the Online Chinese project adopts the traditional cognitive apprenticeship approach (Collins *et al.*, 1991) as a model of instruction. It aims to help the learners transmit knowledge using modelling, coaching, scaffolding, fading and exploration (Du *et al.*, 2005; Jonassen, 1999; Kuo, 2005).

Similarly, cognitive apprenticeships are representative of Vygotskian "zones of proximal development " in which learners' tasks are slightly more difficult than learners can manage independently, requiring the aid of their peers and instructor to succeed. Cognitive apprenticeships reflect situated cognition theory (Brown, 1989).

In light of the theories above, the Online Chinese project designs the target of the training programme by using Goal-based scenarios and constructs cognition ability backed up with Anchored Instruction to deal with realistic problems and carries out the training programme based on perception of the theory of Cognitive Apprenticeship. This aims to achieve the objectives of the programme as is described in the following (Kuo, 2005):

- Focus on Form

The Online Chinese project emphasises, as Long and Robinson (1998) put it, a focus on form. In contrast to traditional teaching methods (such as the Communicative Teaching Method), the online Chinese project is a popular method accepted by many teachers in formal instruction over decades. The Communicative Teaching Method, however, only focuses on meaning and the Online Chinese project emphasised the significance of teaching grammar. This is as a result of a substantial amount of evidence which reveals the constraints on adult learners acquiring a foreign language by simply exposing them to the target language (Ellis, 1985). The Online Chinese project online programme has revisited the importance of grammar instruction. Larsen-Freeman (2002) gave his support to this by stating that grammar allows flexibility for language learners to express more complex meanings, such as explaining a notion or proposing an idea. Thus grammar carries meaning and use in a foreign language, rather than being only a formality. It directs adult trainees to pay more attention to linguistic forms, implicitly or explicitly, when they are engaged in negotiating, comprehending or producing meaning in the target language (Doughty and Williams, 1998).

- Focus on Consciousness-raising

Ellis (1994) advocates consciousness-raising, a language-learning process that can draw a learner's attention to linguistic features before producing them.

This is possible because consciousness-raising tasks do not involve a learner's language production and are directed by the explicit knowledge of the language features presented. The Online Chinese project takes this into account by supplying a consciousness-raising task as the scenario-guessing exercise in the modelling stage at the very beginning of each lesson. Scenario-guessing is an exercise that encourages learners to predict what will happen in the scenarios with texts that connect to sounds and pictures. This will help learners to attain language learning objectives, such as vocabulary and sentences intended for use in the later stage in a learning context provided for them, associating sounds and visual aids with possible meaning from the texts. When the students proceed to the vocabulary exercises after scenario-guessing, some of the information in the scenarios becomes what Krashen (1981, cited in Ellis, 1994) termed "learnt knowledge", which monitors and facilitates the accuracy of language output in the next vocabulary exercise. Targets for learners' further learning will be built upon that learnt knowledge that learners have internalised.

- Focus on Communicative Drill

The Online Chinese project instructor facilitates a language activity that allows learners to produce target vocabulary and sentences. This activity is designed on the basis of what De Keyser (1998) called the "communicative drill". The concept of this derives from the cognitive perspective that learners can maintain knowledge in the working memory by using the target to convey meaning in the sense of mechanical, meaningful and communicative training. The training would lead to the automatic use of the target linguistic feature. The scaffolding stage, one of the five methods to transmit knowledge and based on in-class activities, has been conducted to assist the implementation of De keyser's communicative drill, where the instructor can facilitate and observe learners as they accomplish tasks in an environment that is both learner-centred and based on language communication (Kuo, 2005).

4.6 Discussion

4.6.1 UK guidelines and its practice

UK guidelines for managing foreign language training programmes have provided us with a useful model to be followed. It is noted that facilities, training needs and pedagogy have been acknowledged as the basic elements to ensure foreign language training can be effectively undertaken. Particularly, pedagogy has provided a practical approach to learning the target language through the real world, and therefore it requires training programmes to focus on learning through actual content-based work. This is basically supplying availability to Chinese partners where demand lies in access to the real English-speaking world with teaching closely related to learners' working experience.

We have noted that there is a debate among UK trainers as to the value of language learning to trainees if taking into account the global use of English (Hagen, 1999). There also has differences of opinion as to the usefulness of foreign language skills to trainees who have them in terms of both how far the skills go and to what use they might be put (Hegan, 1999; Knowles, 2006). Additionally, what are the detailed learning objectives, how to define them, and how they are designed to achieve and also fit in both Chinese and English educational cultures for running programmes in the context of strategic management? (Mintzberg, 1988). There is abundant controversy among British programme providers and these perspectives have also led to a dilemma in innovation for training programme management. These views include:

- On one side, the international success of British businesses is often said to be restricted by low levels of trade partner's English skills, which leads to a perception that it is necessary for those trainees to be proficient in their foreign languages (CILT, 2003; Hagen, 1999).

- On the other side, foreign language ability is largely considered to be more important as a "bridge to culture" than as a tool for communication taking place in the middle of international trading exchange (Johnson, 2008; Shanahan, 1997).

Williams and Chaston (2004) point out that there is a lack of consensus as to whether the linguistic skills of trainees from companies and organisations bring about international success, but there is recognition that foreign language proficiency may facilitate a "more general cultural sensitivity".

These debates and arguments not only lead to the dilemma whether language skills and cultural awareness can only be explored and developed so that they can set up a potential channel to build up links with international business. These doubts actually arouse concerns that foreign language qualifications which many foreign language training providers have been focusing on might be an important element to develop for the language trainees, but does it cover everything that companies and organisations from China really need? Is it the only benefit those companies and organisations are intending to achieve?

To answer these questions, we are inevitably concerned with the sustainability a strategic managerial programme needs to possess (Mintzberg, 1988). In view of this, it is unrealistic to ignore the unsustainable views that the guidelines propose. Generally there are two folded objectives for a language training programme as far as the context of sustainability is concerned. One aims to develop programmes to raise awareness of communicative language skills (Johnson, 2008); and the other is to maintain collaborative relations in the long run in strategic management for both training providers and clients (CILT, 2003). At this point, however, programme guidelines and relevant programmes have neglected to attach importance to maintaining training programmes into a sustainable strategy. As the foreign language itself is usually regarded as one of the "controllable factors", it needs to be converted into the "uncontrollable" in the context of international educational management.

4.6.2 Two existing programmes

Nevertheless, both task-based learning and the online Chinese project have provided us with a literature which inspires us to examine what essential elements and components need involving when devising a tailored model for Chinese adults. According to Chinese adult's learning style and the background of learning English in China (see literature review in chapter two), in the sense of pedagogic design, attention needs to be drawn to incorporating Focus on Form into teaching for Chinese adult staff, and equally on Communicative drill and consciousness raising because Chinese adults have been used to the traditional learning which usually starts with forms and then communicative drill (Hu, 2005a; 2005b). At the same time, they also show us that they are inappropriate if they are applied to training programmes with a Chinese cultural background in terms of how to evaluate the learning objectives prior to the implementation of a training programme and how to assess the learning outcomes.

To explicitly illustrate the gap existing in the current two programmes, they are compared and synthesised in terms of the following aspects (see Table 4–1).

A task-based learning or content-based programme is designed for foreign language learning for business purposes only and it requires of participants to achieve the five C's – communication, culture, connections, comparison and communities. The goal of achieving the five C's is to help adult learners to become autonomous learners and at the same time train them in developing linguistic awareness or language knowledge rules. Apparently, the programme as such is designed to heavily emphasise the outcomes relating to foreign language abilities only, as it requires explicitly description of the task and content intended to be learnt prior to the launch of the programme. However, it ignores motivation, an essential factor which incentivises learners to engage totally with the training to ensure the positive effects of the programme. Nevertheless, the Online Chinese project puts more emphasis on the issue by addressing the mismatch between participants' motivation and the objectives designed. The highlighted points are as follows:

- Enhancing materialisation of the need of learners by determining clear target skills throughout the training
- Situating learning in realistic problems to overcome the 'inert' knowledge problem
- Exploring problems learners might encounter and then transmitting knowledge into actual skills for solving problems

It is observed that on the one hand, a task-based and content-based programme is an innovation in creating a more effective training programme for distance learning. On the other hand, it is also a new challenge for the instructors who either have to manage carefully between two different classrooms or take on a heavier workload than usually required for conventional programmes. However, the instructors thus became mainly facilitators and coordinators of the project, which was otherwise autonomously conducted by the learners (Banaoury, 2006).

In fact, the participants of the task-based and content-based programme had mixed feelings about the improvement in their language competence. This is shown in the investigation conducted by Banaoury (2006) in the almost equal distribution of responses from the participants of "somewhat" and "yes" when asked if they had improved their language and presentation skills through training using the task-based and content-based programme designed by the University of Pennsylvania. Most interesting of all is, however, that when asked to comment on the positive aspects of the project, the learners mentioned the value of appropriate expressions to address concrete and specific topics of concern to each individual, the use of language for correspondence, an improvement in business vocabulary, an improvement in the linguistic ability to introduce oneself and an improvement in the style of communication in the foreign language (*ibid.*).

Banaoury (2006) continued to point out that after the investigation the learners overwhelmingly indicated that through this project they had learned how foreign companies where the target language is spoken work and operate. Meanwhile, he also found that learners expressed concerns that their learning objectives were not fully met, and surprisingly they were subsequently willing to acquire more skills and related knowledge and technologies other than language qualification. However, the programme apparently does not anticipate these demands from trainees. Moreover, there are some learners who had little knowledge about the target foreign language they learnt and said, negatively, they had not learnt much more. So it seems as if there is a paradox as far as the effectiveness of the programme is concerned in particular for the management of this type of training programme.

Table 4–1 below highlights the positive and negative points from comparison between task-based and content-based programme and the Online Chinese project.

4.6.2.1 Strengths

- *Shortening distance* – both projects employ "distance learning" (Bates, 1997), which could be seen as an alternative approach to resolving the problem of distance when learning is engaged; this technology facilitates greatly the mutual learning of virtual teams about each other.
- *Technology application* (Sethi, 1994) – the level of appreciation of the technology applied in both programmes facilitates the ease of communication which is particularly important for adult students who are working on their business language.
- *Enhancing communication skills* (Charles, 2002) – both projects have greatly empowered learners on several levels: language development,

cultural and cross-cultural knowledge, negotiating skills and business acuity.

- *Learner-centred learning* (Hutchinson, 1987) – both also achieve the goal of task-based and content-based activities which require the learner to perform them autonomously. It is worthy of the time and effort put into them by adult learners.
- *Multiple strategies* (Madeline, 1990) – both projects require commitment, high motivation, time, mental energy, self-confidence and multiple coping strategies both on the instructors' and on the participants' sides.
- *Learning objectives allocation* – the participants have an opportunity to choose which company they are going to study, so it helps them to define the objectives precisely and hence solve the problems based on the intended content-base (Anon, 2006).

4.6.2.2 Weaknesses

- *Assessment* – It is difficult for participants to assess the outcome of how much they have learned from such an experience because there are no specific assessment criteria being utilised.
- *Language skills improvement* – In such projects, language recycling activities are designed to achieve to improve language skills through distance technological assistant. However it is impossible to achieve a substantial improvement on language ability skill because distance technological assistant cannot provide authentic language environment. Therefore, it is impossible to fix or repair what might have been heard or read, which is vital to improve foreign language ability for adult learners (Ellis, 1985; Jaramillo, 1996; Krashen, 1981).
- *Distance* – distance learning creates difficulties in organizing and managing the programme effectively and finding solutions due to space

distance as well as time difference.

- *Technological facility* – having to face the high technological equipment required for distance learning, according to the feedback from participants (Babanoury, 2006), also triggers the problem of lack of involvement in the programme. Most adult students displayed some reluctance in engaging themselves in the project.
- *Learning environment* – the most difficult part that both instructors and participants felt hard to adhere to were the directions or objectives they were intended to follow because communication among them was effected with the help of a technological tool, instead of sharing something of a more personal nature, like their travel experiences or their special interests in life.
- *Facility-dependent* – Although the project was originally conceived to display an important technological innovation as a case, the success of the project was not clear. This is largely due to the shared understanding that such a foreign language training programme does potentially rely on technological facilities but is not just a matter of bandwidth, cameras, protocols and video-servers. It actually matters to learners which learning devices are used and what the appropriate one is to match their learning targets and learning needs.
- *Time consumption* – it will normally take a much longer time than the usual time allocated to general foreign language training programmes, which is definitely a constraint on the degree of flexibility. The aim was to provide more options for those who have limited time and are keen on arriving at proficiency in the short-term.
- *High cost* – Additionally and most importantly, the level of technology demanded for this model is extremely high both in the cost of investment in facilities and in the qualifications needed to be able to operate it. This depends on which firm, surely.

4.7 Summary

To summarise, this chapter has critically reviewed the guidelines for UK training providers in an attempt to demonstrate the rationale for designing and running a foreign language training programme. It is noted that there is potential for UK training providers to provide a quality-assured training programme through collaborative strategy in terms of the aspects of professionalism, facilities, training needs analysis and pedagogy. However, it also has a potential lack of sustainability due to it focusing on developing communicative competence only rather than expanding to wider range of skills such as work-related skills that trainees demand, converting an 'uncontrollable' component to 'controllable' status (Manolova and Manev, 2004).

Meanwhile, the review has also taken a close look at two up-to-date and representative programmes. Attention has been drawn to their theoretical background which underpins and boosts the influence of the programmes. The significant language training approaches highlighted in the programmes are actually consonant with the prevalent approaches for the development of current language training programmes in the world and can shed light on creating novel modes different from other competitors' strategies. It is hoped that these approaches can be incorporated into any training programme managed for Chinese adults who are intending to study English as a foreign language. Nevertheless, it is also essential for researchers to take a close look at and analyse the existing programmes in an attempt to reflect on innovation in the management of foreign language training. In practice, they still have weaknesses which need to be improved for future purposes, despite their advantages.

Table 4–1 **Outcome of comparison between two programmes**

Programme	Facility requirement	Model	Content Learned	Language outcomes	Other abilities required to develop	Cultural factors	Theoretical features	Sequence of implementation
Skill-based and content-based	High-technology	Online and long-distance	○ Using authentic materials ○ Internet background resources ○ Audio archived materials	○ Using authentic materials ○ Internet background resources ○ Audio archived materials	○ Linguistic awareness ○ Knowledge of rules of syntax, discourse and appropriateness ○ Solve problems independently (learner-centred learning)	Not addressed	Not addressed	○ Case self-creation ○ Case discussion ○ Information exchange ○ Questions determined and solutions addressed through presentation
Online Chinese Project	High-technology	Online and long-distance	○ Language and cultural awareness ○ Courses designed for developing MBA students	○ Defining skills throughout the training before implementation ○ Cognitive ability ○ Enhancing grammar ability	○ Negotiation ○ Communication ○ Consciousness-raising ○ Learner-centred learning	Not addressed	○ Goal-based scenarios ○ Anchored instruction ○ Cognitive apprenticeship	○ Goal designed and skills identified ○ Identify facts ○ Start training

Source: Author's research

Chapter 5　Theoretical Framework

5.1　Introduction

In this chapter, a theoretical structure is presented based on the information which is illustrated in the literature review of the previous chapters. The research will document the sources used in the previous chapters in order to identify the problems throughout the analysis of a series of references. In the meantime, a number of related concepts are to be discussed, so that the research will be incorporated into a structured interrelated idea. These endeavours are expected to generate an innovative model for managing foreign language programmes through an international communication approach. The intention of this is to provide an accessible approach to illustrate the relationship between several interrelated concepts which are integrated in the novel proposed model. The model will be designed in accordance with the current trend of international cooperation with Chinese partners, coping with culture issues and meeting the objectives of Chinese organisational development scheme, with the aim of developing a language training model at a strategic level. In addition, this chapter will also highlight the research propositions which are intended to address the key elements derived from the proposed model. To achieve this, the research starts in this chapter by synthesising interrelated ideas which will pave the way to generate a theoretical framework for the research.

5.2 Definition of Strategy

Strategy aims to provide development direction for organisations, and can be a carefully developed plan or a combination of plans and opportunities (Capon, 2008). Lynch (2006) presents his definition of strategy by identifing the core areas of strategy as being analysis, development and implementation. Johnson (2005) and Lynch (2006), however, go on go to develop the idea of strategy by defining five key elements of strategic decisions: sustainability and maintaining change, distinctiveness, creating links, developing a range of differenct customers and creating clear vision. These propositions have added new meanings to the definition of strategy that strategy needs to adjust according to the change of contexts (Capon, 2008).

Mintzberg has also made a significant contribution to strategy by presenting his 5Ps and forms of strategy. Mintzberg (1987) suggests that strategy should have five Ps, namely, plan, ploy, pattern, position, and perspective. In addition to Mintzberg's perception of strategy, Capon (2008) thinks of strategy in terms of a long-term plan. Strategy is actually drawn up by the organisation in order to meet its objectives. This common approach to strategy is reflected in many definitions of strategy, which often suggest that strategy be developed prior to implementation. Mintzberg (1994) makes the point that this view is limited and a wider perspective of strategy is often useful to leaders and managers charged with providing strategic direction and strategy for an organisation.

Mintzberg (1988) views strategy as a stream of decisions containing patterns. Two strategies are included in this sense: intended strategy and realised strategy.

Figure 5–1 illustrates the process of generating a strategy which usually arises from the planning and intent of an organisation or company and from decisions and patterns which emerge, and ends up with realised strategy (Capon, 2008; Mintzberg, 1988).

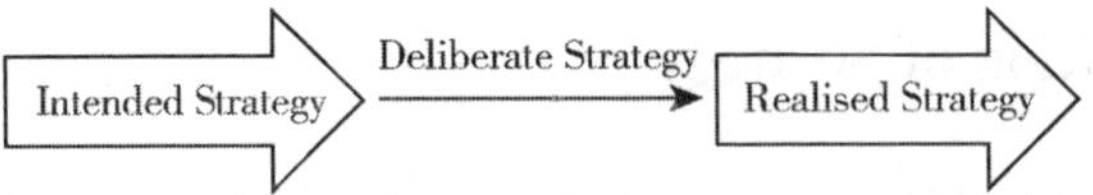

Figure 5–1 '5Ps for Strategy'. (Source: Mintzberg, 1987)

5.3 Defining strategic projects

Following the theory of strategy mentioned above and the literature in Chapter 3 demonstrating the definition of a project and five objectives for project management, the research now needs to clarify how to define a project and what principles are to be followed when defining a strategic project.

As Chapter 3 discussed, project definition initiates the project and therefore relates the work of the project to the orgnaisation's developing objectives. It needs to be strategic, intergrative and tactical. To achieve this, it is necessary to state the training company's or organisation's requirements as well as individual learners' learning targets, to identify the facility expected to satisfy them, and to identify the work required to construct the facility. Management of a strategic project is categorised into two levels: one is to define the individual learning project and another is to define the company's or organisation's training objectives.

The following three requirements should be defined within these two levels (Turner, 1993).

Firstly, the purpose is a statement of the foreign language need to be achieved by the project. It may be a problem to be solved, an opportunity to be exploited, a benefit to be obtained, or the elimination of an inefficiency in terms of related skills in the current workplace. All of these learning needs have to be derived from the strategic objectives of the parent organisation. So the assessement in the end will come back to reflect the purpose. The statement of the purpose should be clear and precise, and should contain both quantitative and qualitative measures. Once the project is underway, it will become the mission of all those involved in the project, both as project team members and as resource providers. It can be regarded as a powerful motivating force if it is seen to be worthwhile and beneficial to the individual's professional development, and can help to build cooperation (Anderson *et al.*, 1987; White, 2004).

Secondly, the scope needs to be defined because it describes the way in which the purpose will be satisfied. The scope will take responsibility either within the project or outside the project (Turner, 1993). The inclusions of the scope indicate the how people draw up the definition and how they reach their targets (Anderson *et al.*, 1987).

Thirdly, It is essential that the objectives are likely to deliver the benefits and also address the question of how they are to be attained (Anderson *et al.*, 1987; Turner, 1993).

In terms of timescales, we accept Turner's (1993) arguments in which he stresses that the definition of a project usually contains a statement of the expected timescale but he would take the rough expected timescale as targets for learning. He stesses it is important to be goal-directed, aiming to achieve the target and scheduling the work appropriately, rather than allowing a theoretical time calculation to influence the effectiveness of individual learning.

5.4 Planning at a strategic level

A project having been defined, the next stage is developing a breakdown of the structure of the work (Collier & Agyei-Ampomah, 2009). The requirements for planning this stage can be decribed as follows (Norton, 2007):

- Show how the intermediate products, or deliverables, build towards the final objectives of the project.
- Set a stable framework, fixed goal-posts, for the project team, and thereby provides a common vision.

Turner (1993) states that because only one set of intermediate products delivers the required final objective of this project, the plan at this level can be made stable. This can be a powerful motivating tool, giving the project team such as training programme providers as well as clients a common vision. To build a common vision, it should present a clear picture of the strategy for the project. To achieve this, those identifying the training needs will communicate the overall strategy of the project upwards to the project sponsor and programme providers to ensure the principles of good project management will be carried out in the programme implemenation.

5.5 Requirement for effective evaluation

Everything covered until now has brought the research to the point where a project is supposed to work effectively as training. However, as the work is done a project must ensure that it achieves the planned results and that it delivers the facility to the specification to which it is designed, within the scope of defined objectives thought to be worthwhile. In view of this, evaluation, such as control and monitoring, is structured and introduced into the process by which we check progress and take action to overcome any deviations from the plan. There are four essential steps to the control process (Meighan, 1991):

- Plan future work and estimate performance.
- Monitor and report results.
- Compare results to the plan and forecast future results.
- Plan and take effective action to recover the original plan, or to minimise the variance.

In the context of this research, more importance is attached to effective evaluation reporting to ensure the hypothesed training project is effective. According to Turner's view (1993), an effective training project should be consistent in its reporting mechanisms. Effective reporting or evaluation should satisfy the following criteria: evaluation should be made against the plan; should have defined criteria for control of the training project; be easy to administer; and reports should be made at defined intervals (Megginson, 1995; Turner, 1993).

However, Lingham *et al.* (2006) argue that no one model of evaluation is suitable for all programmes. To evaluate effectively, it is essential to have a better understanding of the nature of a programme, its purpose and other aspects such as culture, needs and purposes. This research investigates a new model of evaluation which suits an international projects involving Chinese partners.

5.6 Developing international projects

Jessen (1988) and Turner (1993) consider international projects to be a special kind of project because they involve collaboration between two countries and discuss the cultural differences that can arise between the collaborating nations. They argue that this kind of project seems to highlight cultural differences and, as a result, have a high rate of failure, almost always being more costly, more time-consuming and less profitable than originally envisaged. For 30 years, people have tried to find an answer to this problem, but projects have continued to be far from satisfactory on both sides, with increasing opposition from both sides to further projects: the funding training project customers feel that the money given and the goodwill extended are misused and misinterpreted; the training project providers feel that the money offered demands intolerable adjustments to meet the terms and conditions set by funders, which seriously conflict with their own way of thinking and performing (Mckeen, 1997; Jessen, 1988).

This antagonism arises from different views of the two stakeholders (Turner,1993). It can be seen in terms of decision making. The training purchaser side views itself as sponsor, and primary decision taker; the recipent partner views itself as owner, and the funding country as merely a funding agency. The training customer side desires to be primary decision taker but the training projects provider imposes most control in running the programme. However, a greater problem arises through cultural differences between the two sides and the two different countries, which may mean they take a radically different approach to managing international training projects. The training providers often try to impose their approach to learning and teaching, because they have greater experience of project management, but this may not be appropriate in the cultural environment of the recipient nation; indeed the training recipients are most able to decide their own best interests arising from training programmes (Turner, 1999).

Addionally, the different views of needs and ownership described here create two problems of cultural fit on international projects (Turner, 1993; Atkinson, 2001):

- The problem of organisation

It has previously been shown that certain organisational structures and planning procedures seem to support effective training programme management better than others, and certain information and communication systems seem to be more effective at achieving objectives that satisfy both the training providers and clients, as well the training project itself (Nadler, 1994).

As illustrated in the previous chapters, effective project management has all four stages under the control of one company or organisation. This enables that organisation to set the basic rules for developing the right type of training programme for their staff in accordance with their development schemes, with particular emphasis on convincing all levels of management of the advantages of proper management, such as foreign language training for staff in context. However, the role of developing an international collaboration programme is far more complex than that a national normal one, and this needs to be recognised by higher levels of management (Johnson, 2005; Jessen, 1988). Turner (1999) maintains that thisproblem is more prevalent in developing countries which are struggling to import many techniques simultaneously.

Too many projects have been initiated in China as a developing country with thc best of intentions from all parties involved, but gradually have faded because the project managers involved have not established a workable organisation with adequate definition of responsibility combined with proper lines of communication (Jiang, 2008; Zhao, 2001). Particularly in an environment where the participants have different values, different learning styles, different attitudes and cultural norms, these problems can quickly be magnified (Lynch, 2006; Turner 1993).

- The problem of effectiveness versus efficiency

The importance of understanding cultural difference has been recognised, but how to balance effectiveness and efficiency has challenged managers. The main reason is a problem of measurement. While the implications of running a training programme are readily measured, the other relevant factors such as motivation, communication, progress and outcomes are more difficult to assess. It is generally assumed that a sound training provider with developed facilities, broad experience and a higher level of administration should be effective, but the purpose of administration must be to ensure that higher performance and effectiveness are obtained (Gareis, 1990).

The term effectiveness is not easy to define; productivity is an easier parameter to observe, defined as the quantitative relation between outcome of production against input of personal efforts (Kerzner, 1984). However, productivity in this respect must be given a simple indicator, commonly understood by both sides (Sadri, 1995). Its measurement must be good enough to establish mutual confidence for partners and identify the training needs and matched outcomes in particular sectors. Turner (1993) also stresses that the more complex an environment is in development projects, the more difficult it is to attribute productivity measures to particular projects, as they can often mean different things to different people in different contexts. The Westem models promote planned structural changes and procedural effectiveness (Johnson, 2005). However, this can often lead to serious misconceptions about what should constitute proper assessment of training programme success in Chinese culture where a results-driven attitude is dominant (Kumar *et al.*, 2005; Wang, 2004). In addition, one must address how to identify accurately which of the possible macro and micro adaptations within educational settings in the light of outcomes of assessment will be effective in interactions with programme partners. Research has failed to resolve whether optimal results are achieved when the learning objectives are systematically matched or mismatched, to either training providers or clients or both (Cranton, 2000; Hale, 2000).

5.7 Generating a novel project for this research

5.7.1 Initial research

In order to relate these theoretical issues to what actually exists in the real world (Gruber, 1993), some initial research needs to be carried out (Walliman, 2001).

5.7.1.1 Rationale for initial research

To facilitate the achievement of the objectives and highlight the direction of the research that follows. A pilot study was conducted within the field. Most importantly, draft questionnaries were tested out in the field (Davies, 2007).

The research started by carrying out interviews with 11 employees. A semi-structured questionnaire was designed for the interview (see Appendix B). The initial research attempted (Davies, 2007; Silverman, 2004) to:

- Build up confidence in carrying out large scale data collection later in the main study;

- Provide valuable insights for the researcher because few secondary resources are available;
- Assist in shaping the overall design of the study;
- Identify relevant factors impacting on implementing foreign language training programmes for Chinese organizations;
- Obtain valuable data in the hope of exploring the issues more in-depth later in the main study.

5.7.1.2 Analysis of initial research

The pilot study as described below revealed some of the actual needs and issues faced by three Chinese companies in China. The managers were mostly from three different companies: No. 4 Oil Production at Changqing Oil Company China, Ningxia FAJ Bearing Joint Venture and Intel Technology Development (Shanghai) Co. with large presences in northwest China and Shanghai. The reasons for undertaking interviews within these three companies were the availability of human resources managers who were in charge and accessible and for the valuable information they were able to provide. Questionnaires were designed with 10 questions aiming at collecting primary data about experiences in conducting language programmes, perspectives on managing them and views on future management (see Appendix B).

Data was collected through interviews, and analysis was conducted using traditionqualitative methods. To improve the validity of data collected from the responses, views were sought from experienced managers, not inexperienced ones, and from managers working in joint ventures or companies with multicultural experiences. Eleven managers from diverse companies were interviewed.

These managers were asked about their current jobs, their sources of information and their business units. Questions were designed to focus on specific variables and were intended to collect information about organizational history, operational structure, and prescriptions about strategic planning in terms of foreign language training for staff. These questions also sought to elicit description of the implementation of foreign language training, performance management and challenges faced within the history of the company, as well as companies' vision and missions on language training programmes for their staff in future. This was done in an attempt to capture potential elements and managerial factors needed for successfully managing a programme in this context. Based on the needs identified, appropriate executive development and management of foreign language training programmes and a valid approach can be created to facilitate the development of the necessary skills, needs and relevant knowledge. Commentaries given by some of the managers interviewed have been highlighted below.

- Interview with managers working for No. 4 Oil Production, Changqing Oil Company China

No. 4 Oil Production at Changqing Oil Company is a large company in China, and works on oil exploration and production with 11,500 employees and about 3000 technical professionals in total. It is one of the top 500 largest companies in China.

An interview was conducted to investigate the effectiveness of foreign language training programmes which have been managed by the company over the past five years. Three interviewees involved are senior managers in the company and have been in charge of and engaged in employees' training for about seven years. When asked in the interview about the purpose and needs of the relevant training programmes, he said that,

"(w)ith the increasing expansion of collaborative business with the outside world, the company has been aware of the urgent need for talents with foreign language skills. In particular the company needs to recruit

more talent not only with foreign language proficiency but also with broad knowledge of techniques which could be used in practical work. Because of this and over the past five years, the company has invested RMB 0.1billion in employees' training. It aims to foster 1000 talents with skills to enhance multicultural communication. There are about 31 foreign language programmes with 66 classes jointly run with local universities and college institutes. As many as 1107 people, mostly senior specialists and managers, have attended the training in an effort to improve their English ability..."

"Generally speaking, the purpose of foreign language training for staff is to help them update technique knowledge currently used in oil exploration and production and also to attempt to put our company in a state ready to face up to more business challenges from abroad. But current issues challenging the company, based on the evaluation of language training programmes over the past few years, are that the training is not running effectively in accordance with what we really need or that it is off-target to some extent. On the one hand, we need staff to get their foreign language ability improved, and on the other hand, we'd like them equipped with more advanced and up-to-date information and techniques.This results in the problem that we are unable to find an appropriate school or institute where tutors are capable of providing a programme aiming at both sides because these schools and institutes so far don't have tutors specialising in the field, although they have good foreign language proficiency..."(from transcription of the interview of Mr. Li Shen)

Cao (2001) holds the same view as Mr. Li in his research on the position of foreign language training within the "Eleventh Five-year Project" of China's Oil Company. He highlighted the objectives of foreign language training undertaken by many companies over past years and concluded that the objectives of every language training programme became more specific, focused on more detailed fields, like English for oil exploration, English for geography, English for natural gas production, etc. In terms of participants attending language training programmes, he continues that apart from senior managers or project managers, increasing numbers of technical experts and workers have become involved, a new trend which is likely to become main-stream in the future. As far as foreign language training is concerned, Cao points out that a combination of local and overseas forms of training is a likely tendency and training will be laying emphasis on both language acquisition and cutting edge advanced technology (*ibid.*).

The rationale for this study is based on the "Eleventh Five-year Project", a support project launched by China's Oil Company in which it aims to send about 8000 people, mainly senior managers who are responsible for cross-cultural business management, for foreign language training for at least 5 years.

- Interview with managers from Ningxia FAJ Bearing Joint Venture

Ningxia FAJ Bearing Joint Venture is a medium-sized company in Ningxia and has been collaborating in business with Germany, Israel and other countries over the past 5-10 years. It is an excellent example of a medium-sized business seeking to develop a more advanced system of management. They have understood that to participate successfully in competition with other companies requires not only a high quality and competitive service but also an appreciation of an international communication strategy (Mintzberg, 1988, 1994).

As chairman of the human resources department, the interviewee has seen the deficit in management of foreign language training programmes managed over the past five years. He commented that:

> *"(g)enerally speaking, foreign language training programmes managed by our company have often been interrupted. There have been two main reasons causing this problem. One is financial insufficiency and another vital reason is being short of facilities that can be used in*

undertaking the foreign language training ..."

As far as the objectives of language training being managed for employees within the company are concerned, he continues that:

> *"(b)eing a joint venture company, it is potentially vital for us sustaining foreign language training for our staff since they are encouraged to communicate with partners in various aspects. In particular, technical professionals are the major participants required to take part in training because they need to exchange views with foreign partners based on technical development and system management. Apart from this, improvement of senior managers' ability to negotiate, communication, decision-making and skills of overseas investigation is equally important for the design of a foreign language training programme..."*

In the meantime, he has witnessed a real problem that occurred in a previous programme and that exists in a current programme.

> *"We generally send staff involved in training to university institutes nearby. The programme is normally aimed at improving staff's ability in listening to, speaking and writing the foreign language. As a result, we have been aware of drawbacks because of this. It obviously appears that lots of participants are still not able to deal with the work required for language-related working skills. This is largely due to the fact that the training programme is at a tangent and impractical. It is unlikely that it is a proper programme designed for training staff that meets our company's needs, especially technical needs.In addition, it has not found an appropriate and effective approach to examining the outcomes of the training programme."*

It might take a period of time for a research institute to generate an effective approach to manage foreign language training that combines foreign languages and technical accessibility. As a result, this will leave Ningxia Bearing Company to contemplate – as so many companies are doing – a lost opportunity to compete in international business because these general programmes that were previously carried out are frequently unsuitable and ineffective from the corporate perspective, since they are unfocused, designed without reference to the communication needs of the organization and its technical area. In brief, many programmes are not flexible and inclusive(Gross and McDonald, 1998; Kealey, 2009).

- Interview with executive from Intel Technology Development (Shanghai) Company

Mr. Yang is an assembly package design manager with Intel Technology Development and has been working in this position for 14 years. Intel Technology Development Shanghai has been managing foreign language training programmes for their staff for about 12 years, "but the company has had the experience of suspending training for a year as a result of internal management accounting issues." remarked Mr. Yang. In terms of feedback about the programmes done before, he continues,

"(a)ll programmes have proved to be successful because they have enhanced work efficiency and broadened the communication with branches of the company located in different countries across the world. It is very unfortunate that we have not designed an effective system for evaluation of language programmes, neither pre nor post. As a result, investment in programmes to some extent has caused the company substantial waste because there are no objectives of programme management. How to assess the outcomes of a training programme is another challenge for us. No one

ever proposes an approach which is suitable for us."

In terms of what language skills staff currently need, he said that,

"(o)n many occasions, such as in meetings, in negotiations and in settings requiring spontaneous speaking managers will rely heavily on listening and speaking skills, but I think reading and writing might be more important than the former two skills since they are being regularly used for our office work. We have put more emphasis on work and technical related training."

As far as managing foreign language programmes through an international communicative strategy is concerned, he mentions that if those staff with high work commitments had to be off work for a while, it will affect companies badly. He also noted that training staff abroad might be difficult to control and evaluate. His company has been considering a model international communicative channel integrating technology provision and foreign language proficiency.

- Research on business organisations in Shangdong province, China

In addition to primary data collected through interviews, secondary data relevant to the challenges faced have also been examined at. Wang Zhongxin is a professor at the School of Foreign Languages, Shandong University, China. He investigated the challenges faced by about 35 business organizations in Shangdong province. His 2007 Review analysed the key challenges facing companies in that region.

"(i)t is impossible for a company to manage properly without the assistance of an advanced strategy of management and a high technical level. Learning from the experience of developed countries is one of the

major channels, but this is not only based on foreign language education; more emphasis should be laid on updated technology and technique. What successfully managed companies and enterprises in markets nowadays are greatly concerned by is how to transfer the new knowledge into the productive workforce. With this in view, we are not expecting staff taking part in foreign language training only to aim at increasing vocabulary, improving communication skills and remembering grammatical patterns, because previous research has indicated that although language skills are essential for performing daily activities within companies and enterprises, there are still some other aspects of development required to be potentially focused on. What the real need for China's companies and organizations at this certain stage is, is to obtain and access specific and more focused technology development and global economic involvement." (Wang, 2007)

Referring to staff's language proficiency, he argues that,

"(t)he overall level of staff's foreign language proficiency is rather low. This is largely caused by a deficit impact from university language education where students are mainly trained by examination. Language ability obtained within the classroom has not been explicitly acknowledged as a distinctive area of communicative management demanded by many companies. As a result, many of China's companies and enterprises have to invest in staff's professional development in an attempt to fill the gap caused by unsuitable and insufficient language education within universities and help them to be qualified for their work as soon as possible."(ibid.)

As far as the models of foreign language training for China's companies and organizations are concerned, Wang also notes,

"(f)oreign language training programmes need to be variable and

flexible based on specific needs of every job requirement. Because of work diversity, there is a big difference among many people who are doing different work. We have to understand that the objective of foreign language training for company's staff will take foreign language as a tool or medium used to improve staff's technical skills rather than over-emphasise language itself, so a good foreign language training programme should be designed for double purposes by starting with a foreign language training and then following with underlying technical development." (ibid.)

"Apart from this, companies and organizations need to trust other institutes running language training programmes. The reason is that companies and organizations do not have a lot of time and facilities to carry out training independently. However, they are able to make full use of facilities available in other departments, including institutes abroad, where trainees from different companies and organizations not only are able to obtain professional training but also enjoy a useful learning environment. This no doubt will assist them to develop new ideas, approaches and perspectives."(ibid.)

Wang's research has identified two problems that impact on an effective language training programme. Examining these issues will help lead us to a better solution in the design of an effective training programme.

5.7.1.3 Summary of initial research

Although not many companies, only 27.2%, ever discarded the programmes they used, many others are still greatly concerned whether they are going to carry on with those used at present. This is largely due to perceived effectiveness of the training programme. When asked about the challenges faced, many issues were highlighted (see Table 5–1). The primary challenge many organisations are facing within China is the lack of useful facilities including relevant foreign language resources. As a result, it is impossible to produce personnel trained with both practical skills and language abilities intended for use at work and to create a language environment in order to improve business or technical-based language ability.

About 95% of interviewed managers demonstrated positive attitudes towards managing foreign language training programmes for their staff, showing a tendency towards a common view that Chinese organisations are looking for an effective foreign language training programme which is available for immediate use through cross-cultural strategic management. What is noticable is that many managers believe there is no substitute for overseas training. Two managers from Shanghai Intel Company argued that no amount of in-country training beats seeing what other countries look like and how they operate. One human resources manager from Ningxia FAJ Bearing added that overseas training should not be limited to only language training and foresee that "expanding the language training course to tour a plant or firm nearby during the course of training programme might help Chinese employees understand how their own plant operations can be improved." (from the interviewee)

Table 5–1 Results of initial research

Implementation of foreign language training	Results
Years since started	5-10 years in average
Programmes ever discarded	27.2%
Outcomes	18.2% positive, 54.6% negative and 27.2% uncertain
Who needs training	90.9% technical personnel and managers
Increasing business opportunity	90.9% positive answers given
Applied strategy	27.3% positive and 72.7% negative
Toward international strategy	only 36.3% ever thought of the option
Ideal duration for a training programme	27.3% preferred long-term and 72.7% short-term
Skills needed	Foreign language ability, communication and negotiating skills, leadership and new work-related skills
Challenges	Suitable and effective programme are not available, i.e. evaluation

Source: Author's research

Managers were also asked what other challenges they experienced when managing past programmes. The answers can be summarised in four points:

- Many programmes are impractical due to the design of training curricula which do not meet the required needs and skills at work places.
- Both training customers and providers are inexperienced and lack knowledge of training management.
- Lack of an effective and efficient language environment that can enhance learners' independent learning.
- Ambiguity in learning targets and objectives either for individual learner or training companies.

From the summary provided above, and in accordance with theories as mentioned in earlier paragraphs of the chapter, i.e. to manage an integrative, managerial and tactical project, two themes recur:

- The necessity to moderate the current training programmes for Chinese managers and staff in order to carry out the companies' development mission;
- The need to respect Chinese learning needs, learning style and cultural values (Hofstede, 2001; Xie, 2008; Zhao, 2010).

At first glance, these goals may appear contradictory, but in fact they are not. What ultimately is required, as many Chinese managers have said, is for foreign training programme providers to recognise the differences between Western countries and Chinese management methods. While the demands of running a business in the PRC can make establishing and maintaining a cohesive training programme difficult, companies that have been managing training programmes regularly find the efforts worthwhile (Melvin, 2008). Additionally, a fact that could be concluded from the interviews is that, as one of the interviewees indicated, "Chinese managers are thirsty for new ideas, new tools and new information." (from interviewee Mr. Li Shaowei)

In sum, the design of a programme can integrate language, culture, and workforce-related specific content learning, which can be taken as the basis of formulating programme curriculum. Following the interviews above, an enhanced model of programme should be composed of a statement of goals, objectives, and learner needs. A main objective is the development of English language ability for a specialised purpose, namely, work-related skills development. This objective is not limited to developing knowledge of a particular part of the English language, it also addresses the skills requried to use the language in particular contexts – to use English to learn more than techniques and will enable the learner to function in a mutilingual and multicultural communication environment.

5.7.2 Awareness of influential factors

Better understanding of cultural differences would reduce the cost of transactions associated with behaviour and uncertainty (Walsh and Wang 1999; Zhao, 2001). However, to achieve this can be particularly challenging (Ireland, 1991). This challenge can be a struggle both for training programme providers and clients. To deal with these challenges, there are some influential factors to which attention needs to be drawn.

- Cultural awareness

We have argued that Chinese culture is profoundly influenced by Confucianism (see Chapter 2), which not only affects daily management, but also affects the training process. Developing training strategies is usually a challenge to traditional Chinese adult foreign language education.

Practitioners as well as academics have clearly begun to recogise that 'talk' in its broadest sense is central to the conduct of business at all levels, as Harries and Bargiela-Chiappini comment (1997):

> *"... there are in existence a number of definable sub-generic types of business discourse, e.g. negotiations, meetings, service encounters, some of which have been studied much more frequently and intensively than others and from different perspectives..."*

Evidently, these comments still apply to Chinese companies and organisations when encountering challenges of how to seamlessly engage with overseas firms. There is much literature on the notion of language-based communication research which encompassess shared company values and attitudes (e.g. Baron and Walters, 1994; Deal and Kennedy, 1982; Hampden-Turner, 1990), as the presence of a number of competing managerial 'discourses' may create tension within a company and even cause conflict (Watson, 1996). Smith put forward the view that:

> *"(w)hile there may be some universialities to the organisational structures required around the world, the differing national cultures within which organisations are located frequently give those structures substantially different meanings. Working effectively across cultures is therefore not simply a matter of applying the skills found to be most effective within the culture of one's country or organisations. It requires also that one can understand and cope with the process of communication and decision-making in settings where these are achieved in a different manner."* (Smith, 1992, p. 25)

Smith concludes that "we have at present only a very partial understanding of how cross-cultural problems are best addressed." Firth (1995) underpinned this view by pointing out that the difficulty of access to real data from companies and organisations has almost certainly become a hurdle to the development of the field.

Confucianism mainly deals with human relationships. Confucianism can be found in every aspect of life and heavily impacts on different kinds of work. Chinese managers differ greatly from Western managers in their attitudes toward decision-making, for example, a notion regarded as a sense of risk. With high uncertainty-avoidance (Hofstede, 1994) Chinese managers usually lack an adventurous spirit and a sense of risk-taking. They dare not make immediate decisions if they feel the circumstance is uncertain, which may deprive them of the opportunity to compete in the market. In most cases, they would like to make comparatively safe and less risky decisions at the expense of the business opportunity (Fan, 2004). It is understood by many Chinese people that the purpose of decision-making is to avoid risk and uncertainty so that a harmonious environment would be created (Child and Warner, 2003).

Apart from this traditional philosophical culture, we should not ignore the basic system of the People's Republic of China – a system that Chinese people have been following for over 60 years, which could be termed as social culture. This system features a one-party governing political system and power has resided firmly with the central government and with the Chinese Communist Party. This feature of the Chinese political system has remained fundamentally unaffected by the economic reforms (Huang, 1996). It also has the feature that leaders at every level in any company and organisation, whether promoted, or removed and sacked, have been essentially subject to party authorities at a higher level. This characteristic is socially accepted as the uniqueness of socialist management and culturally in line with Confucianism – human relationships should be built up through fidelity to superiors, one of the five virtues Confucianism proposes: benevolence, righteousness, propriety, wisdom and fidelity, although this is changing as younger managers emerge (Levinshon, 2007; Yu, 1999).

- Managerial strategy

Finding the right balance between prescribed management techniques and sensitivity to Chinese worker's training needs and managers desires may be the key to successful foreign language training programme management. Management style is an area of significant difference between Chinese and Western countries (Zhao, 2001). The challenges of management education for Chinese staff is essentially to address the disconnection between the current training management models used in many university business schools and the actual foreign language skills and other actual work-related skill demands (other than foreign languages only). It has to explore a strategic approach that may bridge the gap between Western management theories and the characteristics of Chinese training management.

With the surge in popularity of training programmes such as task-based and content-based, and the Online Chinese project (see Chapter 3), there is no evidence to show that these training programmes have successfully improved the language skills and developed required abilities crucial to Chinese companies and organisations in order to compete in the global market. The heated debates on how to develop an appropriate foreign language model for Chinese staff have overshadowed the need to rethink existing approaches, and to experiment with a new model.

Some suggest that Western methods of management education will not be successfully applied to training Chinese staff unless these cultural values are taken into account (Braun & Warner, 2002; Berrel, *et al.*, 2001; Chee, 2002; Liu, 2006). However, this is only partly true. Whilst a better understanding of Chinese cultural values and managerial strategy will inspire Western educators to adjust their educational managerial strategy and facilitate the process of knowledge transfer. There is a growing tendency to move toward a mixed management approach in which foreign and Chinese elements, Western and Eastern theories are blended; they employ foreign management theories to bridge domestic management goals. At the same time, Western education management needs to actively adapt its managerial strategy by respecting Chinese managerial culture in order to address the West-East divide (Chen, 2011).

5.7.3 Identifying the focus of the research required

The following research aims to address the pitfalls within the previous literature.

Table 5–2 below shows the gaps the research needs to address in terms of a range of aspects including foreign language needs analysis, training needs analysis, learning and teaching method, cultural factors, perception of training management and project-based foreign language learning programme.

Table 5–2 Identifying the focus of the research needed

Category	Chinese training demands	Western training providers	Gaps to fill
Foreign language needs	Foreign language skill Work-related skills	Foreign language skills only	Individual needs analysis Work-related skills
Training needs	Problem solving abilities	Communicative abilities	Problem-solving abilities
Learning & Teaching Method	Need to create innovative pedagogy Need to enhance the quality of learning Responsibility for group (Hofstede, 2003) Teacher-centeredness (formal instruction) (Ip, 1996)	Less diversity of programmes Individual committed (Hofstede, 1993) Autonomy learning style	A new model to enhance individual learning and combination of focusing form and individual directed learning
Cultural factors	Confucianism – *Ren, Yi* and *Li* Paternalism Harmony	Contract-orientation Manager in control Self-interest, self-actualisation (Hofstede, 1994) Universalism Information-oriented	A creative model to respect each factor from two cultures
Perception of training management	Project sponsorship Issue of project ownership Technology and information oriented	Implementation in control Issue of project ownership Language skills only (uncontrollable)	To address the problems of ownership and provide technology and informational based training programme To develop a new innovative evaluation mechanism

Continued Table

Category	Chinese training demands	Western training providers	Gaps to fill
Project-based foreign language learning	A great challenge	Task-based and content-based Online Chinese project	Develop a blended project model to enhance work-related skills learning through a foreign language trainingprogramme

Source: Author's research

- As far as foreign language needs are concerned, there is an apparent gap between clients and providers. According to the initial research, it is assumed that Chinese partners aim not only just to develop foreign language skills but also other work-related skills which may be useful in the company's further development. This necessitates raising awareness of how to manage individual needs analysis and also balancing it with work-related skills. It also has to be justified in the research that follows.
- Training needs will be based on developing problem solving abilities to help trainees perform more professionally and function skillfully in an international multicultural environment after their training programme. Apparently there is a gap in this respect as many progammmes available so far focus on development of communicative abilities such as training basic language skills of listening, speaking, reading and writing but have neglected developing the problem-solving ability increasingly demanded by Chinese companies and organisations.
- Apart from this, attention needs to be drawn to pedagogical innovation where the need is emphasised to creatively incorporate western learning and teaching theory into Chinese learning styles to speed the learning process and encourage the learner to achieve deeper levels of understanding from learning by doing (Oxford, 1990). This innovation needs to make sure it allows Chinese learners to become more self-

directed, and teaching strategies should be more flexible in combining a focus on form and formal instruction.

- Managerial behaviours need to balance Western and Eastern cultures. Training programme managers need to reach agreement on ownership in order to provide technology and informational oriented training which Chinese organisations demand; however, availability of appropriate training is surprisingly rare. In this sense, a strategy to evaluate a training programme via cross-cultural management is vital to the success of a programme.
- In addition, to take advantage of the western theory of project-based foreign language learning and tailor it for Chinese staff and managers, one needs to ensure the quality of training is available.

5.7.4 Objectives of the study

To address the questions highlighted in the above, the research aims to create a novel model of a programme which can contribute to management education and mangement development in China, which in turn will test the transferability of management models developed in the West.

Liu (2006) summarises after his research into comparison of models of management education from different cultures that whilst a better understanding of Chinese cultural values may inspire Western training programme providers to adjust their teaching and learning as well as managerial styles and facilitate the process of knowledge transfer, such knowledge does not translate into the necessary skills and competence for learners to confront the everchanging environment.

In accordance with this and the reality of learning and training needs for Chinese staff members from companies and organisations, in order to remedy the shortage of appropriate models tailored for training Chinese staff and managers, the aim of the research is to balance East and West in the area of management education through cross-cultural communicative strategy by attempting to:

- Incorporate project-based foreign and second language learning theory into training management and particularly use it to train Chinese managers and staff members through an international communicative strategy, that adequately reflects the reality of workplace culture.
- Combine western learning style with Chinese learning style to ensure effective teaching and learning for Chinese adults through an interactive communicative training programme.
- Propose a novel model which takes account of key elements of how to stimulate Chinese learners' improved performance.
- Develop a novel model by blending and updating the task-based and content-based learning programmes and the Online Chinese project.
- Generate a novel model which takes the influence of Confucianism into account to ensure implementing the programme will satisfy Chinese training needs.

To achieve these objectives, a model programme has to be created on the basis of employee's work experience, so that it contributes towards developing individual learning tasks, as well as enhancing the development of organisations in a related aspect such as knowledge of technology, technical skills improvement, international communicative competence development, etc. In do doing, it is hoped that the project will achieve the intended task. In other words, a main objective for this project should entail creation of an initial training objective scheme which attempts to improve the staff's foreign language ability for a specialised purpose, namely, work-related requirements. This objective is not limited to developing knowledge of a particular part of the foreign language, it also addresses the skills required to use the language in particular contexts (Orr, 2002). Therefore, the process of individual project formulation should closely relate to the employee's existing knowledge and experience which has to be integrated into the organisation's development objectives.

In addition to placing the emphasis on building up individual learning projects, the next main objective is to focus on the process of implemenatation of the project which will help to generate a complete map of the programme model. To determine the effectiveness of the implementation of a programme, many researchers (e.g. Alon and McIntyre, 2005; Bechett 2006; Turner, 1993) have identified that an innovatative programme has to capture the essence of foreign training programmes for learners which could focus on several common threads:

- Complex endeavours to do work which creates changes.
- Mixed objectives, especially constraints of quality and time.
- The frequent involvement of people throughout any participanting organisations.
- The evaluation of project needs effectively and creatively.

So the project can be divided into two-tier levels (see Figure 5-2 and 5-3). The first tier is to look at how staff are effectively managing to achieve their learning tasks through an individualised approach. The process of creating their own learning objectives can be seen as individual project-based creation. The individual learning objectives consist of foreign language proficiency improvement, work-related skills and other relevant abilities required by their organisations. The second tier of the project attempts to generate a model that is used to implement the programme for training Chinese staff.

This proposed model is designed as a cycle, as the whole project is designed to begin with the first tier project and end with the second. Completing the second tier project is intended to lead to re-generation of the first. So the project triggers the management of the training programme by beginning with identification of staff foreign language needs, which is essential to the success of implementing the training programme.

At the same time, the model attempts to respond to and address the concerns highlighted in the interviews when the initial research was conducted.

They include effectiveness, motivation, triggers, self-esteem, true needs and quality assurance.

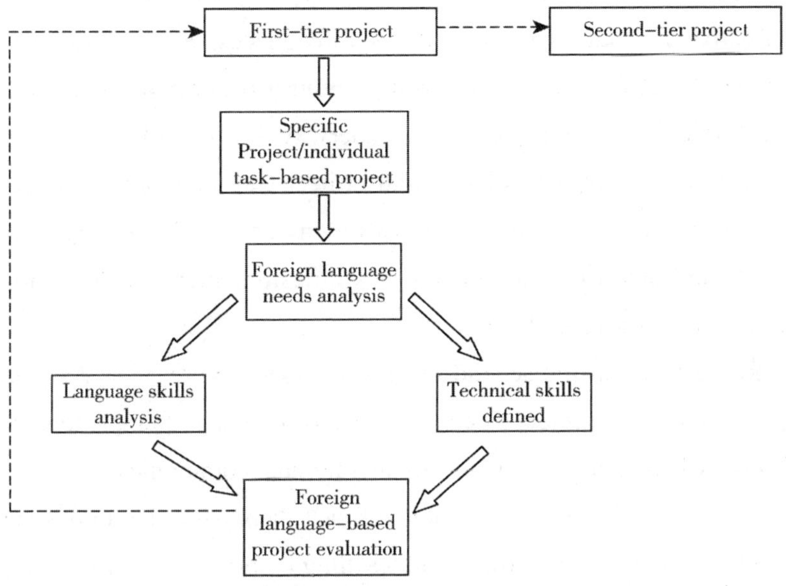

Figure 5–2 First-tier project (FTP)

Source: Author's diagram

Time needs to be devoted to the first stratified project before a project is set out because this is essential in determining a successful programme. It relates to strategies for successful implementation. The task of the first stratified project aims to look at what foreign language skills are needed by individual staff and at the same time it aligns with technical skills defined according to the requirement of the workplace. Stoller (1997) states that the planning of an approach to address either foreign language needs or technical skills largely determines how successful the project will be. It is common knowledge that time spent planning a project is time well spent, yet we consistently spend too little in a project's early stage, failing to consider adequately the range of issues that will subsequently cause problems. The data collected through interviewing Chinese managers in initial research and from other sources in previous chapters have also explicitly shown deep concerns because problems often occur in managing training programmes for Chinese staff. As Beckett (2006) and Turner (1993) stated: one needs to think more effectively about what will influence the success of one's project at the early stage. Apart from this, uncertainty about a programme will inevitably introduce high risk once the project is underway. In view of this, the first-tier project of building a trainee's individual project and its approval is becoming increasingly important as it determines the success of launching a training programme and therefore play the role of a milestone plan which results in the second-tier project derived later.

Then we come to the second-tier project (see Figure 5–3). As explained above, the second-tier project – seen as a macro-project – attempts to generate a novel model which is used to launch an international communication programme aiming at training Chinese staff. In this respect, theory-framing draws upon the social-cultural tradition of learning and teaching – "project-based learning" – an inseparable part of learning which will be carried across the whole programme. This theoretical orientation of project-based foreign language learning and teaching refers to the assumptions of engaging in time-limited projects to achieve pre-specified or emergent performance objectives, which have been initially formulated in the first tier project, to make sure the implementation of the programme facilitates individual and collective learning (Cohen, 1991; Smith & Dodds, 1997). This is also in line with the action learning writings of Somekh (2006) who theorised that learning resulted from the interaction between programmed instruction and the spontaneous questioning that arises from the interpretation of experience. In view of this, particular attention will be drawn to identify aspects of training participants' work experience gained from working in their own organizations.

Looking back at the literature review and initial research, it is possible to highlight the following elements demonstrating the actual needs from Chinese companies and enterprises and the crucial dilemma faced by them as a consequence.

- Training needs analysis – what kind of programme model is appropriate for Chinese staff in the context of Chinese education background and the company's administrative management system? There are concerns about how much language knowledge as well as other related work-based skills the trainees can acquire and how much knowledge could be immediately helpful to the development of their organisations.
- Motivations – what the influencing factors are for triggering the launch of a programme and what motivates staff learning.
- Maintaining self-esteem – how to enhance the self-esteem either of companies and organizations *per se* or of individual participants.
- Effectiveness and Quality assurance – how is the quality of the training programme maintained? How are the outcomes of the training programme evaluated to guarantee effective quality assurance?

In order to respond to and therefore deal with these challenges properly, the research proposes a novel model (see Figure 5–3 Second-tier project) in an attempt to meet actual training needs and to specify the different stages with various conditions that should be present for an effective learning programme. The programme model will be implemented at the same time internally and externally, and can be seen as both planning graphic and project report or diary stages. Moreover, this second-tier project is proposed in an attempt to cope with the key issues highlighted above as training needs analylsis, motivation and triggers, maintenance of self-esteem and effectiveness and quality of service assurance.

- Training needs analysis

Current efforts in managing programmes have been vigorously opposed

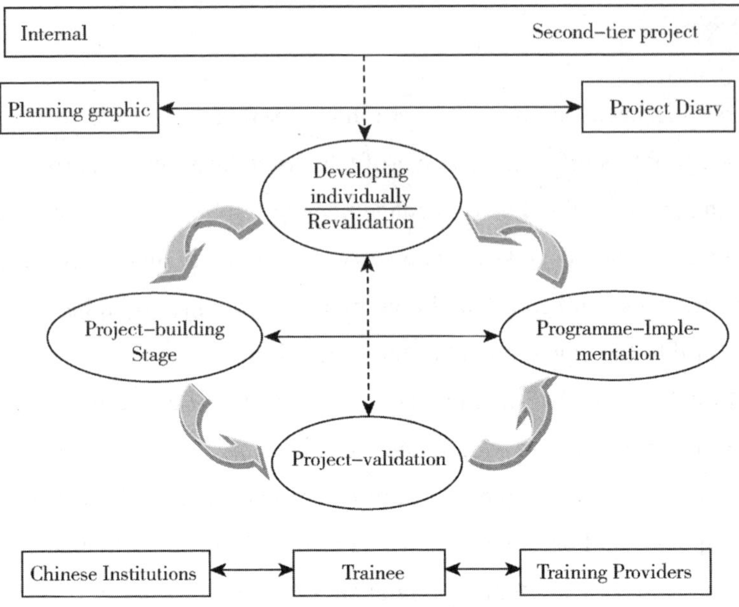

Figure 5–3 Second-tier project (STP)

Source: Author's diagram

by some people within the profession (Child, 2003; Liu, 2001; Stephen, 1998). They believe those models featuring Online Chinese and task-based learning cannot guarantee anything more than the application of general and rather elementary criteria of training programme itself. To be a professional development programme, according to Vieira (2004), every individual learning objective needs to meet two criteria: i) a body of knowledge that is targeted for learning and continuously upgraded; ii) a commitment to achieve learning goals. What is more, to manage a cross-cultural training programme, the emphasis will be placed even more on identifying the real learning tasks, which in turn will give learners a clearer direction they should follow. This not only helps the trainee to build up learning objectives or learning tasks but also to convince the managers from different companies and organizations of the targets they want to achieve (Weiss, 2003).

• Motivation and triggers

The model is incorporated with four components which are situated at its heart. It intends to answer the questions of how to maintain the effectiveness of the programme, and it is also hoped that this model will meet the concerns that come from Chinese managers in the initial interviews. The innovative model starts with development, project-building and project-validation stages which characterise the first tier project. This initial stage of project building designed for the purpose of motivating learners will be mainly undertaken internally, which means it will take a period time for staff to identify their language abilities and create a work-based project, so that the motivation and triggers for training taking place later on would be secured.

But what draws our attention is that the first stage of project development and the third stage of project-validation do not mean the work would be put into action independently without assistance from training providers. On the contrary, this work always requires significant involvement on the part of trainees to make sure the training individuals are effectively and properly motivated throughout the training. It is hoped that jointly evaluating staff's individual projects can preserve individuals' motivation generated at the initial stage so that the quality of programme implementation is sustained.

• Maintaining self-esteem

In addition, this appraoch also maintains the self-esteem either for Chinese training organisers or for training providers, surely important for saving Chinese "face" culture in particular (Wong, 2007). On the other hand, jointly validating and revalidating the training programme will provide further collaboration activities between partners, as there will thus always be "a good start and a happy end" (a four-word Chinese phrase '*shan shi shan zhong*' regarding keeping a good relationship between two partners. This requires both parties involved committing as much responsibility at the onset as they do at the end to ensure a sound quality and a happy outcome).

- Effectiveness and quality of service assurance

The second-tier project is the core stage where the objectives of learning for individual staff are to be established. Every objective, whether in terms of language skills or technical skills based on their own workplace, should be precisely allocated and highlighted, and jointly validated afterwards. This will ensure the effectiveness at the implementation stage and therefore assure the high level of training outcome, based on the project-planning stage. In terms of quality assurance in implementation, the relevant approaches are important such as periodical reports and project diary in order to make sure the training programme stays on the track fixed during the level one stage and also maintains a transparent channel of negotiation between managers from Chinese companies and organizations and training providers. This is particularly important because trainees are always playing the role of a friendly envoy. To some extent this might be very helpful for sustainability of programme management in the context of relationship with Chinese partners, but there is still a risk that any discordant notes from trainees could destroy established loyalty or mutual trust. So keeping partners informed about the progress of the training programme becomes extremely important in order to maintain Chinese partners' self-esteem and relations while the training programme is taking place whether internally or externally. Apart from this, keeping the negotiation between managers from two sides and keeping diary reports are essential because training managers from suppliers and partners will use up-to-date feedback for the assurance of training quality.

To summarise, the proposed model (see Figures 5-2 and 5-3) builds upon the project-based foreign language learning theory proposed by Beckett (1994). In previous chapters 2 to 4 existing literature in connection with foreign language training programmes for Chinese staff and managers has been scrutinised to determine where the effective model fits the needs. No literature references or research reports were found that provide any evidence on how a model provides an appropriate approach to fill existing gaps to train Chinese companies and organisations in terms of above four problems. In addition, little is known about specific learning model with regards to effectiveness and the appropriateness of managing training programmes. Managers worry about the effectiveness of training programmes and whether the training content and training outcomes could bring more profits and benefits. This research therefore serves as a seminal first step in creating a framework for developing training model using foreign language teaching and learning as a passport to international collaboration. As such it provides a theoretical and practical contribution to knowledge.

5.7.5 Propositions and hypotheses

The combined use of research propostions and research hypotheses in this thesis needs some clarification. Dillion *et al.* (1994) and McDaniel & Gates (2001) argue that a hypothesis is an assumption or a guess that the researcher makes about some characteristic of the sample population.

Willemse (2004) defines a hypothesis as an assumption to be tested with the objective of making statistical decisions based on a scientific procedure. It is an attempt to determine when it would be reasonable to conclude, from an analysis of a sample, that the entire population possesses a certain property.

Cooper & Schindler (2008) also argue that the immediate purpose of exploratory research is usually to develop hypotheses or questions based on the reality that research uncovered. This attempt is for further research. They define a proposition as a statement about concepts that may be judged true or false if they refer to observable phenomena. They also point out that when a proposition is formulated for empirical testing, they refer to it as a hypothesis. So the proposition in the context of this research should be also taken as a hypothesis as it is to be tested through a questionnaire.

5.7.6 Testing the two-tier levels model

The following research propositions or hypotheses cover the main areas addressed by the research instruments (to be discussed in Chapter 6) and provide a framework for testing two proposed frameworks and for organising the resultant research results and conclusions that will be discussed in the following chapters.

The propositions or hypotheses only apply to the research subjects, namely, those managers from Chinese companies and organisations who actually sponsor a training programme at a certain point. And also those staff members who have ever participated in the programme and to some extent will be involved in future programme management.

If asked about the primary reasons triggering Chinese business institutions' decision to develop a foreign language programme for their staff, one possible answer might be that foreign language training is merely the channel or medium for managing an international foreign programme. However, the ultimate objective behind a training programme is to help companies' and organisations' development, from business profit increase or improved operational management in general, to a specific step forward within a particular work group, such as staff personal technical skills.

To address this demand, the research model at the same time develops an international communication strategy that requires three essential components from a foreign language programme – an international training provider, trainees and Chinese administrative managers (see Figure 5–3) to work collaboratively and effectively on the programme. It is obvious that the project is potentially emphasising the pre-preparation stage or planning graphic as the figure above indicated, which consists of developing foreign language project (Beckett, 1999; 2006), a project-building stage and a project-validation stage. No matter which stages the programme has reached, the three parties have to make sure that they communicate effectively with each other.

The proposed first-tier project and second-tier project consists of:

(1) Building-up of a specific project (Turner, 1993) or individual task-based project (Goldstein, 2002)

- Individual language skills demands
- Technical skills defined (Littrell, 2002, 2005; Liu, 2001)
- Foreign language-based project evaluation (Sanchez, 2004)

(2) Project-based training programme

- Project-validation – jointly validating
- Programme implementation – consistent with learning demands defined previously at the project-building stage and sticking to the project diary (Kealey, 2009; Kolb, 1991)
- Programme evaluation – joint evaluation

(3) Other related factors

- Intercultural communication (Lynch, 2006; Nordhaug, 2003)
- Motivation of learning (Beckett, 2006; Smith 1985; Whiddett, 2002)
- Trigger for running the training programme
- Learning and teaching strategy (Liu, 1997; Wu, 2001)

To guide the stated purpose of the study, the following research propositions (P) have been made and will be examined further:

P1 – P4 are related to addressing the first-tier framework – building-up an individual task-based project.

P1. Chinese companies will embrace a foreign language training programme if it starts by creating a project individually and independently prior to actual implementation.

The findings for this proposition address the importance of the project creation and building-up stage taking place prior to implementation of a programme within a Chinese company or organization which are of interest to and appropriate and meaningful for both partners.

P2. An effective individual project would be created and welcomed by Chinese companies if it is based on learner's language skill needs and technical skills related to the work place.

The propositions will reveal the participants and managers' attitudes to the necessity of launching a foreign language training programme and also play a role in determining the effectiveness of the programme implementation.

P3. Chinese companies are interested in launching a foreign language training programme if it aims to enhance professional skills and technical ability.

It is hoped that actual foreign language needs of companies can be identified, so that the research can address issues of innovation in managing a training programme – professional skills and technical ability are vital to ensure the success of managing a foreign language training programme for Chinese staff. These are also the elements any foreign language programmes need to emphasise more. It also leads to further consideration as to whether it could indicate a shift in training management from a focus on language proficiency to a focus on professional skills and technical ability.

P4. Chinese companies and organisations would like to launch a foreign language training programme if it aims to develop communicative, reading and writing abilities and cultural awareness.

The question considers the role of training programmes for Chinese employees and what actual needs they are demanding in terms of language proficiency, training orientation, which could motivate managers to run a training programme.

P5 – P8 are related to the second-tier framework of programme implementation and evaluations.

P5. Chinese employees will be more interested in foreign language training programme if the pedagogic style is to combine formal instruction and self-directed learning.

The questions regarding this proposition address operational issues. How can a teaching procedure be managed in alternative models of course delivery? What factors might not be avoidable? In addition, the statement attempts to explore what teaching approaches are useful in improving adult foreign language learning and skill development.

P6. Foreign language training programmes will be of more interest if they aim to develop the trainees' ability to solve problems which closely relate to their real work.

The proposition is to explore more abilities to be developed in the programme but more emphasis will be placed on the ability to develop as a goal of the solution of practical problems. This is about attitudes and intention towards the programme design and packages of outcomes set by both Chinese training managers, trainees and training providers.

P7. Chinese staff and managers will be more interested in training programmes if regular reports about the progress of trainees and ongoing negotiation over course content is required to be incorporated into the training programme.

Reflection on this proposition addresses proper ongoing evaluation approaches to be used to maintain and sustain cross-cultural training programmes for Chinese partners.

P8. Quality of the programme will be assured if Chinese managers and programme providers are jointly involved in the evaluation either at the stage of generating the learning project or at the end of the programme.

Attitudes toward the proposition will look at the degree of Chinese partners' involvement and the determination of the outcome of the quality of the training, and also better approaches to evaluation. It also looks at the management of the relationships between the learner, the training supplier and the programme partner.

5.8 Summary

To summarise, a range of relevant theories including the definition of strategy, how to define a strategic project, theory of planning at a strategic level of a training programme and how to make effective control of a programme, as well as how to look into the problems arising when developing an international project have been discussed in this chapter. All of these relevant concepts have been incorporated in a structured way so as to shed light on generating a novel project for the purpose of this research. In order to give the proposed model a sound basis in reality, the research has explored the gaps that exist in reality through conducting and analysing the initial research in which 11 interviews with managers from different Chinese companies and organisations were carried out. Findings generated from the initial research have revealed the reality challenging current training orientation and have thus inspired the research to hypothese possible solutions on the basis of acknowledging the influential factors and gaps identified.

Two-tier levels projects have been proposed and 8 propositions to test the hypothesised models are also constructed. The following chapter will discuss the methods that are used to justify the validity of the novel model.

Chapter 6 Research Methodology

6.1 Introduction

In this chapter, research methodologies appropriate to undertaking the research and investigation are considered. The research first discusses the research philosophy and reviews the method that was used to develop the research from chapter two to chapter five, and then look into the survey design in terms of sample, measures, and procedures which are used to justify the research propositions.

6.2 Ontology and Epistemology

It is essential to ascertain ontological and epistemological decisions before carrying out a research project (Collis and Hussey, 2003). They point out that reflection on their ontogical views enables researchers to identify what happens in the actual world and how one sees reality (Creswell, 2003; Davies, 2007). This will in turn enable researchers to identify their epistemology. If one identifies principally with the idea that there are macro-realities in a project, researchers are more likely to think that large-scale research will generate useful knowledge (Blaikie, 2000). However, if a researcher is more persuaded by the existence of micro-realities, then s/he should demonstrate a preference for localised investigation which seeks to penetrate issues more deeply. While thinking of these, this will help to clarify the methods by which the data will be collected and analysed; to recognize whether the chosen design could help to meet research objectives and address the research hypothesis (Easterby-Smith *et al.*, 1991). Similarly, Saunders *et al.* (2000) state that before carrying out research, it is essential for researchers to identify the underpinning philosophies. Thus, the researcher will first clarify the ontological position of this study and explan how the researcher regards the entities investigated in this study and what the nature of the exsiting reality of the study.

6.2.1 Ontology

Ontology is the consideration of being: what is, what exists, what it means for something to be (Carson *et al.*, 2001; Packer, 2000). It concerns with the nature of the reality to be investigated (Bryman, 2001). Essentially there two major ontological positions – scientific positivist research and non-scientific interpretivist research (Saunders *et al.*, 2003).

Positivism is based on observations of external reality and is considered as the best way of invesitigating human and social behaviour (Easterby-Smith *et al.*, 1996). Positivism holds that the social world exists externally and its properties could be measured through objective methods. Hussey and Hussey (1997) argued that positivism is founded on the belief that the study of human behaviour should be conducted in the same way as studies conducted in the natural sciences. This is based on the assumption that social reality is independent of us and exists regardless of whether we are aware of it or not, as investigating reality according to the positivist approach has no effect on reality itself. Furthermore, according to positivists, the researcher can establish causal relationship among the variables under investigation by reducing phenomena into simple elements that facilitate formulating and testing hypotheses, which would allow the prediction to occur, and offer causal explanations too (Easterby-Smith *et al.*, 1991; 1996; El-Kot, 2001; Hussey and Hussey, 1997).

Interpretivism was developed as a result of observations and creative thinking, rather than through a logical and rational application of scientific method (Easterby-Smith *et al.*, 1991; 1996). Hussey and Hussey (1997) argued that interpretivism relates to phenomenology, which is based on the assumption that every phenonmenon that can be observed is unique, and this uniqueness is important for undertaking research in a scientific manner. Phenomenology is concerned with understanding human behaviour from the participants' own frame of reference (*ibid.*, p.52). Besides, Easterby-Smith (1991) also stresses that reality is socially constructed rather than subjectively determined; people may place many different interpretations on situations and it is the role of the interpretivist to make sense of it (Saunders *et al.*, 2003). Therefore, researchers should try to evaluate the meaning of and reasons for what actually happened in the real world by assessing different experiences, which allows for gathering natural not artificial data from data resources available and helps contribute to evolution of new theories (Davies, 2007).

These two alternatives work in an opposite way – positivism deductively and interpretivism inductively (Creswell, 2003). Positivism examines the examined reality objectively which is independent of observers; whilst interpretivism investigates the examined reality based on people's perceptions with observers involving in data analysis (Saunders *et al.*, 2007). Crotty (1998) regards these two major ontological positions as being located at either end of a continuum which starts with positivism and ends at interpretivism or vice versa.

Bryman (2007) advocates that deciding ontological orientation depends on how researchers see the entities of the study – whether it is an objective entity that is measured externally or a subjective entity that is based on perceptions of social actors, or both. This study initially investigates the external and objective reality that impacts on a language training programme in practice in order to identify where the gap lies. This understanding allows the researcher to critically review the relevant literature. Meanwhile, people's beliefs, feelings and attitudes on the programmes are majorly investigated in order to shape the research propositions. This is because reality is regarded subjectively to reflect aspects that are deeply rooted in individuals' consciousness (Saunders *et al.*, 2003; Silverman, 2004). These individuals in this study refer to managers and staff from Chinese organisations who have engaged and participated in foreign language programmes. At a later stage, the research examines and tests the hypothesised innovative model through investigating those participant's views and positions in their actual work situations where the entities investigated are socially constructed (Bryman, 2007). Hence, the researcher regards the nature of this study as one of multiple realities which entails not only the investigation of external and objective reality but also internal and subjective perceptions from subjects of this study (Saunders *et al.*, 2003).

Based on this clear ontogical position, the researcher decided to employ pragmatism as the mode of enquiry, in which both traditions of research philosophy – positivism and interpretivisim, are utilised. Pragmatism embraces the two extremes of positivism and interpretivism with an effort to gain a profitable result for data collection (Pansiri, 2005). The positivism emphasises quantitative methods as opposed to interpretivists' qualitative approaches. Pragmatism has been hailed as the foundation of mixed-method research (Tashakkori and Teddlie, 1998; Teddlie and Tashakkori, 2003a). Mixed-methods have been defined as those studies involving the collection or analysis of both quantitative and qualitative data in a single research in which the data are collected sequentially. It also involves the integration of the data at one or more stages in the process of research (Creswell *et al.,* 2003, p. 212). Creswell further argues that, instead of methods being important, the research problem is the most important issue and each individual research has their own choice regarding the methods, techniques and procedures of research that best meet their needs and purposes (Pansiri, 2005, p. 198). Pragmatism embraces both points of view of positivism and interpretivism and is oriented towards using both qualitative and quantitative methods (Tashakkori and Teddlie, 1998). Therefore, the research advocates using mixed-method methodology as the researcher tends to base knowledge claims on pragmatic grounds and employs strategies of inquiry that involve collecting data sequentially to best produce desired outcomes (Creswell, 2003).

6.2.2 Epistemology

Epistemology is the systematic consideration, in philosophy, of knowing: when knowledge is valid, what counts as truth (Carson, *et al.*, 2001; Packer, 2000) and how the data could be acquired (Creswell, 2003). Essentially, epistemology attempts to identify properties by virtue of which beliefs are justified and counted as knowledge (Bernecker, 2006). Based on the ontological position of this study discussed in section 6.2.1, the research aims to clarify what this study counts as valid knowledge.

Firstly, in order to generate a context for understanding the reality of a foreign language training programme for Chinese employees, considerable observation and critical thinking were carried out through interpreting the causality of the deficit of current exsiting training programmes and investigating the views from programme managers. This attempt is based on the researcher's view that the reality in this sense is socially constructed and has been critically examined by previous research. The vaild knowledge can be obtained from both the previous studies in the area and experienced managers engaged in educational management. Inductive method was largely used in this sense in order to provide qualitative data following the principle of interpretivism.

Then, the research was designed to utilise the perceptions from both staff and managers enabling the main investigation to investigate training participants' behaviour and reality. The deductive method, in line with the principle of positivism, was employed to demonstrate the justification and quantitative data obtained allowing the research to see simple numerical figures for start and end points. Due to both Chinese staff and managers who are potiently selected to participate in foreign langauge training programmes, knowledge is counted as a product of the experience, attitudes, history and actual needs of the participants; thus can be discovered 'out there' based on their attitudes (Bryman, 2001).

Moreover, pragmatically, using quantitative method is the best approach to collect data from a large-scale observed population, staff participants in this study, because self-administered questionnaire and representative sample could be adminstered (Bryman & Cramer, 2001). In addition, quantitative method enables participants to provide their thoughts and opinions quickly to tackle time and budget problem (Creswell, 1999; Field, 2009).

Later, in order to gain more vaild data, the follow-up in-depth inteview was needed to explore the details to find support for the observations and conclusions (Creswell, 2003; Saunders *et al.*, 2003). The subjective ontological position which allows using qualitative technique was resumed for this regards. An informal and relaxed atmosphere created in the semi-structured interviews enabled the researcher to understand participant's attitudes, actions, and reactions toward issues of divergent perceptions between staff and managers (Creswell, 1999; Newman, 2008).

In summary, the sufficiency of the data according to different data sources or data collection methods allowed the researcher in this study to identify and elicit aspects of investigation for the same situation and the same time with multiple sources of evidence in order to find answers for the research objectives. In addition, using a mixture of both qualitative and quantitative data sources helped stengthen the credibility of findings and ensured the trustworthiness of both qualitative and quantitative findings (Davies, 2007; Newman, 2008).

6.2.3 Triangulation

Triangulation refers to the use of a variety of methods in one project with a view to exploring the research question from different angles (Davies, 2007) and is the most common and well-known approach to mixing methods (Crewell, 2007; Crewell, *et al.*, 2003). It is widely acknowledged that there are advantages in using multiple methods of investigation in exploring a given research topic. These different perspectives or 'triangulation' as it is referred to, offer the researcher an all-round and explicit picture of the topic discussed (Coolican,

1999; Hayes, 2000). The purpose of this design is "to obtain different but complementary data on the same topic" (Morse, 1991, p.122) to best understand the research problem. The intent in using this design is to bring together the differing strengths and non-overlapping weakness of quantitative methods with those of qualitative methods (Patton, 1990).

This research project involves the use of four types of triangulation (Bryman 2008).

- *Data triangulation*, which entails gathering data through different sampling strategies such as interviews with managers and questionnaire surveys to both managers and staff.
- *Investigator triangulation*, which refers to the use of 4 researchers in the field to gather data and another 4 people with a bilingual background to transcribe and interpret data.
- *Theoretical triangulation,* which consists of the use of four statistics of tests from PASW 18 and Nvivo 8 in interpreting data.
- *Methodological triangulation,* which involves of the use of semi-structured interviews and quantitative-based questionnaires.

Apart from this, the design of the research methodology also follows the current popular trend using mixed methods (Creswell, 2009) to create the triangulation of the research. It includes:

- Literature research
- Quantitative empirical research
- Qualitative empirical research

For literature research, desk work including reviewing the previous research retrieved from the library databases, websites, newspapers and documental papers was carried out with a view of exploring the existing gap to be filled or the specific questions that remained unanswered in the past. The aim of doing this part was to serve several purposes. Firstly, it critically investigated the outcomes previously arrived at in order to gain an overall understanding of the relevant components integrated into proposing an effective foreign language programme for China's trainees. Secondly, the researcher reviewed the literature and used it to provide evidence for the purpose of the study and the underlying problem addressed by the appropriate research methodology.

For the second and third empirical research referred to in this project, the researcher intends to use a mixed-methods research approach. Tashakkori and Teddlie (1998; 2003a) argued in favour of this design approach that if a research proposition has been generated and confirmed by two or more independent measuring approaches, the uncertainty of its interpretation is greatly reduced. And they believed that the most persuasive evidence comes through using more than one approach to an investigation. Creswell (2007) illustrates this by putting forward the view that in designing and conducting mixed-methods research, researchers need to know the alternative stances on world views and mixed-methods research and need to be able to articulate the stances they are using. Tashakkori and Teddlie (2003a) suggest that at least 13 different authors embrace pragmatism as a worldview or paradigm for mixed-methods research. Surely, all of these actually support the view that the two sets of findings may be inconsistent, but as Kenneth (1994) observed, such an occurrence underlines the problem of relying on just one measure or method. In view of this, the research has been designed so as to enable data triangulation (Bryman, 2001; Creswell, 1999) so that slices of data at different times on a variety of people are gathered.

6.3 Scheme of research methodology

The research is aimed at developing an effective model of foreign language training and offering the international communication managerial approach for Chinese adult language learners in light of China's actual needs. Two-tier levels of model have been proposed in the previous chapter. It is time to justify them. To achieve this goal, the following procedures have been designed for the research to follow.

- *Procedure one* – To investigate where foreign language training gaps are and where the need lies within China's organisations and companies. This procedure also identified existing shortcomings in current practices. Meanwhile, it explored the necessary interrelated theories which underpin the research to generate the theorised proposals in an effort to solve the practical problems in the field of education management. Reflecting on this research, the previous chapters 2 to 5 have constructed the framework of the intended theory using the principles of interpretivism through widely reviewing secondary data from relevant resources. This has also been accompanied by collecting the primary data generated from the interviews with managers during initial research. This as a result leads the research to interpreting primary and secondary data and puts forward the intended theory for further investigation. The design of this procedure is based on the premise that an exploration of a phenomenon – in the sense of this research, an issue relating to existing training programmes and an approach to resolve it, is needed. The design begins qualitatively (Creswell *et al.*, 2003).
- *Procedure two* – Based on the literature review and findings from the initial research, the researcher developed the research propositions and established research questions to be addressed. In this phase, the research looked into relevant theories and narrowed down the perspectives in order to generate a theory interconnecting the themes (Creswell, 2007). This is in line with what Creswell mentions that in qualitative research, inquiries are "up front" and identify how their experiences and backgrounds shape the interpretations they make through the coding and theme development process (*ibid.*). The hypothesised model will be considered as the main part of the contribution to the knowledge of foreign language education

under a certain set of circumstances that will be justified in the later stages of research.

- *Procedure three* – As noted previously, the author chose to use mixed methods. This method is designed to explore the issue sequentially and consists of two distinct steps: quantitative followed by qualitative (Creswell *et al.*, 2003). In this design, the author first collects and analyses the quantitative data and in turn investigates the attitudes of both managers and staff towards the proposed models. The qualitative analysis that follows is intended to help explain, validate, elaborate or enrich the quantitative results obtained in the first step. The second, qualitative step builds on the first. The rationale for this approach is that the second step is to numerically support and validate the results of the first quantitative work and the following stage of the qualitative data and their subsequent analysis results in a deeper understanding of the research problem. The intent of this procedure is that the quantitative step is emphasised; and qualitative analysis is to qualitatively generalise the quantitative results (Creswell, 2007). In addition, it should be noted that the remaining chapters of the research will use the principle of positivism to deductively investigate what is actually going on in the real world. Therefore, the overall framework of research methodology for the present project is depicted within Table 6–1 below:

Table 6–1 Scheme of research methodologies

Chapters	Chapter 2, 3 and 4	Chapter 5 and 6	Chapter 7 and 8
Objectives and content	Literature review	Theoretical framework Research methodology	Objective 1- to define where the need lies and where the deficits are within education management Objective 2- to identify existing shortcomings in current practices Objective 3- To justify the significance of the implications of a project-based foreign language training programme for Chinese employees Objective 4- To develop the ability of foreign language training suppliers to establish a management strategy for project-based language training

Continued Table

Chapters	Chapter 2, 3 and 4	Chapter 5 and 6	Chapter 7 and 8
Research Philosophy	Interpretivism	Interpretivism	Positivism
Research Design	Qualitative and inductive	Identify themes Hypothesis-generated	Mixed-methods (Qualitative and quantitative); and deductive analysis
Methods	Secondary data collection and critically review initial research	Qualitative and inductive	Numerical questionnaires survey, and subsequent qualitative interviews

Source: Author's research

6.4 Quantitative research design

To test the propositions, as in line with the natural science, the research employs the null hypothesis at the outset of the experiment (Bryman, 2001; Pallant, 2005). In statistics, the typical null hypothesis, at the outset of the experiment posits that no difference exists between the control and experimental groups. The null hypothesis plays a major role in testing the significance of differences between variables and it requires the research to collect data and measure how likely the particular set of data is (Howitt& Cramer, 2008). To collect the evidence to prove the propositions in this research, the rejection of null hypothesis will be examined considering if the data does not contradict the null hypothesis, then only a weak conclusion can be made; namely that the observed data set provides no strong evidence against the null hypothesis (Fisher, 1966).

The use of rejection of the null hypothesis, while widespread, offers several grounds for arguments in other disciplines as to its opposite – retaining null hypothesis, for example, *unit root test* – as often appeared in the literature of economics and finance (Dickey & Fuller, 1981; Kapetanios, 2005), and as well as *type II error* – as often used in examining drug effectiveness in pharmaceutical research (Wuensch, 1994). The null hypothesis in the former is that a *unit root* is present. If that hypothesis is rejected, one can estimate the series of the difference stationary; whilst if the presence of a *unit root* is maintained, then one should predict the series of the trend stationary model (Dickey & Fuller, 1981). While, the null hypothesis in the later is defined as failing to reject a false null hypothesis – in a sense to conclude that the drug is safe when in fact it is not. In contrast, for pragmatists, as contended by James (2000), 'truth' means the same thing as it means in science and 'truth' is the name of whatever proves itself. Powell (2001) also supports that a true proposition is one that facilitates fruitful paths of human discovery, and should be retained. So, the way to prove that the propositions in the research are true needs to be via a process of enquiry and data collection through examining the null hypothesis to each proposition. For practical purposes, the rejection of the null hypothesis is employed in this research.

6.4.1 Sample

Eight companies and organisations from Western China were selected for the survey. They are Ningxia Schaeffler Bearings Company, Bank of China (Ningxia Branch), China Chamber of International Commerce Yinchuan, Chamber of Commerce, Industrial and Commercial Bank (Ningxia Branch), OrganisationDepartment of Ningxia, Ningxia University, Intel Technology Development (Shanghai) Co. and China Oriental Group. Seven of them are situated in the northwest of China; the area is seen prospectively as "a crucial area for building a moderately prosperous society in an all- around way in ten and fifteen years", according to China's 12th Five-year Plan (Xinhua, 2010). One organisation from Shanghai is considered to be one of China's major 'growth engines' (Ou *et al.*, 1996), and it was the one that was only involved in the initial research. Four companies from the samples were state enterprises and another four were private enterprises. All of them have been included in the survey based on the selective criteria that they have business links with other countries and also they have schemes of foreign language training and have experience of managing foreign language training programmes for their staff over past 10 years. Besides, the sample was heterogeneous (Gillespie and Mileti, 1981). It comprised a variety of industries and services. This provided the degree of freedom necessary for testing research propositions, following the approach of Pugh and Hickson (1976) and successor studies (see Beyer and Trice, 1979). Their organizational researches achieved a degree of sample diversity that only a few cross-national studies match (Miller, 1987). Subsequent research confirmed that theories and causal models of organisational structure are applicable to samples of very different organisations (Schlevogt, 2002), which suggests that findings from this research may also apply to a wider set of organisations.

6.4.2 Questionnaire Design

The research largely followed Wittington's framework (2001) and adapted the design of the questionnaire's structure from adapting Basuki (2009). There were three reasons for this choice. First, Wittington and other scholars developed a wealth of theoretical insights on investigating strategy orientation (Berger & Milem, 2000) and management practice, as well as the relationships between these scales and various antecedents (Schlevogt, 2002). Secondly, Littrell (2002) implemented a staff and manager satisfaction survey, using a five-point Likert-scale technique for data collection. This forced-choice 'disagree – agree' technique was repeatedly used by many researchers looking into Chinese management (e.g. Littrell, 2002; Schlevogt, 2002). Thirdly, as will be demonstrated below, the psychometric properties of the various items adapted by Basuki (2009) are well validated.

The questionnaire was designed for both staff and managers. Each of them consisted of three sections totaling 64 questions, and the staff's questionnaire was comprised of 30 questions and the manager's questionnaire 40 questions. Both questionnaires cover the same questions with same styles but different genres of expressions designed to address the same variables. The staff's questionnaire covered their attitudes, reflections and biographical details; and in the manager's it covered socio-demographic background, attitudes and behaviour and biographical details as well. Closed questions were used in most cases, including either 5-point Likert scales or multiple-choice. A Likert five-point scale was designed and used as (1 = strongly disagree, 2 = disagree, 3 = neutral, 4 = agree and 5 = strongly agree). In addition, there were several open-ended questions to inquire whether respondents would like to receive details of the main findings of this study or whether they would like to participate further in the project. The descriptive statistics for both staff and manager questionnaires are as follows: multiple-choice questions (n = 13); multiple-item scales (n = 43); open-ended questions (n = 7). The average response time per questionnaire was 10 to 15 minutes. Meanwhile, for consistency, straightforwardness, and to ensure that the questionnaires could be completed relatively quickly, all statements were presented in the same format (Bryman, 2004). Furthermore, two versions of questionnaires in both English and Mandarin Chinese with the same format were designed to be ready for the Chinese respondents' preference.

To ensure appropriate methodological design of the questionnaire, four people with strong academic backgrounds within the same area and who were qualified to make appropriate judgments for the questionnaire were engaged in the process of questionnaire design and helped to work on designing the pattern, proof-reading, moderation and validation of the questionnaire. In addition, all the items were translated into Chinese and pilot-tested to ensure comprehensibility. The principle of relevant theory was followed to make sure the accuracy of the interpretation (Poland, 1995).

6.4.2.1 Questionnaire for Staff

The questionnaire for staff consists of two parts. Part A concerns the participant's attitudes and reflections, including 24 questions. These were designed as a representative mix which contains individual project design and content of individual project aimed to investigate both the hypothesised first-tier project (FTP), and the proposals of developing a project individually, project validation stage, implementation and revaluation.

For the FTP, items relating to the project created individually and independently included defining the individual's learning needs and the time needed which determines the necessity of individual project creation (items Q1, Q2); the content of the individual project including the needs analysis characterized by correlation of foreign language skills and professional effectiveness, work-related skills and individual project assessment, as well as motivations (items Q3, Q4, Q5, Q6, Q7, Q13 and Q14).

For the second-tier project (STP), the items consisting of evaluation of the individual project, implementation and revaluation characterised by joint assessment (items Q8, Q23, Q24), communicative and foreign language skills and cultural awareness (items Q9, Q10, Q11, and Q12), worked-related skills and problem-solving (items Q18, Q19 and Q20) and pedagogy and on-going assessment (items Q21 and Q22).

Part B consisted of the questions which concern the participants' personal details (that is, gender, age, educational background and their general attitudes towards the research.)

6.4.2.2 Questionnaire for Managers

The questionnaire for managers consisted of three parts. Part A is concerned with the background of the company and organisation where the participant is working, and included nine items, which were designed to collect data about the surveyed organisations' form of ownership, their sector of the economy, the scale of the business, the percentage of graduates employed, percentage of training employees, the length of time foreign language training offered and duration of the programmes.

Part B concerns the managers' attitudes and reflections, including 25 items which were designed to address the hypothesised first and second-tier level project.

For the first-tier project, items with five statements were designed similar to the staff's questionnaires, with the same issue as a focus but largely different in tone to be consistent with the managers' status. These mainly involve the individual project constructed in the beginning stage of the training programme (items Q1, Q2, Q3, Q4 and Q10).

For the second-tier project, items involved individual project evaluation (items Q11, Q12), implementation (Q13, Q14, Q15) and re-evaluation (Q16, Q17), as well as some other aspects which are highly likely to be determined by the managers such as programme preference (Q7), decision-making (Q8) content of programme design (Q5, Q6, Q9), programme management (Q18, Q19), communicative ability (Q20), cultural awareness (Q21), actual language needs analysis (Q22), formal instruction (Q23), self-managed learning approach (Q24) and work-related foreign language training (Q25).

6.4.3 Pilot study and validation

The pilot study in this research refers to so-called feasibility studies which are a small scale version, or trial run, done in preparation for the major study (Polit *et al.*, 2001). However, a pilot can also be the pre-testing or 'trying out' of a particular research instrument (Baker, 1994). Teijlingem (2011) demonstrates the importance of carrying out a pilot study saying that one of the advantages of conducting a pilot study is that it might give advance warning about where the main research project could fail, where research protocols may not be followed, or whether proposed methods or instruments are inappropriate or too complicated. Schlevogt (2002) also added that the purpose of the pilot study was to discover possible weaknesses, ambiguities, and other problems such as acceptability, ease of completion, reliability, and reproducibility of the questionnaire (Taylor *et al.*, 2001) in the survey research design and to correct them before full-scale data collection. Following common practice, the questionnaire and administrative procedures were pilot-tested with an effective sample size (n = 5), including participants from the target sample and professional researchers involving in designing the questionnaires. This sample size approximated to 1% of the level of respondents included in the final sample, as recommended in the literature (Sarantakos, 1993, p. 206). The researcher evaluated the results of the pilot according to its objectives.

6.4.4 Data collection method

This study collected its data from China. To ensure better quality and proper validity when conducting a survey in China, careful design is required to conform to local customers and circumstances. Because the Chinese government actually does not allow foreign organisations to conduct a questionnaire survey without government permission (Li, 2003), the questionnarie survey at organisation level was very difficult. A plethora of previous research in China often had the limitations of small sample size, of failure to control industrial differences and of very low response rates (Schlevogt, 2002). Moreover, the questionnaire surveys have relied heavily on self-reporting items, which often lead to common source bias and distorted questionnaire measurements. So, to improve the quality of data on the attitudes to training programmes through an international communicative strategy, the study adopted the key informant method (Phillips, 1981; Schlevogt, 2000a), as recommended when necessity dictates.

Schlevogt (2000i) explained that the key informant method entails selecting a knowledgeable informant in one or more organisations and asking them to play the role of a link to introduce the researcher to the managers who have expertise in the area that the research is intended to explore. It is assumed that the informant's role either provides him with comparatively specialised knowledge or that he is in some other respect representative of the unit. The term 'informant' is distinguished from 'respondent'. The latter reports on personal attitudes rather than on how the survey was conducted (Schlevogt, 2002).

The questionnaire was conducted through the informants for the companies and organisations investigated who distributed the well-bound standardised questionnaire to the respondents; every respondent answered the questions individually, and then returned the completed questionnaire to the informant directly. For the sake of validity and objectivity (Black, 1999), all respondents were allowed to take the questionnaire away so that they could fill it on their own without intervention of other people and without too many time restrictions (Black, 1999; Bredget, 2006). Usually they were given one to three months to work on them. There were 10 respondents who emailed the completed questionnaire back due to their time availability and work commitments.

6.4.5 Operationalisation and measurements

The research used an eclectic and creative approach (Stufflebeam & Shinkfield, 2007), choosing operational definitions and scales from earlier studies such as Basuki's and developing new ones where necessary. Wherever possible, the study adopted standard definitions and well-validated scales that had strong theoretical grounding and, through frequent application and replication, were shown to possess desirable psychometric properties (Kiresuk, Smith and Cardillo, 1994). Only by using this approach, which is commonplace within the research, can findings be compared with international data from other studies and knowledge accumulated (De Vaus, 2002). This approach follows common usage in the research literature. As noted by Churchill, Gilbert and Peter (1984), when at all possible, the research should use existing measurement scales or adapt them for its research purposes. The unnecessary use of new scales makes it difficult to compare and aggregate findings (Segars, 1997).

Since a novel model with two-tier levels was proposed, it is appropriate for the research to test and validate it. However, the concept concerned in the model looked very broad, thus serious consideration was given to the possibility that it comprised underlying dimensions which reflect different aspects of the concept in question (Bryman *et al.*, 2001). Very often it is possible to specify those dimensions on a *priori* grounds so that possible dimensions are established in advance of the formation of indicators of the concept.

Denzin's (2009) approach to the measurement of concepts viewed the search for underlying dimensions as an important ingredient. Similarly, Hall (1968) developed the idea of 'professionalism' as a consequence of his view that members of professionshave a distinctive constellation of attitudes to the nature of their work.

To design the research by establishing the possible dimensions reflecting the concept that is to be measured is in line with Denzin's approach (Denzin, 2009) to the measurement of concepts. He proposed that initially the research forms an image from a theoretical domain. This image reflects a number of common characteristics which denote the tendency for the researchers to have a deeper understanding of the concepts in relation to the management of the training programme and in each case a concept starts to be formed from those common characteristics. At the next stage, concept specification takes place (Bryman, 2001). We need to be aware that the concept specification stage is very useful because it not only reflects and captures the full complexity of concepts, but also serves as a means of bridging the general formulation of concepts and their measurement (*ibid.*).

6.4.5.1 Dimensions of concepts

Based on the literature reviews, the dominant elements or key concepts to be identified are a novel two-tier level model that significantly determines managing the programme. The first-tier project comprises of three stages:

- Individual task-based project
- Needs analysis of a foreign language
- Individual project evaluation

It should be noted that foreign language needs analysis actually consists of language skill demands analysis and technical and professional skills analysis.

The second-tier project (STP) encompasses four stages of programme management which determine the outcome as well as the implementation of training management.

- Building up an individual project
- Project validation
- Programme implementation
- Project evaluation

Looking at the concepts mentioned above, there are seven underlying dimensions which actually reflect the nature of these dominant elements. The research looked into these concepts to see whether they statistically support the reality of the existence of the innovative model.

6.4.5.2 Operationalisation and measurements

An overview of the constructs, operationalisation and measures used in this research is presented in tables 6-2, 6-3 and 6-4 below. These tables include detailed information on the procedures used to justify the proposed model, which is composed of two-tier levels. Based on Bryman and Cramer (2001) underlying dimensions derived from models examined were identified. Meanwhile, key elements relevant to each dimension have been synthesised, which consist of six essential elements (see Table 6–2).

Table 6–3 and 6-4 provide an overview of how the research attempts to test the proposition using established variables and appropriate statistic tests either for the staff questionnaire or the manager's questionnaire. To define and determine which statistical test is approriopate for the purpose of justification of each identified variable, four professional experts from Solent University in the field of statistics were involved in examining their suitablity.

Table 6–2 **Overview of constructs**

	First-tier Project	Second-tier Project
Objectives	Objective 1 and 2 – to identify training needs and existing programmer's deficits	Objective 3 and 4 – to test and analyse the hypothesised training model
Main Dimensions	Individual project	Innovative foreign language training model (including validation of individual project and assessment)
Key concepts	Building specific individual project Foreign language needs analysis Foreign language-based project evaluation	Project validation Programme implementation Evaluation
Underlying dimensions	Language skills demands and technical and work-related skills defined Foreign language-based project evaluation	Joint assessment Regular report (as a means of assessment) Joint evaluation
Research Proposition/ Hypothesis	P1. Chinese companies will embrace a foreign language training programme if it starts with a project created individually and independently prior to actual implementation. P2. An effective individual project will be created if it is based on learners' language skills needs and technical skills related to the work place. P3.Chinese companies are interested in launching a foreign language training programme if it aims to enhance professional skills and technical ability.	P4.Chinese companies or organizations will likely trigger a foreign language training programme if it aims to develop communicative, reading and writing abilities and cultural awareness. P5. Chinese employees will be more interested in foreign language training programmes if the pedagogic style is to combine formal instruction and self-centred learning. P6. Foreign language training programmes will be of more interest if they aim to develop the trainee's ability to solve problems which closely relate to their real work. P7. Chinese companies and organisations will be more interested in training programmes if there is the requirement of regular reports about the progress of trainees and on-going negotiation in course content incorporated into the training programme. P8. For the purpose of effective quality assurance, Chinese managers and programme providers will be jointly involved in the evaluation either at the stage of generating the learning project or at the end of the programme.

Source: Author's research

Table 6–3 Research operationalisation and measurements for staff (Source: From this study)

Level of arrangement	Construct/Variables	Operationalization	Types of scale	Items (Staff)	Measuring techniques
First-tier project	Individual project (IP)	Degree of attitudes to individual learning needs, learning target, foreign language needs and work-related foreign language	5-point Likert	5 (Q1, Q2, Q3, Q4 and Q10)	One sample Kolomogorov Smirnov test
First-tier project	Work-related skills (WRS)	Degree of attitudes to foreign language needs and work-related skills	5-point Likert	2 (Q5 and Q13)	Related-Samples Wilcoxon Signed Ranks Test
First-tier project	Foreign language needs assessment (FLNA)	Degree of attitudes to foreign language needs assessment	5-point Likert	1 (Q6)	One sample Kolomogorov Smirnov test
First-tier project	Joint assessment of individual project (JAIP)	Degree of attitudes to evaluation by training providers and organisations	5-point Likert	3 (Q7, Q8 and Q23)	Kolomogorov-Smirnov test
First-tier project	Language communicative ability (LCA)	Degree of attitudes on what skills need to be developed through training	5-point Likert	1 (Q9)	Correlation coefficient
Second-tier project	Cultural awareness (CA)	Attitudes on developing cultural awareness in training programme	5-point Likert	1 (Q11)	Correlation coefficient
Second-tier project	Foreign language skills (FLS)	Skills intended to be improved	5-point Likert	1 (Q12)	Correlation coefficient
Second-tier project	Formal instruction (FI)	Degree of attitudes on formal instruction and informal lessons	5-point Likert	2 (Q15 and Q16)	One sample Kolomogorov Smirnov test
Second-tier project	Self-managed learning (SML)	Degree of attitudes on self-managed learning	5-point Likert	1 (Q17)	One sample Kolomogorov Smirnov test
Second-tier project	Problem-solving ability (PSA)	Degree of attitudes on developing foreign language ability only or problem-solving ability	5-point Likert	3 (Q18, Q19 and Q20)	One sample Kolomogorov – Smirnov test
Second-tier project	Regular reports (RR)	Degree of attitudes on how to monitor the learning progress; suggesting monthly report	5-point Likert	2 (Q21 and Q22)	Kolomogorov- Smirnov, Effect size
Second-tier project	Joint assessment (JA)	Degree of attitudes on proposing joint assessment from both training providers and organization managers	5-point Likert	1 (Q24)	Kolmogorov – Smirnov test

Source: Author's research

Table 6–4 **Research operationalisation and measurements for manager**

Level of arrangement	Construct/Variables	Operationalisation	Types of scale	Items (Manager)	Measuring techniques
First-tier	Individual project (IP*)	Degree of attitudes on individual learning needs, learning target, foreign language needs and work-related skills	5-point Likert	Q1, Q2, Q3 and Q10	One-sample t-test analysis
First-tier	Work-related language skills (WRS*)	Degree of attitudes on development of practical vocational skills and general language skills	5-point Likert	Q4 and Q7	Related Sign test
First-tier	Training needs analysis (TNA*)	Degree of attitudes on what real needs the trainee demands	5-point Likert	Q7	Frequencies analysis, One sample Kolomogorov – Smirnov test
Second-tier	Language communicative ability (LCA*), cultural awareness (CA*) and foreign language skills (FLS*)	Attitudes on the preference of learning content	5-point Likert	Q7 and Q9	One sample Kolomogorov – Smirnov test, One sample t-test
Second-tier	Formal instruction(FI*) and self-managed learning (SML*)	Attitudes on the combination of formal instruction and self-managed learning	5-point Likert	Q23 and Q24	Wilcoxon Signed Ranks test
Second-tier	Problem solving ability (PSA*)	Degree of attitudes to the ultimate goal of managing a training programme	5-point Likert	Q25	One-sample t-test
Second-tier	Regular reports (RR*)	Degree of attitudes on how to monitor the learning progress; suggesting monthly report	5-point Likert	Q11 and Q12	Frequencies analysis and Mann-Whitney U test
Second-tier	Joint assessment (JA*)	Degree of attitudes on proposing joint assessment from both training providers and organization managers	5-point Likert	Q16 and Q17	Frequencies analysis and Mann-Whitney U test

Source: Author's research

6.5 Qualitative Research Design

This section outlines the qualitative research design, covering questionnaire design, the choice of companies, validation and sampling.

6.5.1 Questionnaire design

A semi-structured questionnaire for qualitative data collection was designed; it consists of three sections with 12 questions covering a wide range of aspects relating to explored issues. The major consideration in using semi-structured interviews is that in survey research using questionnaires it is considered desirable to standardize the interview situation for all respondents – same briefing, same questions and also for the interviewer to respond to each interviewee as a unique person, and to allow, indeed encourage, interviewees to expand on topics as they wish and to raise topics of their own. Making a close trusting relationship with respondents may be regarded as a benefit (Bradburn, 2004; Gomm, 2009). In addition, all the items were translated into Chinese and pilot-tested to ensure comprehensibility. The translation followed the principle of relevance framework (Meng, 2000). In translating, the principle of relevance was kept because it governed the selection of context and guided the inference of intention (Cao, 2007; Meng, 2000).

6.5.2 Choice of companies

According to Leeuw *et al.* (2009) and Gomm (2009), the key issue for sample surveys is how the researcher can select and sustain statistically representative samples. They further claim that statistical representativeness is the basis for an important form of generalisation.

The companies and organisations were mentioned in a previous section 6.4. The objective in selecting these companies was to obtain more qualitative data and real-world richness, which supplemented the quantitative findings.

The Chinese companies were selected because they were judged to be typical examples in terms of ownership mode and geographic location. Many of them are medium-sized and large companies and organisations and were chosen because of the economic potiential to run foreign language training programme through an international communicative strategy. Among these companies and organisations, Ningxia Organisation Department, one of the important departments in charge of training cadres and controling personnel assignments in China, was very secretive and tightly controlled as it is the key organisation responsible for every single application to establish links with foreign countries and it also has sent five groups of leaders to the USA, New Zealand and Australia for a one-year programme of training over the past five years. The interview had to be solicited in writing and be approved at an interdepartmental meeting.

The qualitative data were collected mainly through interviews with top managers or executives and archival data which they were prepared to make available.

6.5.3 Validation and reliability

Validity for this research means a relationship of accuracy between the responses and the reality the responses were intended to capture: construct validity (Gomm, 2004). The higher the level of the validity is, the more accurate and meaningful the measured results are (Garson, 2007; Wortzel, 1979). Since looking into the effectiveness of each company and organisation's training programme relied mainly on primary data, the research followed the methodological guidelines recommended for empirical research to avoid bias including co-operation bias, self-serving bias, social desirability bias (Gomm, 2004) in an effort to construct a higher degree of validity.

Kirk and Miller (1986) define reliability as 'the degree to which the finding is independent of accidental circumstances of the research' (pp.41-42). Silverman (2001) also points out that checking the reliability is closely related to assuring the quality of field notes, audio recordings and guaranteeing public access to the process of the productions involved. Following these theories, the research invited four volunteers with bilingual backgrounds to transcribe and re-transcribe the interview recordings (Matheson, 2007).

6.6 Research fieldwork

In-depth interviews with the company's CEO and other top managers were undertaken within eight companies and organisations in Ningxia Province, who acted as key informants. The general structure and semi-structured questionnaire were used as the interview guide and the point of departure for the discussion. Interviews as usual had to be set up in advance through e-mails and phone calls as a result of the interviewees' busy schedules. Nevertheless, booking interviews with those top managers or CEOs with a high political position turned out to be difficult, and an agreed appointment often took a few weeks or even a few months to set up. In order to get hold of the managers who are actually the best person to be interviewed, the researcher had to make all efforts through the networks to contact these top managers and CEOs. This resulted in many delays before travelling to meetings. Many companies and organisations are scattered across different cities, which necessitated much travelling. To conduct interviews adverse weather sometimes had to be overcome, including on one occasion heavy snow, which even made the trip dangerous.

The informants were visited in their offices and the probing questions were asked to collect evidence for each major component relating to training management. All interviews were recorded. Interviewees were asked for permission and each was asked to sign the 'Consent for Voluntary Participation' (see Appendix A). Interviews were targeted, focusing directly on the key issues to be examined in the research, and provided many insights. However, some bias may result from poorly constructed questions, the characteristics of the informant, and inaccuracies because of the poor quality of recording. Further inquiry was sometimes necessary afterwards.

6.7 Comparison between the managers' and staff's attitudes

In order to test the novel model proposed by this research, it was also designed to investigate the different attitudes from both managers and staff. To achieve this, the research mainly focused on collecting primary data from both managers and staff using quantitative questionnaires, and then planned to go in-depth to explore more answers from interviews with managers. The design of the methodology followed the principle of mixed research methods (Creswell, 2009; Newman & Ridenour, 2008) and also achieved the purpose for research triangulation (Flick, 2009).

6.8 Summary

In conclusion, this chapter introduces the research framework, inferences and designed procedures of how to conduct the justification for the research propositions. In outline, procedure one mainly focuses on objective 1: to define where the need lies and where the gaps are within education management; and objective 2: to identify existing shortcomings in current practices. Procedure two is to focus on the method of addressing objective 3: to explore a novel programme model with two-tier levels. And procedure three is aimed to design a mixed research methodology used to seek the answer for objective 4: to analyse and justify the hypothesized training model. Meanwhile, key concepts i) building specific individual projects; ii) foreign language needs analysis; iii) foreign language-based project evaluation; iv) project validation; v) programme implementation; vi) re-evaluation; and underlying dimensions: i) time used for building individual project; ii) definition of language skills demands and technical skills; iii) foreign language-based project evaluation; iv) joint assessment; v) regular diary reports; vi) joint re-evaluation have been derived from the proposed two-tier projects and are synthesised and highlighted (Bryman & Cramer, 2001).

Statistical tests such as reliability test, Spearman Correlation coefficient, Kolmogorov-Smirnov test, one-sample t-test sign test, Wilcoxon Signed Ranks test and Mann-Witney U test were used to analyse the data collected from both staff respondents and manager respondents. The reliability was used to test internal consistency of the sets of questions for each dimension. The Spearman correlation coefficient was used to identify and quantify the relationships between the measured variables. Kolmogorov-Smirnov, one-sample t-test and sign test were used when the researcher decided to look into the attitudes of either staff or managers depending on various correspondent data property and its distributions. Whereas, Wilcoxon Signed Ranks test and Mann-Whitney U test mainly examines the result of the comparison between staff's and manager's attitudes with the aim of probing into the in-depth research questions, which are explored in the qualitative interviews.

Design of both quantitative and qualitative questionnaires has been detailed and summarised in this chapter. Meanwhile, samples, reliability and validity and research fieldwork were also discussed to make sure that the research had been undertaken following appropriate guidelines in order to achieve optimal data accuracy (Silverman, 2004).

Chapter 7 Data Analysis

7.1 Introduction

This chapter contains five sections which aim to describe the quantitative and qualitative analysis undertaken in the research.Section 7.2 demonstrates the quantitative data analysis, which introduces the properties of the data, the recoding, the values, and reliability analysis and test results of each question from the quantitative questionnaires for both staff and managers. The comparison between managers' and staff's data is illustrated in section 7.2.9. The qualitative data analysis based on the data collection through interviews with managers is illustrated in 7.4. Finally, a summary of the test results is provided in section 7.5.

7.2 Quantitative data analysis

7.2.1 Results of data collection

Two hundred and ten questionnaires for staff were sent to eight companies and organisations and 136 responses were received, a return rate of 64.7%. Of the eight questionnaires for managers, 8 came back, with 100% rate of response. This high response rate confirmed Harzing (1996) justification that to increase high rates of response in an international research is not only to pay a careful attention on the understanding of two different cultures (Mullen, 1995), but also to a strategic personal approach. On the cover of each questionnaire, it was explicitly explained that this research is an international study, which possibly generated an enthusiastic response from the Chinese respondents. The reason for such high response rates was possibly because the research followed survey techniques proposed by Bruce *et al.* (2009). firstly, It consists of sending an invitation message in the hope of establishing personal relationships with informants who will then be entrusted to play the role as the gate-keepers. Secondly, regular meetings are organised to explain the project goal, describe the timeline and explain sensitivity to mechanisms for ensuring anonymity and ease of participation. Finally, the importance of the survey was illustrated and stressed by informing participants that this was a research project conducted in the setting of an international background, which had drawn much attention from participants.

7.2.2 Recoding the values of variables

Due to the cultural factors which affect the people's actions in response to the questions posed to them, Chinese people are generally likely to follow the majority's attitudes by saying "yes" or "nodding heads" (Ip, 2009; Littrell, 2002). By doing so, they attempt to avoid making mistakes which might attract blame from their superiors (Keller, 2005). In view of this, the researcher has carefully designed the questionnaires in order to make them varied in a way that responses from either Chinese managers or staff who are likely to say yes to everything (yeasayers) or no (naysayers) (Bryman *et al.*, 2001) do not end up with an extreme score. While designing the questionnaire, some questions have been worded with negative tones rather than positive tones. Specifically, the researcher has worded five questions assessing the importance of creating individual projects and on-going monitoring in the negative. These five questions for staff are: *1) It is not important to define the individual's learning needs clearly; 2) I don't think it needs time to conduct my foreign language needs analysis before the programme of training starts; 3) There is no correlation between improving foreign language skills and developing my professional effectiveness; 4) I don't care if a foreign language training programme is closely related to my work-related skills or not; and 21) I am reluctant to report my progress because I think it destroys my motivation.*

For managers, questionnaires are devised based on the same concept. Six questions that are worded in the negative are: *2) I believe that it will be effective if my staff attend a training programme without setting a learning target; 4) The ultimate goal of managing a foreign language training programme is to develop language skills only; 6) I think a foreign language training programme leading to a degree, is not a crucial factor for a successful training programme; 10) Developing an individual project is unnecessary for my staff before they attend a language programme; 12) Regular reports from staff about their progress are not important to maintain successful learning; and 13) The training provider's involvement in the process when staff set their learning objectives is unnecessary.*

All of these questions above were drafted in the questionnaire in order to help the respondents take them seriously and base their answers on what they actually think. Doing this also draws the attention of our respondents to what we are trying to accomplish.

These questions are answered in terms of a five-point Likert scale ranging from 1(strongly disagree) to 5(strongly agree). When analysing the data, it is necessary to recode the answers to the negatively worded questions (Bryman & Cramer, 2001), so that 1 becomes 5, 2 becomes 4, 4 becomes 2, and 5 becomes 1.

7.2.3 Choice of statistical tests

A variety of statistics tests including reliability analysis, Kolmogorov-Smirnov (K-S) test, correlation coefficient, one sample t-test, two related samples test, and non-parametric sign test are used, depending on the purpose of addressing the diverse questions derived from the research propositions. The reliability analysis is used to test the internal consistency of the sets of questions for each dimension. It is also necessary to review the measures property of the collected data, so the test of goodness-of-fit of the data has been conducted in order to identify whether the data collected were normally distributed or non-distributed. This would help the researcher to decide which kind of statistical test could be used to test the statistical significance of the data. Finally, based on the result of the K-S test which indicates that the data collected were non-distributed, a Mann-Whitney U test will be used to compare the attitudes from both staff and managers concerning the addressed questions.

7.2.4 Reliability Analysis

Cronbach's alpha was used to measure internal reliability and inner consistency of the questions. According to Nunnally (1978), McKinley *et al.* (1997), and Cronbach, Lee and Shavelson (2004) an alpha value between 0.70 and 0.98 indicates high reliability, while a value above 0.6 is acceptable for exploratory research. In this research, the results of measuring internal reliability for each item of the staff responses lie in the range of 0.766 to 0.787 (see Tables 7–1 and 7–2: Cronbach's alpha value for staff and managers). This result has indicated that the internal consistency of all dimensions is high enough to be acceptable so that the questions will be reliable to test the properties of the variables.

Table 7–1 Cronbach's Alpha value for staff (n = 133)

Variables	Quantity of questions	Cronbach's α
Individual project (IP)	5	0.783
Work-related skill (WRS)	2	0.778
Foreign language needs analysis (FLNA)	1	
Joint assessment of individual project (JAIP)	3	0.771
Language communication ability (LCA)	1	
Cultural awareness (CA)	1	
Foreign language skills (FLS)	1	
Motivation (Mot)	1	

Continued Table

Variables	Quantity of questions	Cronbach's α
Formal instruction (FI)	2	0.777
Self-management learning (SML)	1	
Problem-solving ability (PSA)	3	0.776
Regular report (RR)	2	0.784
Jointly assessing objectives (JAO)	1	

Table 7–2 Cronbach's Alpha value for managers (n = 10)

Variables	Quantity of questions	Cronbach's α
Individual project (IP*)	4	0.846
Work-related skills (WRS*)	1	
Foreign language need analysis (FLNA*)	1	
Joint assessment (JAO*)	2	0.786
Language communication ability (LCA*)	1	
Cultural awareness (CA*)	1	
Foreign language skills (FLS*)	1	
Formal instruction (FI*)	1	
Self-management learning (SML*)	1	
Problem-solving ability (PSA*)	1	
Regular report (RR*)	2	0.842

7.2.5 Demographic data analysis

The demographic data from the questionnaire included gender, age, and number of working years, as well as information about the respondent's position in the organisation and the nature of the business (see Table 7–3).The surveyed companies and organisations were all medium or large size, state-run, and with more than 1000 employees, nearly 25% of whom were graduates; all of the surveyed companies and organisations had already run foreign language training programmes over five years and nearly 10% of employees had received, or will receive language training. Ninety per cent of staff respondents and 100% of managers had received a first degree. More than 81% of staff respondents have more than two years of work experience and all managers in the survey have worked for the current organisation more than 15 years, so are very experienced. For details, please see Table 7–3 staff sample.

Table 7–3　　Staff sample properties (n = 133)

Biographical details	Category	n	Percentage (%)
Gender	Male	69	51.9
	Female	64	48.1
Age	30 and under	63	46.6
	31-40	42	31.6
	41-50	26	19.5
	50 and above	2	1.5
Educational level	Vocational and technical college level	2	1.5
	2 or 3 years college level	12	9.0
	Bachelor Degree	91	68.4
	Master Degree or Higher	28	21.1

Table 7–4　　Manager sample properties (n = 10)

Biographical details	Category	n	Percentage (%)
Gender	Male	7	70
	Female	3	30
Age	31-40	3	30
	41-50	6	60
	51-60	1	10
Educational Level	2 or 3 years college level	1	10
	Bachelor Degree	6	60
	Master Degree or Higher	3	30
Position in organisation	CEO	2	20
	Manager and above	8	80
Working years	6-10 years	1	10
	11-15 years	1	10
	15 years or more	8	80

Continued Table

Nature of Organisation	Category	n	Percentage (%)
Ownership	Public sector	8	80
	Private sector	2	20
Scale of business	Medium and above	10	100
Percentage of graduates	26% – 50%	2	20
	More than 50%	8	80
Training participants	Technical personnel	9	90
	Managers	1	10
Percentage of trained employees	6%-10%	2	20
	More than 10%	8	80
Length of running foreign language training	Less than 5 years	1	10
	5 years or more	9	90

7.2.6 The agreement and mean of each question

The agreement and mean of each question staff (n = 132) and manager (n = 10) is shown in tables 7–5 and 7–6 below.

Table 7–5 The agreement and mean of each question (staff)

No. of questionnaire	Agreement (low → high) 1 = Strongly disagree 2 = Disagree 3 = Neutral 4 = Agree 5 = Strongly Agree					Median	Mean±SD
	1-n(%)	2-n(%)	3-n(%)	4-n(%)	5-n(%)		
IP1	1(0.8%)	8(6.0%)	5(3.8%)	81(60.9)	38(28.6)	4.00	4.11±0.791
IP2	2(1.5%)	9(6.8%)	16(12.0%)	82(61.7%)	24(18.0%)	4.00	3.88±0.835
IP3	2(1.5%)	13(9.8%)	11(8.3%)	70(52.6%)	37(27.8%)	4.00	3.95±0.944
IP4	2(1.5%)	11(8.3%)	10(7.5%)	84(63.2%)	25(18.8%)	4.00	3.90±0.855
IP5	0(0%)	25(18.8)	5(3.8%)	82(61.7%)	21(15.8%)	5.00	3.74±0.943
WRS1	1(0.85)	2(1.5%)	6(4.5%)	54(40.6%)	70(52.6%)	4.00	4.43±0.721
WRS2	8(6.0%)	38(28.6%)	16(12.0%)	65(48.9%)	6(4.5%)	4.00	3.17±1.084
FLNA	1(0.8%)	13(9.8%)	8(6.0%)	73(54.9%)	38(28.6%)	4.00	4.01±0.900
JAIP1	1(0.8%)	2(1.5%)	13(9.8%)	69(51.9%)	48(36.1%)	4.00	4.21±0.739

Continued Table

No. of questionnaire	Agreement (low → high) 1 = Strongly disagree 2 = Disagree 3 = Neutral 4 = Agree 5 = Strongly Agree					Median	Mean±SD
	1-n(%)	2-n(%)	3-n(%)	4-n(%)	5-n(%)		
JAIP2	1(0.8%)	0(0%)	12(9.0%)	77(57.9%)	43(32.3%)	4.00	4.21±0.663
JAIP3	2(1.5%)	15(11.3%)	11(8.3%)	80(60.2%)	24(18.0%)	4.00	3.84±0.928
LCA	0(0%)	26(19.5%)	15(11.3%)	60(45.1%)	32(24.1%)	4.00	3.74±1.036
CA	1(0.8%)	24(18.0%)	29(21.8)	51(38.3%)	27(20.3%)	4.00	3.60±1.033
FLS	0(0%)	25(18.8%)	21(15.8%)	50(37.6%)	35(26.3%)	4.00	3.73±1.060
MOT	0(0%)	11(9.8%)	13(9.8%)	87(65.4%)	22(16.5%)	4.00	3.90±0.767
FI1	0(0%)	20(15.0%)	13(9.8%)	75(56.4%)	24(18.0%)	4.00	3.78±0.919
FI2	0(0%)	29(21.8%)	16(12.0%)	52(39.1%)	36(27.1%)	4.00	3.71±1.091
SML	1(0.8%)	2(1.5%)	19(14.3%)	13(9.8%)	78(58.6%)	4.00	3.64±1.262
PSA1	0(0%)	13(9.8%)	8(6.0%)	56(42.1%)	56(42.1%)	4.00	4.17±0.923
PSA2	0(0%)	7(5.3%)	8(6.0%)	70(52.6%)	47(35.3%)	4.00	4.19±0.773
PAS3	0(0%)	2(1.5%)	2(1.5%)	58(43.6%)	71(53.4%)	5.00	4.49±0.611
RR1	1(0.8%)	16(12.0%)	24(18.0%)	84(63.2%)	7(5.3%)	4.00	3.61±0.798
RR2	1(0.8%)	26(19.5%)	20(15.0%)	76(57.1%)	8(6.0%)	4.00	3.49±0.906
JAO	1(0.8%)	15(11.3%)	7(5.3%)	89(66.9%)	20(15.0%)	4.00	3.85±0.842

Table 7–6 The agreement and mean of each question (manager)

No. of questionnaire	Agreement (low → high) 1 = Strongly disagree 2 = Disagree 3 = Neutral 4 = Agree 5 = Strongly Agree					Median	Mean±SD
	1-n(%)	2-n(%)	3-n(%)	4-n(%)	5-n(%)		
IP*1	0(0%)	0(0%)	0(0%)	3(30%)	7(70%)	5.00	4.70±0.483
IP*2	0(0%)	1(10%)	0(0%)	5(50%)	3(30%)	5.00	4.00±0.943
IP*3	0(0%)	0(0%)	0(0%)	6(60%)	4(40%)	5.00	4.40±0.516
IP*4	0(0%)	1(10%)	0(0%)	6(60%)	3(30%)	4.00	4.10±0.876
FLNA*	0(0%)	1(10%)	2(20%)	4(40%)	1(10%)	5.00	3.70±0.823
WRS*	0(0%)	0(0%)	0(0%)	3(30%)	7(70%)	5.00	4.70±0.483
RR*1	0(0%)	0(0%)	0(0%)	5(50%)	5(50%)	4.50	4.10±0.527

Continued Table

No. of questionnaire	Agreement (low → high) 1 = Strongly disagree 2 = Disagree 3 = Neutral 4 = Agree 5 = Strongly Agree					Median	Mean±SD
	1-n(%)	2-n(%)	3-n(%)	4-n(%)	5-n(%)		
RR*2	2(20%)	0(0%)	1(10%)	6(60%)	1(10%)	4.00	3.60±0.966
JAO*1	1(10%)	8(80%)	1(10%)	0(0%)	0(0%)	2.00	2.00±0.471
JAO*2	0(0%)	0(0%)	0(0%)	6(60%)	4(40%)	4.00	4.40±0.516
LCA*	0(0%)	0(0%)	0(0%)	6(60%)	4(40%)	4.00	4.40±0.516
CA*	0(0%)	0(0%)	0(0%)	8(60%)	2(20%)	4.00	4.20±0.422
FLS*	1(10%)	3(30%)	4(40%)	2(20%)	0(0%)	3.00	2.70±0.949
FI*	0(0%)	0(0%)	1(10%)	8(80%)	1(10%)	4.00	4.00±0.471
SML*	0(0%)	0(0%)	1(10%)	5(50%)	4(40%)	4.00	4.30±0.675
PSA*	0(0%)	0(0%)	2(20%)	4(40%)	3(30%)	4.00	4.10±0.738

7.2.7 Analysis of staff questionnaire

Research proposition one

Chinese companies will embrace a foreign language training programme if it starts with a project created individually and independently prior to actual implementation.

For the question of whether a foreign language training programme starts with a project created individually and independently, the null hypothesis H_0 is that there is no relationship between starting with individual project creation and increasing motivation for foreign language training programme. There are five measured items (IP1-Q1, IP2-Q2, IP3-Q3, IP4-Q4 and IP5-Q10) in the questionnaire that are actually designed to address the question about *individual project need*. The questionnaire firstly went to staff to test their attitudes over the related questions. Descriptive statistics including means and standard deviation are showed in Table 7–5 above.

The first one (IP1) is looking at whether staff are in favour of the individual project; the second one (IP2) asks whether they need time to create an individual project; the third (IP3) addresses the correlation between improving foreign language skills and development of professional effectiveness; the fourth (IP4) investigates attitudes about the kind of skills staff need to be trained and the fifth (IP5) is on the kind of language skills they need.

To test the question, the research used the K-S test based on the understanding that the test is to examine whether a sample was from a normally distributed population (Black, 1999; Field, 2009). As the research used five items to assess the question, it was preferable and reasonable to combine them into one index (Bryman and Cramer, 2001). Therefore, the five items have been computed using PASW into one addressed variable IP. The histogram of frequency shows that the result lies on the value of 4 which is "agree" (mean = 3.91, Std. Dev. = 0.485, N = 132) (see Figure 7–1). In addition, the outcome of the one-sample Kolmogorov-Smirnov test has indicated that the observed data distribution is significantly different from a normal distribution as the two-tailed significance of the test is very small (0.007), which means a big significance (see Table 7–7). The null hypothesis is rejected. These outcomes actually have supported the research assumption one that foreign language training programmes may possibly start with a project created individually and independently prior to actual implementation.

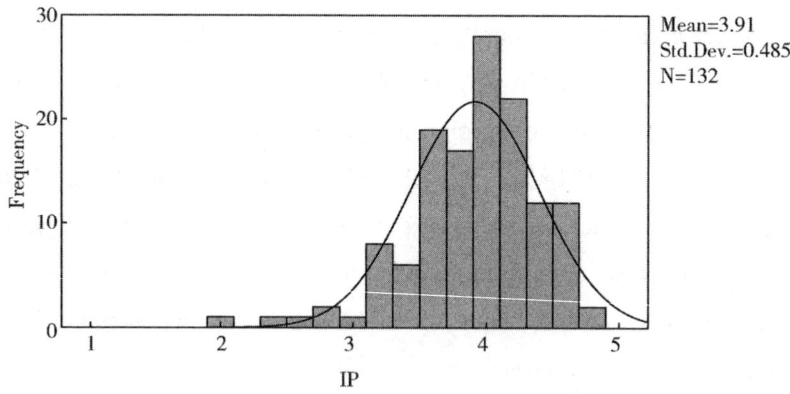

Figure 7–1 Histogram of frequency for IP

Table 7–7 The result of one-sample Kolmogorov-Smirnov test

Null Hypothesis	Test	Mean±SD	Sig.	Decision
There is no relationship between starting with an individual project creation and prompting the management of foreign language training programme	One-sample Kolmogorov-Smirnov test	3.914±0.485	0.007	Reject the null hypothesis

Research proposition two

An effective individual project would be built up if it is based on learners' language skill needs and technical skills related to the work place.

To explore whether an individual project should be specific to staff foreign language needs and work-related technical skills, the answers to the variable of individual project (IP) and work-related skills (WRS1 and WRS2, computerised as WRS) while the creation of staff individual learning objectives was investigated. The research firstly used frequency to examine the outcomes. As indicated in Figure 7–2, the result has shown a comparatively high scale of agreement with incorporating work-related technical skills training into an individual language project (mean = 3.80, median = 4.00 and SD = 0.615). Secondly, as IP has also demonstrated a comparatively higher scale, the researcher decided to use a related sample test to compare whether there is a significant difference between them. If there is no significant difference between them, it can be assumed that technical skills related to the work place are equally important as developing individual learners' foreign language skills. The null hypothesis is the median difference between IP and WRS equals 0.

Table 7–8 Result of comparison between WRS and IP

Null Hypothesis	Test	Mean±SD	Sig.	Decision
WRS is equally important as IP (The median of differences between IP and WRS equals 0).	Related-Samples Wilcoxon Signed Ranks Test	3.80±0.615	0.053	Retain the null hypothesis

N = 132

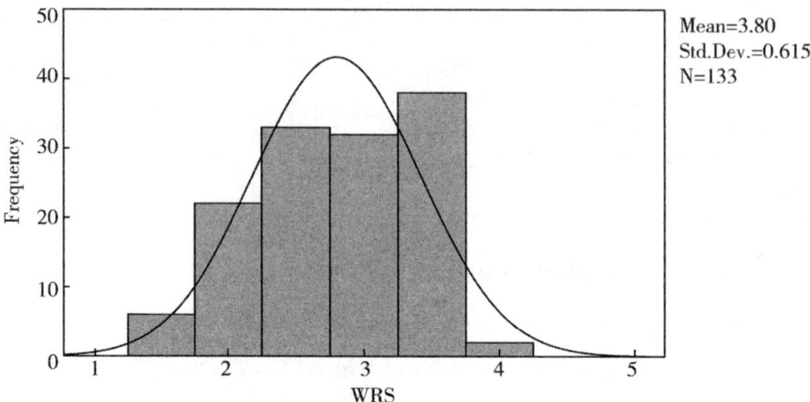

Figure 7–2 Histogram of frequency for WRS

Table 7–9 Result of Wilcoxon Signed Ranks test

WRS – IP	N	Mean Rank	Sum of Ranks	Z	Asymp. Sig.(2-tailed)
Negative Ranks	65[a]	68.25	4436.00		
Positive Ranks	56[b]	52.59	29.45.00		
Ties	11[c]				
Total	132			-1.931[d]	0.053

WRS<IP b. WRS>IP c. WRS = IP d. Based on positive ranks

The Wilcoxon Signed Ranks test compares the number of positive and negative differences between two scores from the same related samples, which are staff members in this case. If two responses for two different variables IP and WRS are similar, then these differences should be normally distributed. The output in Table 7–9 has displayed the number of negative, positive and ties differences. There are 11 ties, 56 positive differences (WRS>IP) and 65 negative ones (WRS<IP). The test also shows there is no significant difference between two means with 2-tailed test (Sig 0.053, stronger than 0.05), which means the null hypothesis has to be retained in that there is no change in one particular direction between two responses.

Research proposition three

Chinese companies are interested in launching a foreign language training programme if it aims to enhance professional skills and technical ability.

WRS1 "*I believe developing an individual project which aims to mix development of language skills and work-related skills is an effective way of implementing foreign language training*" and WRS2 "*The development of language skills rather than work skills needs to be focused on foreign language training programmes run through international collaboration*" were designed to examine the question. WRS1 aims to investigate whether the mixture of developing language skills and work-related skills or a non-mixture of them is an effective way of implementing foreign language training; therefore, the null hypothesis is the mixture of them equals the non-mixture. WRS2 aims to investigate whether the development of language skills only rather than work skills needs to focus on foreign language training programmes, so the null hypothesis is the development of language skills only is equally important as the mixture of developing language skills and work-related skills.

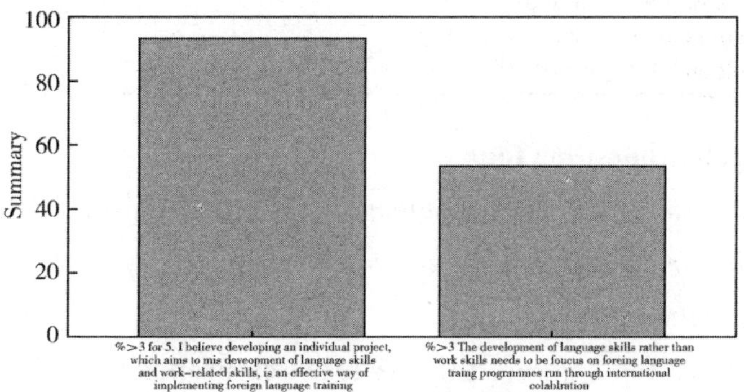

Figure 7–3 Results of WRS1 and WRS2

Figure 7–3 displays the outcomes from the respondents to the two questions. It demonstrates that more than 90% of staff respondents (%>3) support mixing development of language skills and work-related skills, which will result in an effective way of implementing foreign language training;

however, nearly 60% of them (%< 3) do not support the assumption that it focuses on developing language skills only.

The Kolmogorov-Smirnov test was also used to test the null hypotheses of each variable. The result showed that both WRS1 and WRS2 are significantly different after comparing the mean of the estimated (WRS1: mean = 4.43, SD = 0.72, Sig. = 0.000; and WRS2: mean = 3.17, SD = 1.08, Sig. = 0.000). So from the results in Table 7–10, we can reject the null hypotheses for both WRS1 and WRS2. The alternative is enhancing foreign language skills and work-related skills are equally important in managing a successful foreign language training programme run through international collaboration.

Table 7–10 The result of one-sample Kolmogorov-Smirnov test for WRS1and WRS2

Variables	Null Hypothesis	Test	Mean±SD	Sig.	Decision
WRS1	The mixture of developing language skills and work-related skills equals to a non-mixture of them	One-Sample Kolmogorov-Smirnov Test	4.43±0.72	0.000	Reject the null hypothesis
WRS2	The development of language skills only is equally important as the mixture of developing language skills and work-related skills	One-Sample Kolmogorov-Smirnov Test	3.17±1.08	0.000	Reject the null hypothesis

Research proposition four

Chinese companies or organisations are likely to trigger a foreign language training programme if it aims to develop communicative, reading and writing abilities and cultural awareness.

To explore the answers for this research proposition, four questions (measured as LCA, IP5, CA and FLS) were designed in the staff questionnaire. The statistics' descriptive output (Table 7–5) has shown that answers for FLS have a large percentage with a cumulative per cent of 73.3 (with mean 3.73, median 4.00 and SD 1.060), meaning that the observed samples are taking account of the relationship between the organisation's operational success and foreign language skills. For CA, the result of approximately 79.5 (with mean 3.60, median 4.00 and SD 1.033) indicates that the staff respondents place much more emphasis on developing cultural awareness as part of a foreign language training programme. At the same time, the result of IP5 (with mean 3.74, median 4.00 and SD 0.943) reveals that foreign language skills of reading and writing are also embracing the foreign language needs of the staff members. In addition, the result of CA has denoted that there is a stronger positive response for developing the ability to language communication ability (LCA) than to study foreign language knowledge only (with a cumulative per cent of 'agree' of 75.9, mean 3.74, median 4 and SD 1.033).

Table 7–11 Correlations among LCA, IP5, CA and FLS

		LCA	IP5	CA	FLS
Spearman's rho	LCA	1	0.156	0.441^{**}	0.523^{**}
Spearman's rho	IP5	0.156	1	0.122	0.152
Spearman's rho	CA	0.441^{**}	0.122	1	0.423^{**}
Spearman's rho	FLS	0.523^{**}	0.152	0.423^{**}	1

N = 132 $p^{*}<0.05$ $p^{**}<0.01$ $P^{***}<0.001$ Sig. (2-tailed)

In addition, Spearman's rho was used to explore the correlation among these variables LCA, IP5, CA and FLS (see Table 7–11). The analysis showed that LCA was positively associated with CA (value of 0.441 significant at the level of $p < 0.01$), and showed a strong correlation (Cohen, 1988; Pallent, 2005) with FLS (value of 0.523 significant at the level of $p < 0.01$). However, the analysis has also shown less association between individual needs analysis and other variables: language communicative ability, cultural awareness and specific foreign language skills (0.156, 0.122 and 0.152).

These findings, however, are unable to fully answer the research proposition because the analysis also raises another question about what language skills are required to meet the learning needs, as we have found less association between IP5 and other variables (0.156, 0.122 and 0.152). This question actually can be extracted from the research proposition four in an effort to further a more in-depth exploration through qualitative analysis. Therefore, another subscale question of what language skills Chinese companies and organisations actually need should be addressed while analysing the qualitative data later on.

Research proposition five

Chinese employees will be more interested in a foreign language training programme if the pedagogic style is to combine formal instructions and self-managed learning.

FI1, FI2 and SML (measured as Q15, Q16 and Q17) are incorporated in the questionnaire to explore how the variables of computed FI and SML affect the pedagogical approach taken at the stage of programme implementation. As indicated in the table of statistical output for staff (see Table 7–5), a high percentage of FI1 with 'agree' 56.4 and 'strongly agree' 18.0 (mean 3.78, median 4.00 and SD 0.919), FI2 with 'agree' 39.1 and 'strongly agree' 27.1 (mean 3.71, median 4.00 and SD 1.091) and SML with 'agree' 59.5, 'strongly agree' 14.5 (mean 3.71, median 4.00 and SD 1.262) indicate respondents' positive attitudes toward formal instruction as a pedagogic approach for the training programme. Additionally, Spearman's rho was used to explore the relationship between variables of FI and SML. The analysis showed (see Table 7–12) that formal instruction was significantly correlated with self-managed learning, $r = 0.331$, $p<0.01$(1-tailed). Clearly the outcomes of the analysis have positively supported the research proposition that using a teaching approach combining formal instructions and self-managed learning will be better in training Chinese staff.

Table 7–12 **Correlations between FI and SML**

		FI	SML
Spearman's rho	FI	1	0.331^{**}
Spearman's rho	SML	0.331^{**}	1

$N = 132$ $p^{*}<0.05$ $p^{**}<0.01$ Sig. (1-tailed)

To triangulate the data analysis (Bryman, 2008), and to additionally demonstrate the difference between attitudes to using a formal instruction and self-managed learning strategy, the present research also applies the related paired sign test to discover the degree of difference between two responses to two FI and SML.

Table 7–13 **Sign test for FI and SML**

		N	Mean	Std. Deviation	Z	Asymp. Sig. (2-tailed)	Exact Sig. (2-tailed)
FL		132	3.75	0.848			
SML		131	3.71	0.940			
SML-FI	Negative Differences[a]	54			-0.597[d]	0.550	0.551
	Positive Differences[b]	47					
	ties[c]	29					

SML<FI b. SML>FI c. SML = FI d. based on positive differences

The sign test compared the number of positive and negative differences between the two scores from FI and SML (Table 7–13). The outcomes confirm that there is no difference between the two means of responses as there are 29 ties with almost equal numbers of positive and negative difference (negative 54 and positive 47). Additionally, the test also shows there is no significant difference between the two means with 2-tailed test (Sig 0.551, stronger than 0.05), which means we are unable to reject the null hypothesis that there is no change in one particular direction between two responses. Instead we have good evidence for the research proposition that the pedagogic style of a language training programme should combine formal instructions and self-managed learning.

Research proposition six

Foreign language training programmes will be of more interest if they aim to develop the trainee's ability to solve problems which closely relate to their real work.

The variable PSA (problem-solving ability) (as measured by PSA_1 – Q18,

PSA_2 – Q19 and PSA_3 – Q20) is actually designed to explore staff attitudes towards the ability to solve problems relating to their real work. As indicated in the table of statistical output for staff (see Table 7–5), a high percentage of responses to PSA1, with 'agree' 42.1 and 'strongly agree' 42.1 (mean 3.71, median 4.00 and SD 0.923), and PSA2, with 'agree' 53.0 and 'strongly agree' 35.6 (mean 4.17, median 4.00 and SD 0.773), and PSA3 with 'agree' 43.6 and 'strongly agree' 53.4 (mean 4.49, median 5.00 and SD 0.611), indicate the 133 respondents' interest in engaging problem-solving ability in the training programme. These outcomes actually support the proposal that staff are interested in attending the training programme if it aims to develop their ability to solve problems.

The research also intends to ascertain the tendency of the attitudes, either positively or negatively. In other words, it attempts to identify the degree of probability that can be predicted through the gained outcomes in order to make the assertion whether it is positively or negatively supporting the research proposition. In this sense, the null hypothesis is *the attempt to developing the trainee's ability to solve problems is equally significant when designing a foreign language training programme as the absence of the ambition to develop the trainee's ability to solve problems*. So, therefore, the Kolmogorov-Smirnov statistics test was used to look into the significance of difference in determining the actual tendency of the attitudes. To begin with, the three variables relating to PSA (PSA1, PSA2 and PSA3) were computed using PASW. The analysis showed, as indicated in table 7.14 below, that the values are significantly different from a normal distribution since the two-tailed significance of the test is very small (0.000). Meanwhile, Z score 2.18 (rounded up) represents an approximately 98% larger portion and only 1.5% smaller portion of effect size if compared to the established standard normal distribution. This means there is a plausible positive attitude to participating in the training programme if it is aimed at improving the ability to solve problems. Clearly proposition six has been plausibly supported.

Table 7–14 One-sample Kolmogorov-Smirnov test for PSA

Null Hypothesis	Test	Mean±SD	Z	Sig.	Decision
The attempt to develop the trainee's ability to solve problems is equally significant when designing a foreign language training programme as the absence of the ambition to develop the trainee's ability to solve problems	One-sample Kolmogorov-Smirnov Test	4.29±0.597	2.178	0.000	Reject the null hypothesis

N = 132

Research proposition seven

Chinese staff will be more interested in a training programme if regular reports about the progress of trainees and on-going negotiation in course content are incorporated into the training programme.

To address this question, the research was designed to use the variable RR (as measured by RR_1-Q21 and RR_2-Q22) to examine attitudes of staff. As indicated in the table of statistical output of staff (see table 7–5), a high percentage of RR1, with 'agree' 63.2% and 'strongly agree' 5.3% (mean 3.61, median 4.00 and SD 0.798), and RR2, with 'agree' 58.0% and 'strongly agree' 6.1% (mean 3.49, median 4.00 and SD 0.906), indicate that respondents demonstrate positive attitudes towards regular reports and on-going negotiation if employed in the implementation of the foreign language training programme through an international communication strategy. Meanwhile, the Kolmogorov-Smirnov (K-S) test was used to examine whether the sample was from a normally distributed population (Field, 2009). The two variables RR1 and RR2 were computed into RR using PASW as they are looking into the same variable. Moreover, the histogram of frequency shows that around 60% respondents lie on the value of 4, which is 'agree' (see Figure 7–4). In addition, the outcome of the analysis has indicated that the observed data distribution is significantly different from a normal distribution as the two-tailed significance of the test is very small (0.000), which means a big significance (see Table 7–15). The null hypothesis is rejected. Thus the research proposition seven has been plausibly supported.

Meanwhile, effect size of the value obtained has been looked up via "*Table of the Standard Normal Distribution*" (Field, 2009). Z score 3.19 (rounded up) represents an approximately 0.99 larger portion and only a 0.001 small portion of effect size, meaning regular reports and on-going negotiation have largely effected the estimated distribution (Kinnear and Gray, 2010).

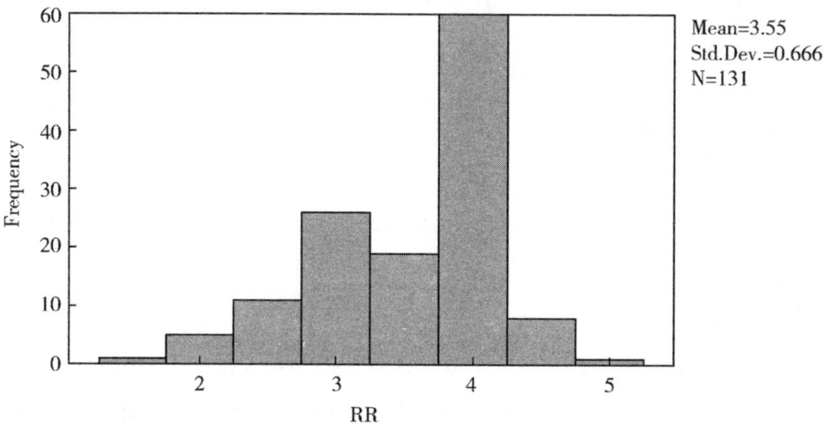

Figure 7–4 Histogram for computed RR

Table 7–15 One-Sample Kolmogorov-Smirnov test for RR

Null Hypothesis	Test	Mean±SD	Z	Sig.	Decision
The requirement of incorporating regular reports about the progress of trainees and on-going negotiation in course content into the training programme is equally significant to a programme without such requirement	One-sample Kolmogorov-Smirnov Test	3.54±0.666	3.19	0.000	Reject the null hypothesis

Research proposition eight

Quality of outcome of the programme will be assured if Chinese managers and programme providers are jointly involved in the evaluation either at the stage of generating the learning project or at the end of the programme.

The variable JAIP(as measured by $JAIP_1$ – Q7, $JAIP_2$ – Q8, $JAIP_3$ – Q23) is actually designed to explore staff attitudes towards the proposed way of evaluating outcomes of the training programme in order to assure its effectiveness when developing the training programme. The research initially proposed that Chinese managers and programme providers should be jointly involved in the evaluation either at the stage of generating the learning project or at the end of the programme. The data analysis has showed, as indicated in the table of statistical output for staff (see Table 7–5), a high percentage of positive responses to JAIP1, with 'agree' 51.9% and 'strongly agree' 36.1% (mean 4.21, median 4.00 and SD 0.739), JAIP2, with 'agree' 57.9% and 'strongly agree' 32.3% (mean 4.21, median 4.00 and SD 0.663) and JAIP3, with 'agree' 60.2% and 'strongly agree' 18.0% (mean 3.84, median 4.00 and SD 0.928) among the 133 respondents. These figures essentially support the proposal that Chinese managers and programme providers should be jointly involved in the evaluation.

The Kolmogorov-Smirnov statistical test was also used to explore whether the results shown above significantly differ from the assumed normal distribution. The null hypothesis is that joint evaluation is equally significant as that without it. Before conducting this, rather than treating the measured items as separate measures, it is reasonable to create a new variable by computing three measuring items, $JAIP_1$, $JAIP_2$ and $JAIP_3$, into one index, JAIP (Cramer, 2001). Meanwhile, the chart below (see Figure 7–5) also displays the positive tendency of the respondents' attitudes on joint involvement in evaluation, and that has given a view of what staff members think of the joint evaluation of learning objectives and outcomes.

Table 7–16 One-Sample Kolmogorov-Smirnov test for JAIP and JAO

	Null Hypothesis	Test	Mean±SD	Z	Sig.2-tailed	Decision
JAIP	Joint evaluation of individual learning needs is equally significant as evaluation that does not include contributions from both sides.	One-sample K-S Test	4.09±0.57	1.75	0.001	Reject the null hypothesis
JAO	Joint evaluation of individual learning objectives is equally significant as evaluation without joint contribution from both sides	One-sample K-S Test	3.85±0.842	4.56	0.000	Reject the null hypothesis

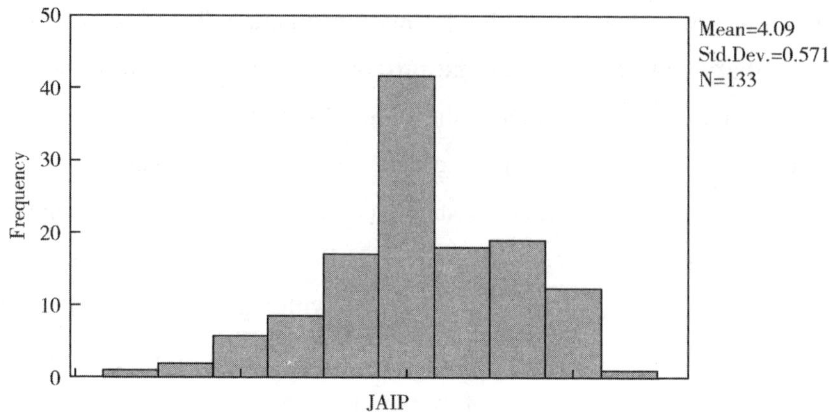

Figure 7–5 Histogram for JAIP

As indicated, the output has shown (see the above Table 7–16) that the values are significantly different from an assumed distribution since the two-tailed significance of the test is small (0.001), which is smaller than 0.05. Meanwhile, the Z score 1.75 (rounded up) represents an approximately 96% larger portion and a 4% small portion of observed data, which is different from assumed distribution. This means there is a plausible positive attitude toward the proposal of joint evaluation. Obviously proposition eight has been partly positively supported by the staff, which means at least they prefer Chinese managers and training providers being jointly involved in the evaluation from the beginning.

An one-sample Kolmogorov-Smirnov test was also used to explore the attitudes of staff regarding the evaluation at the end of programme. The variable JAO (as measured by Q24) is designed to look at how staff reflect on the assumption if the evaluation allows both training providers and organisation managers to get involved in the assessment of learning objectives. Firstly, a high percentage of positive responses to JAO, with "agree" 67.4% and "strongly agree" 15.2% (mean 3.85, median 4.00 and SD 0.842), was given by the 133 respondents to express their attitudes. The Kolmogorov-Smirnov test (see Table 7–17) also provides the results in support of the significance of difference;

since *p* is well below the two-tailed 0.05 level, the difference is significant. This means that the answers from the respondents to the question of involving Chinese managers and training providers jointly in the assessment at the end of the training course will be positive. Clearly another part of the question relating to proposition eight has thus been addressed.

In order to ensure there is a correlation between JAIP and JAO, Spearman's rho correlation coefficient test was used to verify the outcomes through a survey. As indicated in Table 7–17 below, there was a significant relationship between the JAIP and JAO, r = 0.466, Sig. = 000 (2-tailed), which means staff members who prefer joint assessment of their individual project during the first stage will prefer joint assessment of their learning outcomes at the end of programme. Thus, based on the above analysis, the proposition eight is plausibly supported.

Table 7–17 Correlation for JAIP and JAO

		JAIP	JAO
Spearman's rho	JAIP	1	0.466**
Spearman's rho	JAO	0.466**	1

N = 132**. Correlation is significant at the 0.01 level (2-tailed).

7.2.8 Analysis of managers' questionnaire

Reliability Analysis

To begin with, Cronbach's alpha was used to measure internal reliability and inner consistency in the managers' questionnaire. According to Nunnally (1978) and McKinley *et al.* (1997), an alpha value between 0.70 and 0.98 indicates high reliability, while a value above 0.6 is acceptable for exploratory research. In the case of this research, the results of measuring internal reliability of each item among managers' responses range from 0.786 – 0.846 (see Table 7–6), which indicates that the internal consistency of all dimensions produced high reliability, which can be used to test the properties of the variables.

Research proposition one

Chinese companies will embrace a foreign language training programme if it starts with a project created individually and independently prior to actual implementation.

The variable IP* (as measured by IP*1, IP*2, IP*3 and IP*4) is actually designed to explore how managers reflect on the questionnaires. To address this question, the research will firstly measure internal reliability of each item by evaluating the value of Cronbach's Alpha. Secondly, the research used one-sample t-test to look into the difference of the means between the observed sample and the large population, in an effort to address research proposition one.

One sample t-test analysis

Having computerised the results from IP*1, IP*2, IP*3 and IP*4 to be the variable IP*, the normal distribution of the data was tested using PASW. Tests of normality showed that there is no difference between the distribution of observed data and hypothesised data (Sig 0.200 less than significant level of 0.05). This indicates a normal distribution of the data collected, so the researcher decided to use one-sample t test, one of the parametric tests, to compare the means.

Table 7–18 The result of tests of normality and One-Sample test for IP*

	N	Tests of normality(Sig.)	t	Test value	Mean	Std. Deviation	Sig.(2-tailed)
IP*	10	0.200	7.305	3.00	4.30	0.563	0.000

By comparing the means, the researcher initially set the hypothesised mean = 3 after computerising the five items IP*1, IP*2, IP*3 and IP*4 as the mean (neutral = 3) designed for each item in the questionnaire. Thus, the one sample t-test will test the mean of 3 to address the location of observed data. The figures from the one-sample t-test as indicated in Table 7–18 show that the mean of the response attitudes for the individual project (Mean = 4.30, SD = 0.563) was greater than the mean of the hypothesised response attitudes (test value = 3). The test also showed significance beyond the 0.05 level: $t(10) = 7.305$; $p = 0.000$ (two-tailed). The 95% confidence interval on the difference was (0.89, 1.70), which does not include the value of zero specified by the null hypothesis. The obtained results support research proposition one that managers hold positive attitudes on beginning to create an individual project before the training programme.

Research proposition two

An individual project will be effectively created if it is based on learners' language skill needs and technical skills related to the work place.

To address this question, the research actually uses the variables FLNA* and WRS* (as measured by Q7 and Q4) to explore the attitudes of managers. If keeping the original negative tone of FLNA* as designed in the questionnaire, the two measured variables in the questionnaire for managers (*4. The ultimate goal of managing a foreign language training programme is to develop language skills only; 7. I think language training programmes should focus on the development of work-related professional skills as well as general language skills.*) could be accounted for as dichotomous questions because the tones of the two observed variables are totally opposite. Based on the results of the normality of distribution test as indicated in Table 7–19, the data of either FLNA –Q4 or WRS* -Q7 does not show goodness-of-fit in distribution (FLNA*: 0.342 at 0.002 sig level, smaller than 0.05 levels; WRS*: 0.433 at 0.000 sig level, smaller than 0.05 levels). Thus, the research decided to use non-parametric related samples sign test to explore the managers' attitudes on what a training programme should be based on to ensure that an effective individual project is established.

Table 7–19 Tests of Normality for FLNA* and WRS*

	Kolmogorov-Smirnov		
	Statistic	Degree of freedom	Sig.
FLNA*	0.342	10	0.002
WRS*	0.433	10	0.000

The sign test actually carries no assumptions about the original distribution, and the test is also an application of the binomial test, which is suitable for this purpose (Kinnear and Gray, 2010). The results shown in Table 7–20 below show that there are nine negative differences and no positive differences. According to Cohen's (1988) guidelines (for interpreting the effect size index g (Small size: $0.05 \leq g < 0.15$; Medium size: $0.15 \leq g < 0.25$; Large size: $g \geq 0.25$), the output below proves that 90% of participants have shown negative difference scores; whereas the proportion under the null hypothesis is 0.5. Substituting in formula $g = | P - p|$, we have $g = | P - p| = 0.9 - 0.5 = 0.4$ which means a large effect. In addition, a sign test showed a p-value of 0.004 (2-tailed), meaning a significant difference.

These results have demonstrated what the managers' attitudes about the content of building up an individual project actually are. In fact, there is a great deal of disagreement on the proposal that the ultimate goal of managing a foreign language training programme is to develop language skills only; however, there is significant agreement on the idea that language training programmes should focus on the development of practical vocational skills as well as general language skills. The managers' attitudes are indeed consistent with those of the staff as illustrated in the previous results, that they are inclined towards a foreign language training programme with the combination of developing foreign language skills and work-related technical skills. The outcome of this analysis favourably supports research proposition two.

Table 7–20 Related Samples Sign test for FLNA*- WRS*

	Negative differences[a]	Positive differences[b]	Ties[c]	Asymp Sig. (2-tailed)
FLNA*-WRS*	9	0	1	0.004

FLNA*<WRS* b. FLNA*>WRS* c. FLNA* = WRS*

Research proposition three

Chinese companies are interested in launching a foreign language training programme if it aims to enhance professional skills and technical ability.

To address this question, the research used variable WRS* (as measured by Q7) to explore the standpoint adopted by managers. WRS* "*I think foreign language training programmes should focus on the development of work-related professional skills as well as general language skills*" aims to investigate how Chinese company managers view a programme which aims to enhance professional skills and technical ability. So the null hypothesis, without focusing on developing work-related professional skills, equally draws Chinese managers' attention to a foreign language training programme if it focuses on the development of work-related professional skills in a foreign language training programme.

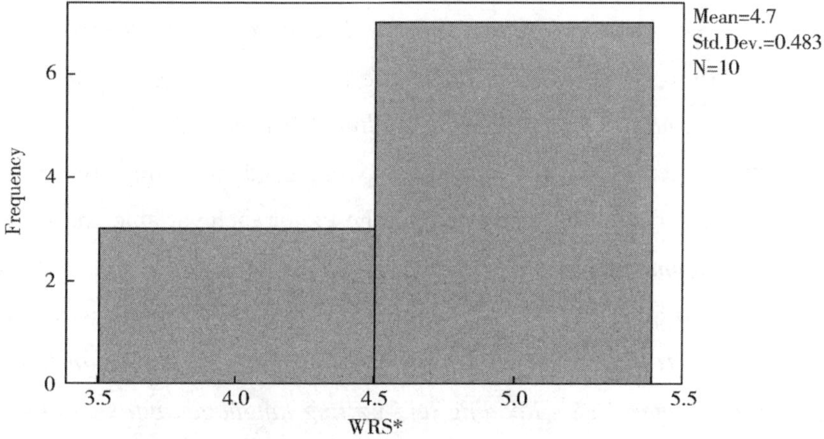

Figure 7–6 Histogram for WRS*

Figure 7–6 shows the outcomes from the responses of the managers. These demonstrate that the majority of respondents fall within the range of 4.0-5.0, which actually agrees with the assumption that language training programmes should focus on the development of work-related professional skills (mean = 4.70, median = 5.00 and Std. Dev. = 0.483).

The Kolmogorov-Smirnov test was also used to statistically test the null hypothesis of the variable. The results showed that distribution of WRS* is significantly different to the estimated distribution with mean 4.7, standard deviation 0.483 and Sig. 0.032. (as shown in Table 7–21). The null hypothesis is thus rejected. The results actually support the alternatives of this research proposition that managers are more interested in a foreign language training programme if it aims to enhance trainees' professional skills and technical ability.

Table 7–21 The results of the K-S test for WRS*

Null Hypothesis	Test	Mean±SD	Sig.	Decision
The distribution of WRS is normal*	One-Sample Kolmogorov-Smirnov Test	4.7±0.483	0.032	reject the null hypothesis

Research proposition four

Chinese companies or organisations will be more likely to trigger a foreign language training programme if it aims to develop language communication ability, reading and writing abilities and cultural awareness.

The variables LCA*, CA* and FLS* were used to explore the opinions within managers' responses. The null hypotheses for each variable are: *LCA* – A training programme focusing on developing the trainee's ability to communicate in a foreign language is equally important as a programme without this objective; CA*- It is unnecessary to be incorporated into a foreign language training programme; FLS*- Reading and writing language abilities are equally useful as those of speaking and listening.*

Table 7–6 shows degrees of agreement on and the mean of each question, with LCA* mean = 4.40, median = 4.0 and Std. Dev. = 0.516; CA* mean = 4.20, median = 4.00 and Std. Dev. = 0.422; and FLS* mean = 2.70, median = 3.00 and Std. Dev. = 0.949. Tests of normality have shown that LCA* Sig. 000, CA* Sig. 000 and FLS* Sig. 0.168, which supports the researcher's decision to use the one sample Kolmogorov-Smirnov test for LCA* and CA*, and the one-sample t-test for FLS* (Black, 1999; Field, 2009).

In Table 7–22, the results of one sample Kolmogorov-Smirnov tests for LCA* and CA* demonstrate that the distribution of LCA* is not significantly different to the estimated one, with mean 4.40, Std. Dev. 0.516, and Sig. 0.110 at the significance level of 0.05; however.responses to CA* are significantly different to the estimated ones, with mean 4.20, Std. Dev. 0.422 and Sig. 0.009 at the significance level of 0.05. Thus, the null hypothesis for LCA* cannot be rejected, but for CA* it is rejected.

Table 7–22 The results of the K-S tests for LCA* and CA*

Null Hypothesis	Test	Mean±SD	Sig.	Decision
The distribution of LCA* is normal	One-Sample Kolmogorov-Smirnov Test	4.40±0.516	0.110	Retain the null hypothesis
The distribution of CA* is normal	One-Sample Kolmogorov-Smirnov Test	4.20±0.422	0.009	Reject the null hypothesis

Meanwhile, the one-sample t-test was used to test FLS* to the set test value 3 as it was set to be the hypothesised mean under the null hypothesis in the questionnaire (Field, 2009). The results in Table 7–23 show that the exact p-value for the sample data is 0.343, which is larger than 0.05 at 2-tailed significance level. This signals that the null hypothesis is retained.

Table 7–23 The results of the One-Sample t-test for FLS

	N	t	Test value	Mean	Std. Deviation	Sig.(2-tailed)
FLS*	10	-1.00	3.00	2.70	0.949	0.343

Research proposition five

Chinese employers will be more interested in a foreign language training programme if the pedagogic style is to combine formal instruction and self-managed learning.

FI* and SML* were used to look into how Chinese managers view the use of a teaching style combining formal instruction and self-managed learning. FI* was designed to investigate the respondents' attitudes to using formal instruction, and SML* was used to explore the opinions relating to self-centred learning. So the null hypotheses for these are: FI* – *the distribution of trainees in my company who prefer formal instruction is normal;* SML*– *the distribution of trainees who are also using the self- managed learning approach is normal.*

Table 7–6 shows the degree of agreement and mean of each question from managers' responses with FI* mean = 4.00, median = 4.00 and Std. Dev. = 0.471, and SML* mean = 4.30, median = 4.00 and Std. Dev. = 0.675. The histogram in Figures 7–7 and 7–8 below shows the frequency for FI* and SML* and reveals there is a high frequency of agreement with the assumptions. Also, the test of normality has indicated that both sets of data are non-parametric (FI*- Sig. 0.000, SML*- Sig. 0.035, lower than 0.5).

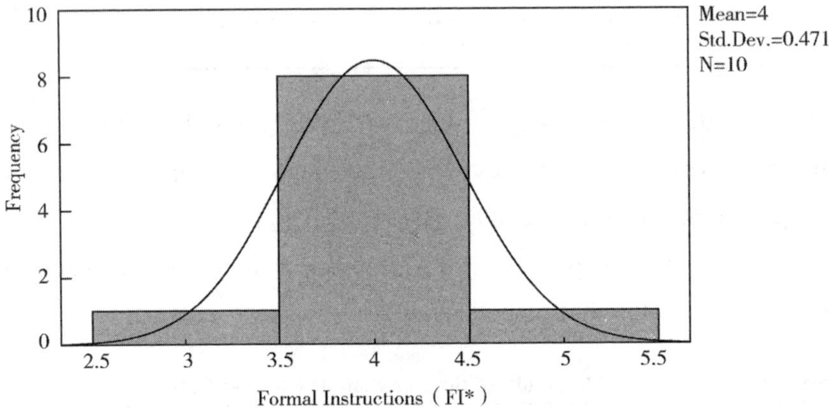

Figure 7–7 Histogram for FI*

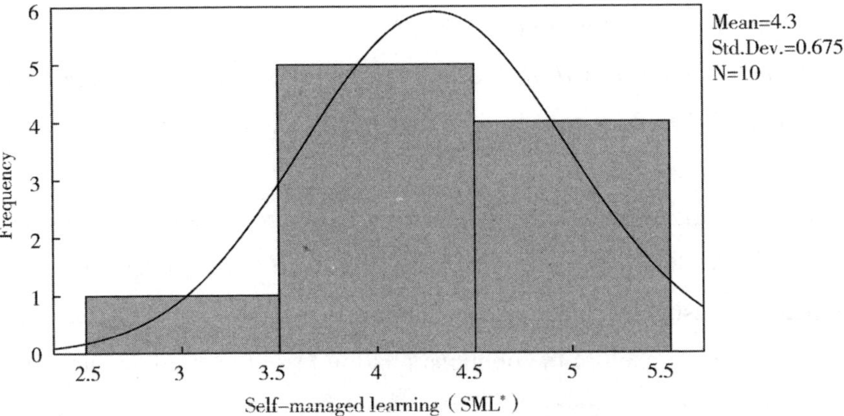

Figure 7–8 Histogram for SML*

Therefore, the researcher decided to use a related sample test to compare their medians. The null hypothesis in this sense is the median of difference between FI* and SML* equals 0. Table 7–24 presents the results of the Wilcoxon Signed Ranks test which actually compared the number of positive and negative differences between two scores from the related samples. There are six ties, three positive differences and one negative. This clearly confirms that there is no significant difference between two medians with Asymp. Sig. (2-tailed) 0.257, stronger than the significant level of 0.05, which means the null hypothesis is retained.

Table 7–24 The results of the Wilcoxon Signed Ranks test for SML* – FL*

SML*-FI*	N	Mean Rank	Sum of Ranks	Z	Asymp. Sig.(2-tailed)
Negative Ranks	1[a]	2.00	2.00		
Positive Ranks	3[b]	2.67	8.00		
Ties	6[c]				
Total	10			-1.134[d]	0.257

SML*<FI* b. SML*>FI* c. SML* = FI* d. Based on positive ranks

The results actually reveal that there is no difference in responses to the question relating to formal instruction and self-managed learning. This indicates that Managers believe the use of pedagogy by blending formal instruction and regular self-managed learning in the training programme would be beneficial for participants.

Research proposition six

Foreign language training programmes will be of more interest if they aim to develop the trainee's ability to solve problems which closely relate to their real work.

To address this question, the research used PSA* (as measured by Q25) to investigate the opinions of Chinese managers. Table 7–6 displays the degree of agreement and mean of each question from the managers' responses with PSA*mean = 4.10, median = 4.00 and Std. Dev. = 0.738. Tests of normality have shown that there is no difference between the distribution of observed data and hypothesised data (Sig. 0.067, stronger than the significant level of 0.05). This suggests that the data collected are normally distributed and are parametric. Therefore the researcher decided to use the one-sample t-test to compare the mean of observed data to three (neutral) in this context, as it is designed as the mean in the questionnaire.

Table 7–25 The result of tests of Normality and One-Sample t-test for PSA*

	N	Tests of normality(Sig.)	t	Test value	Mean	Std. Deviation	Sig.(2-tailed)
PSA*	10	0.067	4.714	3.00	4.10	0.738	0.001

Table 7–25 reveals that the mean of the responses concerning attitudes to developing problem-solving ability in foreign language training programmes (mean = 4.10, SD.Dev. = 0.738) is greater than the mean of the hypothesised test value = 3. It also shows that the significance is beyond the significant level of 0.05: t (10) = 4.714; p = 0.001 (2-tailed). The result has confirmed that there is a significant difference in distribution between the observed and hypothesised data.

Thus, the research proposition is supported according to the data collected from managers.

Research proposition seven

Chinese managers will be more interested in a training programme if it incorporates regular reports about the progress of trainees and on-going negotiation about course content.

The research uses the variable RR* (as measured by RR*1-Q11 and RR*2-Q12 in the questionnaire for managers) to address the attitudes of managers. If we keep both measurements RR*1 and RR*2 with their original negative tones as designed in the questionnaire, both of them (*I review the submission of learning outcomes of each regular member of staff in order to be able to evaluate the subsequent success of the training programme. Regular reports from staff about their progress are not important to maintain successful learning*) can be taken as dichotomous questions as a result of the controversial tones designed for maintaining the subjectivity of the responses (Cramer, 2001).

Due to the abnormal distribution of the collected data for $RR^{*}1$ (Sig 0.003) and $RR^{*}2$ (Sig 0.001) as indicated in Table 7–26 below of tests of normality, which are less than the significant level of 0.05, the research decided to use the non-parametric related samples test to explore the managers' attitudes to regular reporting.

Table 7–26 The results of the tests of Normality and descriptive statistics for $RR^{*}1$ and $RR^{*}2$

	Tests of Normality (Sig.)	N	Mean	Median	Std.Dev.
$RR^{*}1$	0.003	10	4.50	4.50	0.527
$RR^{*}2$	0.001	10	2.40	4.00	0.966

Table 7–27 The results of the Wilcoxon Signed Ranks test for $RR^{*}1$ and $RR^{*}2$

$RR^{*}2$-$RR^{*}1$	N	Mean Rank	Sum of Ranks	Z	Asymp. Sig.(2-tailed)
Negative Ranks	6[a]	4.25	25.50		
Positive Ranks	1[b]	2.50	2.50		
Ties	3[c]				
Total	10			-1.983[d]	0.004

$RR^{*}2<RR^{*}1$ b. $RR^{*}2>RR^{*}1$ c. $RR^{*}2 = RR^{*}1$ d. based on positive differences

The Wilcoxon Signed Ranks test was also used to address the question. The results shown in Table 7–27 above denote that there are six negative differences, one positive difference and three ties. The p-value of 0.004 (2-tailed) indicates a significant difference between these values. In addition, according to Cohen's (1988) guidelines for interpreting the effect of the size index g (Small size: $0.05\leq g<0.15$; Medium size: $0.15\leq g<0.25$; Large size: $g\geq 0.25$), output below depicts that 90% of participants have shown negative difference scores; whereas the proportion under the null hypothesis is 0.5. Substituting in formula $g = | P - p|$, we have $g = | P - p| = 0.9 - 0.5 = 0.4$ which means a large effect.

The outcome of this analysis illustrated above has indicated that for the one hand, the managers' attitudes about the addressed question of regular reporting actually are consistent with those of the staff, and on the other hand, this also positively supports proposition seven. (For this point, it seems the proposition seven would have been supported but it hasn't yet. The discussion on this will come back later in section 7.2.9 comparison of attitudes of staff and managers).

Research proposition eight

Achievement of learning outcomes will be ensured if Chinese managers and programme providers are jointly involved in the evaluation either at the stage of generating the learning project or at the end of the programme.

To explore the attitudes of managers in terms of this question, the research designed the variable JAO* (as measured by JAO*1 –Q16 and JAO*2- Q17) to measure the general tendency toward the proposition of joint assessment. In fact, the statements of Q16 and Q17 in the questionnaire have been designed with opposite attitudes, negative and positive, in an effort to avoid respondent bias (Bernardi, 2006; Hall, 2005; Jackson, 2009), and to maintain the reliability of the questionnaire (Davies 2007). So the two measured variables (*The training provider's involvement in the process when staff set their learning objectives and evaluate their learning outcomes is unnecessary; The training provider and the sponsor should both be involved in assessing the outcomes of the programme because this will be helpful to ensure the training quality)* could be counted as dichotomous variables (Bryman *et al.*, 2001). From the result of the normality of distribution test using the Kolmogorov-Smirnov test as shown in the table below, neither JAO*1 nor JAO*2 achieves goodness-of-fit in the distribution, as tests of normality showed that JAO*1: Sig 0.000 and JAO*2: Sig 0.000, so both are less than the significant level of 0.05. Thus, the researcher decided to use the non-parametric related samples test to explore the answers from the managers. Again, the Wilcoxon Sign test was used for this purpose.

Table 7–28 The results of tests of Normality and descriptive statistics for JAO*1 and JAO*2

	Tests of Normality (Sig.)	N	Mean	Median	Std.Dev.
JAO*1	0.000	10	4.00	4.00	0.471
JAO*2	0.000	10	4.40	4.00	0.516

Table 7–29 The results of the Wilcoxon Ranked test for JAO*1 and JAO*2

JAO*1-JAO*2	N	Mean Rank	Sum of Ranks	Z	Asymp. Sig.(2-tailed)
Negative Ranks	10[a]	5.50	55.00		
Positive Ranks	0[b]	0.00	0.00		
Ties	0[c]				
Total	10			-2.848[d]	0.002

JAO*1<JAO*2 b. JAO*1>JAO*2 c. JAO*1 = JAO*2 d. based on negative ranks

The results shown in Table 7–29 above denote that there are ten negative differences. The p-value of 0.002 (2-tailed) indicates a significant difference between these values. In addition, according to Cohen's (1988) guidelines for interpreting the effect of the size index g (Small size: $0.05 \leq g < 0.15$; Medium size: $0.15 \leq g < 0.25$; Large size: $g \geq 0.25$), output above depicts that 100% of participants have shown negative difference scores; whereas the proportion under the null hypothesis is 0.5. Substituting in formula $g = | P - p|$, we have $g = | P - p| = 1 - 0.5 = 0.5$, which means a large effect.

The outcome has indicated that the managers' attitudes about the addressed question of joint assessment are positive. Therefore, this also positively supports proposition eight.

7.2.9 Comparison of attitudes of staff and managers

In order to further explore the attitudes of staff and managers to ascertain whether both groups have a consistent, similar attitude towards four key elements: i) building up an individual project, ii) project-validation, iii) programme implementation, and iv) project evaluation, the research attempts to compare these attitudes by extracting the variables from the questionnaire which are actually designed to address these four aspects. This attempt aims to ensure the validity and reliability of the responses given by these two groups of people: managers and staff. To do this is to minimise unpredictable and uncontrollable factors such as political or cultural influence so that the research will be firmly grounded.

7.2.9.1 Building up an individual project

The variables IP from the staff questionnaires and the variables of IP*from the managers' questionnaires are the relevant measurable items with which to assess whether both groups are interested in managing an English language programme by initially building up an individual project. The research used the Mann-Witney U statistics test to compare these two groups of responses due to the unusual distribution of the collected data. Table 7–30 below demonstrates the result.

Table 7–30 The results of the Mann-Witney U test

	S/M	N	Median	Mean Rank	Sum of Ranks	Mann-Whitney U	Z	Exact. Sig. (2-tailed)
IP (S/M)	Staff	132	4.00	69.72	9203.50	425.500	-1.895	0.059
	Manager	10	4.20	94.95	949.50			

Due to the scarcity of the data from the managers' questionnaires (N = 10) which is likely to result in poor approximation, it is better to choose an exact test and report the exact p-values for the non-parametric test, rather than the asymptotic p-value (Kinnear and Gray, 2010).

From the output above, we see from the exact p-values that the Mann-Whitney U test shows no significance on a two-tailed test (p-value 0.059, bigger than 0.01).

As a measure of effect size, King and Minium(2003) advocate the Glass rank biserial correlation coefficient r_g, where

$$r_g = \frac{2\ (M1 \mid M2)}{n_1 + n_2} = \frac{2\ (94.5 \mid 69.72)}{132+10} = +0.36 \text{ (rounded up)} \qquad (1)$$

Cohen (1988) offers guidelines for interpreting the value of a correlation:

$0.1 \leq |r| < 0.30$ and $0.01 \leq r^2 < 0.09$ —— small size of effect

$0.30 \leq |r| < 0.50$ and $0.09 \leq r^2 < 0.25$ —— medium size of effect

$|r| \geq 0.50$ and $r^2 \geq 0.25$ —— large size of effect (2)

The results shown in table 7–30 denote that the mean figure for staff (M =

3.9, SD = 0.44) was less than the mean figure for managers (M = 4.2, SD = 0.57). A Mann-Whitney U test showed this difference to be not significant: U = 425.5; exact p = 0.059, bigger than 0.01 (two-tailed). The Glass rank biserial correlation = +0.36, a 'large' effect in Cohen's (1988) classification.

Essentially, both groups, as indicated in the analysis of previous chapters, are in support of the proposal of building up an individual project, as research proposition one suggests. The result of this test has provided evidence that both staff and managers' attitudes toward building up an individual project prior to the implementation of a training programme are consistently identical. So without doubt, building up an individual project prior to actual programme implementation is an approach that enjoys strong broad-based support in generating a foreign language training course through an international communicative strategy.

7.2.9.2 Project validation and project revaluation

The computed variables JAO from the staff questionnaire and the variables JAO* from the manager questionnaire are the relevant measurable items to explore whether both groups are interested in the proposal of joint assessment at either stage of project validation or project revaluation. The research used the Mann-Witney U statistics test to compare the means from these two independent groups of responses in an attempt to test the proposed model.

Due to the scarcity of the data from the managers' questionnaire (n = 10) which is at risk of resulting in a poor approximation, it is suggested that the exact test is chosen and that the results for the exact p-values for nonparametric test are reported, rather than the asymptotic p-value (Field, 2009; Kinnear and Gray, 2010).

Table 7–31　　　　The result of the Mann-Whitney test for JAO

	S/M	N	Median	Mean Rank	Sum of Ranks	Mann-Whitney U	Z	Exact. Sig. (2-tailed)
JAO (S/M)	Staff	132	4.00	70.60	9319.50	541.500	-0.967	0.339
	Manager	10	4.20	83.35	833.50			

From the output above, we see from the exact p-values that the Mann-Whitney U test shows no significance on a two-tailed test (p-values 0.339, bigger than 0.01).

For measuring the effect of the size of this outcome, King and Minium(2003) advocate that the Glass rank biserial correction coefficient r_g be produced (see the formula labelled 1above), and Cohen (1988) also offers guidelines for interpreting the value of a correlation (see also the guideline labelled 2 above). In this case,

$$r_g = \frac{2\ (M1 \mid M2)}{n_1{+}n_3 6} = \frac{2\ (83.35 \mid 70.60)}{132{+}10} = +0.18 \text{ (rounded up)}$$

Thus, we can conclude from Table 7–31 above that the mean number of staff (M = 4.02, SD = 0.56) was less than the mean number of the managers (M = 4.20, SD = 0.42). A Mann-Whitney U test showed this difference to be not significant: U = 541.5; exact p = 0.339, bigger than 0.01 (two-tailed). The Glass rank biserial correlation = +0.18 (rounded up); therefore, there is a medium effect according to Cohen's (1988) classification.

This finding reveals that both staff and managers' attitudes to joint assessment from trainers and training providers at either stage of project validation or project revaluation are consistently indistinguishable, and both groups clearly supported the value of joint panels to assess the learning objectives and learning outcomes from both training providers and organisation managers.

7.2.9.3 Programme implementation

There are a variety of factors as discussed in literature which are integrated into the implementation of a training programme. These are:

- Problem-solving ability (Turner, 1993)
- Regular reports (Meighan,1991; Turner,1993)
- Language communicative ability and cultural awareness (Smith, 1992; Harris, 1996)

- Combination of formal instruction and self-managed learning (Beckett, 2006)
- Decision-making (Child and Warner, 2003)

Problem-solving ability (PSA)

The variables PSA and PSA* are designed to address the attitudes of both staff and managers as to whether training programmes should be implemented with an emphasis on developing the trainer's problem-solving ability. As illustrated in the previous part of quantitative analysis for staff and managers, positive answers have been given by both groups to support the proposal of placing emphasis on this ability as a part of training goals. However, the question is whether their responses have been consistent in order to ensure that the proposed model is justified. To address this question, the research aims to compare two groups of responses using two independent samples test. Tests of normality showed that the data for both appeared to be significantly non-normal (*PSA, Sig.000, $p<0.05$; PSA*, Sig.000, $p<0.05$*), indicating that a non-parametric test has to be used.

From the outputs below (Table 7–32), we can see the exact p-values in which the Mann-Whitney U test shows significance on an exact two-tailed test (p-value 0.269, larger than 0.05), which appears to show no difference between both groups in terms of the preference for developing problem-solving ability. The box plot (see Figure 7–9), however, shows that the median of managers' responses (5.00) is higher than that of the staff (4.33 rounded up). Additionally, there are two extreme pieces of data from staff labelled 27 and 26 which gave negative responses towards developing problem-solving ability.

Table 7–32 **Mann-Whitney U test for PSA and PSA***

	S/M	N	Median	Mean Rank	Sum of Ranks	Mann-Whitney U	Z	Exact. Sig. (2-tailed)
PSA (S/M)	Staff	132	4.33	70.46	9300.50	522.500	-1.117	0.269
	Manager	10	4.50	85.25	852.50			

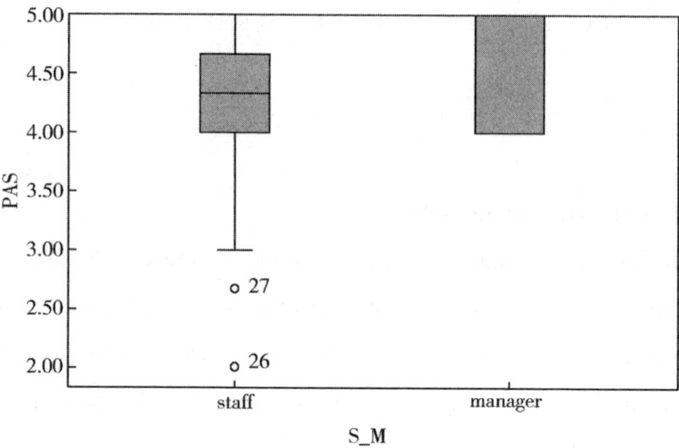

Figure 7–9 Boxplot for S/M comparison

This finding obviously reveals that managers from Chinese companies have a higher degree of preference than staff members in the perception of developing trainers' problem-solving ability although staff are supportive of developing problem-solving ability as well. In other words, the demand for the ability to solve work-related problem is stronger from managers than from staff, although both are in favour of the same requirement.

Regular report (RR)

To compare these two groups of people in terms of their attitudes about regular reports while implementing the training programme, the research uses the computed variables of RR (RR1 and RR2 from the staff questionnaire and RR^*1 and RR^*2 from the managers' questionnaire) to explore whether there is any difference between the two groups of people as to whether they are in favour of regular reports into the implementation of a training programme. This effort is to check the consistency of the attitudes of both groups to ensure the validity of responses.

Taking into account the unusual distribution of the collected data from two groups of people, as the test of normality indicated that both are sig at 0.000 and 0.034 level respectively, less than 0.05 levels, the research decided to use the non-parametric Mann-whitney U test for comparison because the median number is the best figure to allow us to assess the difference in this respect (Cramer, 2001).

Table 7–33 **Mann-Whitney U test for RR and RR***

<table>
<tr><th></th><th>S/M</th><th>N</th><th>Median</th><th>Mean Rank</th><th>Sum of Ranks</th><th>Mann-Whitney U</th><th>Z</th><th>Exact. Sig. (2-tailed)</th></tr>
<tr><td rowspan="2">RR (S/M)</td><td>Staff</td><td>132</td><td>4.00</td><td>72.97</td><td>9558.50</td><td rowspan="2">397.500</td><td rowspan="2">-2.178</td><td rowspan="2">0.028</td></tr>
<tr><td>Manager</td><td>10</td><td>4.00</td><td>42.25</td><td>452.50</td></tr>
</table>

The Mann-Whitney U test is used to determine if the distribution of values either side of a common median differs for two samples (King and Minium, 2003). Table 7–33 has given the output indicating that the medians of two groups are significantly different – exact Sig. (2-tailed) = 0.028, less than 0.05, indicating that the assumption of homogeneity has been rejected. This result is in contrast to the research proposition that either staff or managers areinterested in regular reports where assessment is concerned.

Figure 7–10 below indicates that staff had a mid-range of 50% of responses ranging between neutral (3 = neutral) and agree (4 = agree) lying in the inter-quartile range and they are all below the median; while managers have 50% of responses ranging between agree (4 = agree) and above and they are all above the median. This provides further information about the attitudes of whether regular reports would be highly valued by both managers and staff, or managers only, or staff only. The research will elaborate on this question when the qualitative analysis is undertaken.

Language communication ability and cultural awareness (LCA and CA)

LCA and CA and LCA* and CA* were designed to investigate whether language communicative ability and cultural awareness need to be incorporated into the design of a training programme. The aim of comparing the outcomes from two groups, managers and staff is to examine the consistency of the attitudes from both samples.

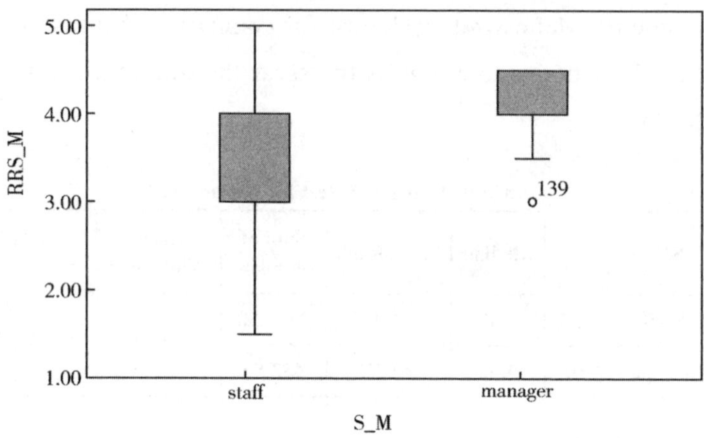

Figure 7–10 Boxplot for RR and RR*

Table 7–34 Mann-Whitney U test for LCA and CA

	S/M	N	Median	Mean Rank	Sum of Ranks	Mann-Whitney U	Z	Exact. Sig. (2-tailed)
LCA (S/M)	Staff	133	4.00	70.28	9347.00	436.000	-1.934	0.057
	Manager	10	4.00	94.90	949.00			
CA (S/M)	Staff	132	4.00	69.89	9225.00	447.000	-1.784	0.074
	Manager	10	4.00	92.80	928.00			

The Mann-Whitney U test was used for this purpose. Table 7–34 above gives the result of the comparison between managers' and staff's responses and it mainly compared the median of both groups. It appears that the perceptions of both staff and managers towards developing language communicative ability and cultural awareness are not significantly different – exact Sig. (2-tailed) = 0.057 and 0.074, both more than 0.05 – signalling that the assumption of the differences from both groups is rejected and the similarity of the responses from staff and manager remains.

To observe the size of the effect, the Glass rank biserial correction coefficient r_g was also measured:

$$r_g = \frac{2\,(M1 \mid M2)}{n_1 + n_2} = \frac{2\,(94.80 \mid 70.28)}{133+10} = +0.34$$

$$r_g = \frac{2\ (M1 \mid M2)}{n_1+n_2} = \frac{2\ (92.80 \mid 69.89)}{133+10} = +0.32$$

These results represent a medium-sized effect for both language communicative ability data and cultural awareness data according to Cohen's (1988) guidelines (it is above the 0.3 criterion for a medium effect size).

Therefore, staff attitudes toward language communicative ability (Mdn = 4.00) did not differ significantly from managers' attitudes (Mdn = 4.00), U = 436.00, Z = -1.934, Sig. (2-tailed) = 0.057, ns, r = +0.34; and also staff attitudes towards cultural awareness (Mdn = 4.00) did not differ significantly from managers attitudes (Mdn = 4.00), U = 447.00, Z = -1.784, Sig. (2-tailed) = 0.074.

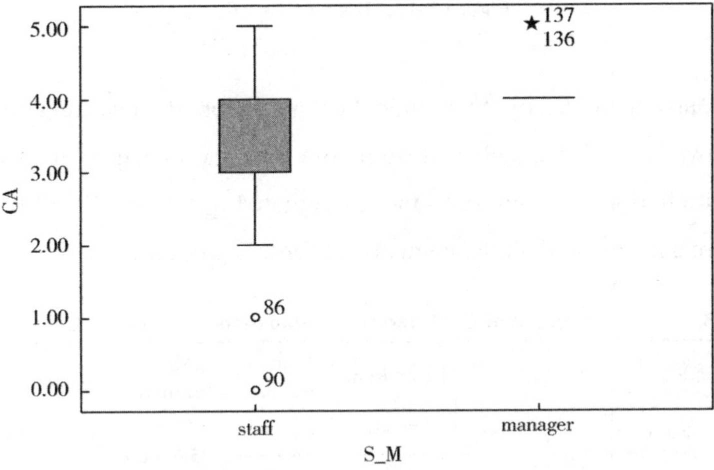

Figure 7–11 Boxplot for CA

Nevertheless, the results as shown in Figure 7–11 and 7–12 for CA and LCA show that there are two outliers with staff respondents and also two extremes with managers' data respectively. For this point, the further research needs to explore in interview analysis.

Combination of formal instruction and self-managed learning (FI and SML)

To address whether there is consistency among staff and manager groups in terms of the attitudes towards the teaching style for a foreign language

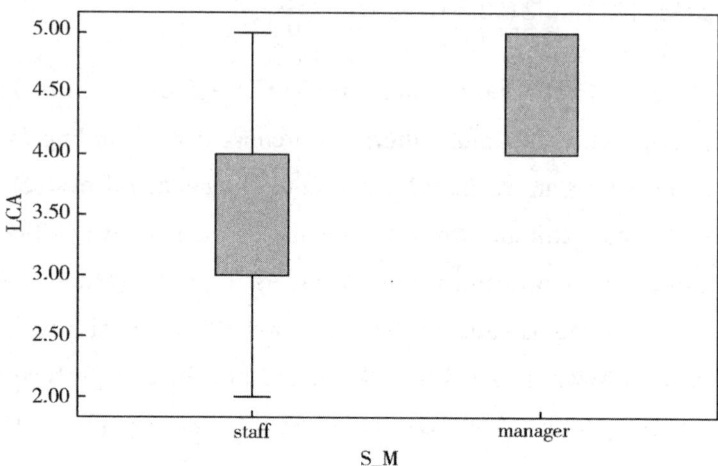

Figure 7–12 Boxplot for LCA

training course managed by international collaboration, the researcher decided to compare two sets of data collected from both staff and managers to ensure there is no contradiction in response to the investigated questions. FI, SML, FI* and SML* were used to conduct the comparison for this purpose.

Table 7–35 Mann-Whitney U test for combination of FI and SML

	S/M	N	Median	Mean Rank	Sum of Ranks	Mann-Whitney U	Z	Exact. Sig. (2-tailed)
FI (S/M)	Staff	133	4.00	70.89	9358.00	580.000	-.654	.520
	Manager	10	4.00	79.50	795.00			
SML (S/M)	Staff	132	4.00	69.77	9209.00	431.500	-2.046	.037
	Manager	10	4.00	94.35	943.50			

Table 7–35 has revealed that the attitudes towards using formal instruction of both staff and manager are not significantly different – exact Sig. (2-tailed) = 0.520, larger than 0.05 – so the hypothesis that the responses from both staff and manager are identical is upheld. However, there was a significant difference between the attitudes on self-managed learning between the two groups – exact Sig. (2-tailed) = 0.037, less than 0.05 – indicating that the attitudes on self-

managed learning between staff and managers are slightly different. At this stage, the need to further explore what actually happens in this context arises; this will be investigated in the interview analysis.

In addition, the boxplot in Figure 7–13 has also shown that more than 50 per cent of managers' responses range from 4 (agree) to 5 (strongly agree); while staff have 50 per cent of responses ranging between 4 (agree) and 3 (neutral), which is lower than the median 4. This also provides us with a few pieces of extreme data collected from staff, representing their disagreement with this pedagogical approach. The result has exposed more information on how the attitudes between the two groups differ. In fact, the manager supports self-managed learning more than the staff does. The research will elaborate on this problem in the qualitative analysis.

Further, the size of the effect was observed through measuring the Glass rank biserial correction coefficient r_g:

$$r_{F1} = \frac{2\,(M1 \mid M2)}{n_1+n_2} = \frac{2\,(92.80 \mid 69.89)}{133+10} = +0.32$$

$$r_{SML} = \frac{2\,(M1 \mid M2)}{n_1+n_2} = \frac{2\,(92.80 \mid 69.89)}{133+10} = +0.32$$

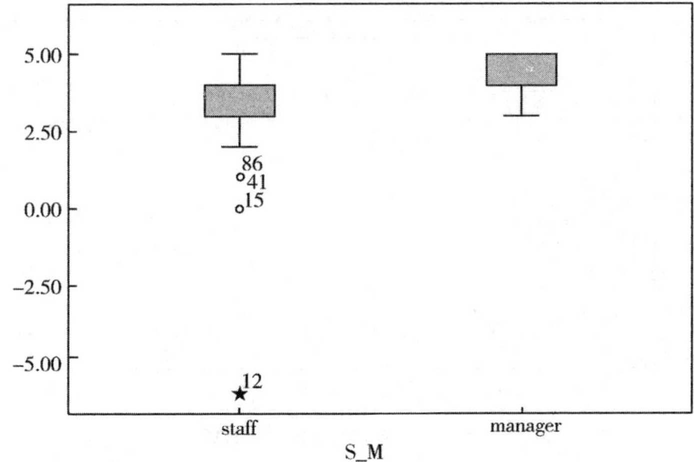

Figure 7–13 Boxplot for the two groups of responses for SML

These results indicate a medium size of effect for both FI and SML according to Cohen's classification (1988).

Therefore, the attitudes of staff towards formal instruction (Mdn = 4.00) did not differ significantly from managers' attitudes (Mdn = 4.00), U = 580.00, Z = -0.654, Sig. (2-tailed) = 0.520, ns, r = +0.12. However, the attitudes of staff towards using self-managed learning (Mdn = 4.00) differed significantly from managers' attitudes (Mdn = 4.00), U = 431.500, Z = -2.046, Sig. (2-tailed) = 0.03, r = +0.34.

Decision-making (DM)

In the managers' questionnaire, the research design also included a relevant item to explore how managers react to decision-making. The variable DM (as measured DM – Q8 in the managers' questionnaire) was investigated using the one-sample Kolmogorov-Smirnov test as no prediction of collected data assumption has been made (Black, 1999).

Table 7–36 The results of the One-Sample Kolmogorov-Smirnov test for DM

DM	Mean	Median	Std. Dev.	One-Sample Kolmogorov-Smirnov Test (Exact Sig. 2-tailed)
	4.00	3.70	0.675	0.015

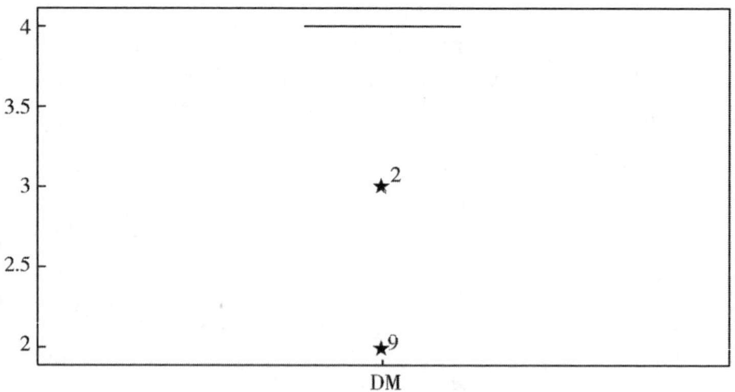

Figure 7–14 Boxplot for DM

The findings in Table 7–36 above indicate that there is a significant difference between explored data and established theoretical distribution (Asymp. Sig. 2-tailed 0.02 and Exact Sig. 2-tailed 0.01, both less than 0.05). At the same time, the descriptive data presents the outcome of the responses of the variable DM with mean = 3.70, median = 4.00, which interestingly displays that managers are reluctant to commence a foreign language training programme themselves even if they anticipate the cost effectiveness of a foreign language training programme; instead, they would suggest such a programme to their superiors. This result has explained that managers are not willing to take such a decision themselves and they would prefer to wait for further guidance from the senior leaders of the companies and organisations.

Meanwhile, the boxplot also presents an outlier, labelled 9, which actually gives us an idea that, based on the gained biographical detail, this response is from a director of a higher education institute in Ningxia, who disagreed that he would suggest cost-effective programmes to others, but stated that he would make his own decision. The power to make the decision in this case is derived from the fact that there is no one else who is able to veto his decision. Another outlier, labelled 2, is actually demonstrating the manager probably follows the nature of Chinese culture which is heavily influenced by the Confucian approach to behave neutrally and not make a decision in a hurry, or prefers to be directed by senior leaders in order to avoid uncertainty (Hofstede, 2003) as discussed in the literature review.

The reasons behind the controversial results revealed in the quantitative analysis will be explored in depth in the analysis of the interviews.

7.3 Findings of the quantitative analysis

In summary, the results obtained from the statistical tests on each research proposition in support of two-tier levels of the innovative model have revealed its effectiveness in major aspects; but have also found it to be unsupportive and controversial findings in certain facets.

The statistical analysis of staff and manager questionnaires in terms of generating an individual project (indicated as IP-IP*) created individually and independently prior to actual implementation has shown the consistency of the answers received from staff and mangers, which as a result was in support of research proposition one. In terms of foreign language needs analysis (indicated as FLNA-FLNA*) and work-related skills (indicated as WRS-WRS*), and how to build up an effective individual project (IP), the results obtained from statistical tests have also supported propositions two and three as responses from both staff and managers are positive and also consistent with each other after statistical comparison. Apart from these, for problem-solving abilities (indicated as PSA-PSA*), joint engagement in the assessment (indicated as JAO-JAO*) and pedagogy including formal instruction and self-managed learning (indicated as FL-FL* and SML-SML*), the results obtained through analysis of both staff and manager questionnaires and the comparison between two groups were positively supportive of propositions five, six and eight.

The results also partly supported proposition four, particularly in the aspects of language communicative abilities. However, they also proved there were absolutely negative attitudes towards the specific needs analysis including cultural awareness (indicated as CA-CA*), specific foreign language skills (indicated as FLS-FLS*) such as reading and writing skills, as the results obtained from statistical analysis of both staff and managers answers have revealed that the null hypothesis had to be retained.

Also, the results for the comparison of two groups further raise the awareness of the research to explore the unaddressed existing gaps in respect of the actual foreign language needs for Chinese companies and organisations. In addition, the results have also exposed the inconsistency between staff and mangers in terms of regular reports (RR-RR*) when the training programmes are under way. It has clearly indicated that managers have higher expectations from this aspect than staff. Therefore, the regular reports needs to be further investigated and addressed in the interviewing data below in order to elaborate the proposition seven.

Apart from this, the results of the comparison of the two groups, however, has caused the uncertainty to proposition five although it was positively supported by the analysis of both groups separately. The analysis of comparing both groups indicates that the attitudes on self-managed learning (SML) between staff and managers are slightly different as a few pieces of extreme data collected from staff were found, representing their disagreement with the suggestion of use self-managed learning. In fact, manager's attitudes support self-managed more than the staff do.

In addition, the results gained in the statistical analysis of decision-making (DM) for managers also proved to be controversial as overall the managers show a preference for Chinese Confucius doctrine, as discussed in the literature review, in that they are normally reluctant to commence a foreign language training programme. However, the two outliers (see Figure 7–14) were also found, standing 20% of total respondents with the small sample size (n = 10), which draws attention to the research and merits a further investigation in the later section 7.4.

In short, the statistical results of the tests were supportive of research propositions one, two, three, six and eight, and partly four, five and seven. The propositions designed for testing the innovative model could quantify the theories based on the proposal of two-tier levels of the training model. The analysis has actually confirmed the theoretical framework in terms of designing a useful training programme for Chinese staff. However, the subtracted questions emerging the controversial answers from staff and managers in the quantitative analysis will be elaborated in greater depth in the qualitative analysis below. These questions are highlighted as:

- What language skills do Chinese companies and organisations actually need?

- Why do Chinese managers and staff reject the proposal of incorporating cultural awareness as a part of a training programme?
- Why is there a significant difference between staff and managers in terms of incorporating self-managed learning into the teaching style?
- Why are staff reluctant with regard to regular reports, but the managers are in favour of it?
- How do managers make decisions with regard to foreign language training programmes?

7.4 Qualitative analysis and findings

7.4.1 Introduction

A number of questions (see above) arose from the findings of the quantitative data that merit further investigation through interviews. Subsequently, interviews with eight Chinese managers from eight representative companies and organisations were conducted to collect more primary data. The exploration of the primary data was based on identifying the possible answers for the four questions posed in the interviews which were related to *the actual needs in terms of foreign language skills*, *culture awareness*, *self-managed learning,regular reports* and *decision-making* in designing an individual project-based foreign language training programme. In addition, another five employees were also involved in the follow-up interviews.

7.4.2 Data collection and analysis

The study learned from Schlevogt's (2002) experiences in undertaking his research on Chinese management:

> *Using mailed questionnaires to collect data was shown to be unfeasible in China. Supposedly because of the low efficiency of the*

postal system and lack of personal interaction, the response rate was extremely low. The quality of the returned questionnaires turned out to be unsatisfactory. There were many missing questions left with blanks, or only 'don't know' answers (Schlevogt 2002, p.323).

In contrast, he preferred using personal interviews and continued:

However, personal interviews elicited a high response rate from CEOs (or their most senior vice-president) and complete responses (*ibid.,* p.322).

Therefore, in order to avoid repetition of his poor experience, the researcher has adopted personal interviews to collect data for this study and it turns out to be a right decision. All eight contacted informants agreed to participate, partly because they thought they could learn from interacting with a researcher from a western university. In addition, difficult sections of the questionnaire with concepts unfamiliar to the Chinese managers could be clarified. Because none of the informants had ever participated in an interview for research purposes or answered a questionnaire, sometimes the researcher had to explain the notion of and reason for the use of the data. The interaction formed between the interviewer and informants significantly reduced the chances to give 'don't know' answers, and instead the interviewees became more talkative when meeting with a Chinese researcher, albeit from abroad. On occasions, informants declined to answer particular questions, claiming ignorance, but most of them were willing to cooperate.

All the participants prior to the interviews in this survey were told of the purpose of the survey and their views and opinions would be used anonymously and treated as strictly confidential. They were treated equally and fairly in the venue for the interviews with a quiet and friendly environment (Fisher, 2004; Manthner, 2002; Saunders and Lewis, 2003).

No question was overlooked during the interviews and a portable IC recorder was used to record all interviews. Three Chinese natives transcribed the recordings, and translations from Chinese to English were undertaken by four Chinese MA students with bilingual language abilities prior to submitting the drafts to an experienced associate professor for approval. The final copy of the transcriptions was examined by two experienced researchers to ensure the highest possible degree of validity had been attained (Silverman, 2004).

Qualitative research is varied and usually also treats as data the records of ideas. NVivo 8 has tools such as free nodes and tree nodes for recording and linking ideas in many ways, and for searching and exploring the patterns and ideas within data and ideas (Richards, 1999). Therefore, the researcher decided to use NVivo 8 to investigate possible answers.

In addition, NVivo analysis provides the research with a tool to organise concepts emerged by coding the interview data, however, to some extents it would fail to interpret the association among these concepts. Therefore, the classical data analysis was necessarily employed to virtually reflect the respondent's attitudes in order to make the research purely objective (Bazeley, 2004; 2007).

7.4.3 Actual foreign language needs

The results of statistical analysis through quantitative research have provided the researcher with a dilemma as to exactly what foreign language skills Chinese companies and organisations actually need. Basically the findings of experiments in terms of individual project-based programmes have been largely and positively emphasised by the attitudes both of managers and staff; however, concerning foreign language skills needed, the respondents gave a variety of answers, ranging from speaking, listening comprehension, reading and writing, which caused the researcher a level of embarrassment because the answers superficially covered all four basic foreign language skills without highlighting the actual specific needs. Richards (1999) explained that tree nodes could be managed in hierarchies of categories and subcategories and could be viewed as a catalogue or system. Bazeley (2010) also clarified that qualitative analysis using NVivo needs to sort and connect nodes into a branching system of tree structured hierarchy to catalogue what kind of things are being considered. To explore the answers in depth and to obtain accurate answers, a tree node (see Figure 7–15) has been coded through analysing the interview data, which includes:

- Organisational development goal
- Productive language skills
- Receptive language skills

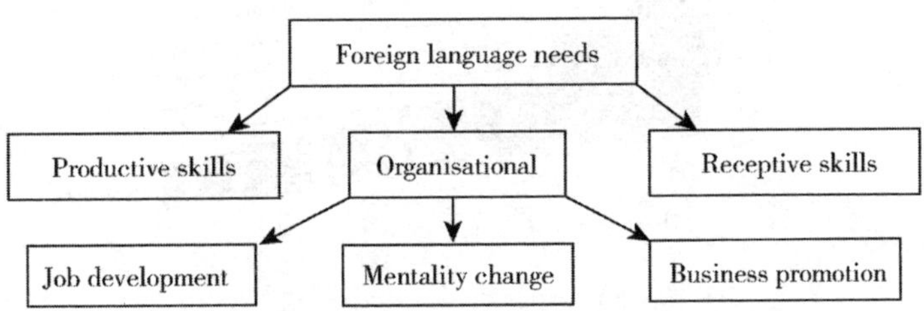

Figure 7–15 Hierarchical coded themes

After coding the relevant references from eight interviews with regards to foreign language needs in Chinese organisations and companies, the findings show (see Table 7–37 below) that seven of the eight companies and organisations with the exception of ICBC stressed that they have given a high priority to foreign language skills development. Foreign language skills can be categorised into productive and receptive skills (Davies, 1976; Harmer, 2001). After coding the nodes of productive and receptive skills, the coded references from the interviews have demonstrated that the actual needs for the interviewed companies are productive skills including speaking and writing skills; as out of the eight interviews, there were seven (approximately 87.5%) coded (see Table 7–37 below and Figure 7–16 below). Meanwhile, all interviewed managers from different companies and organisations expressed their interests in developing productive skills for their employees but only one source from SG mentioned receptive skills (see Figure 7–17 below).

Table 7–37 Summary of coded tree nodes

Tree node	Source	References	Words	Paragraphs	Percentages
Productive ability	8	16	596	15	87.5%
Receptive ability	1	1	40	1	12.5%

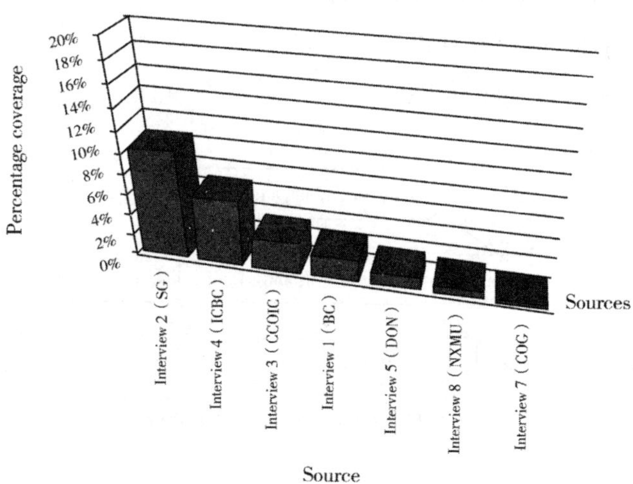

Figure 7–16 Foreign language needs analysis

The answer relating to adopting productive skills as the objective for foreign language training needs was also supported by other highlighted training objectives of the surveyed companies. These training objectives were also coded as free nodes in the analysis and included 'job development', 'mentality change' and 'business promotion'. Under the current developing strategy of internationalisation, many companies such as SG, BC, CCOIC, ICBC, DON, NXU, COG, and NXMU initially provided their views on the objectives of running foreign language training courses. The characteristic themes can be represented through the managers' comments below:

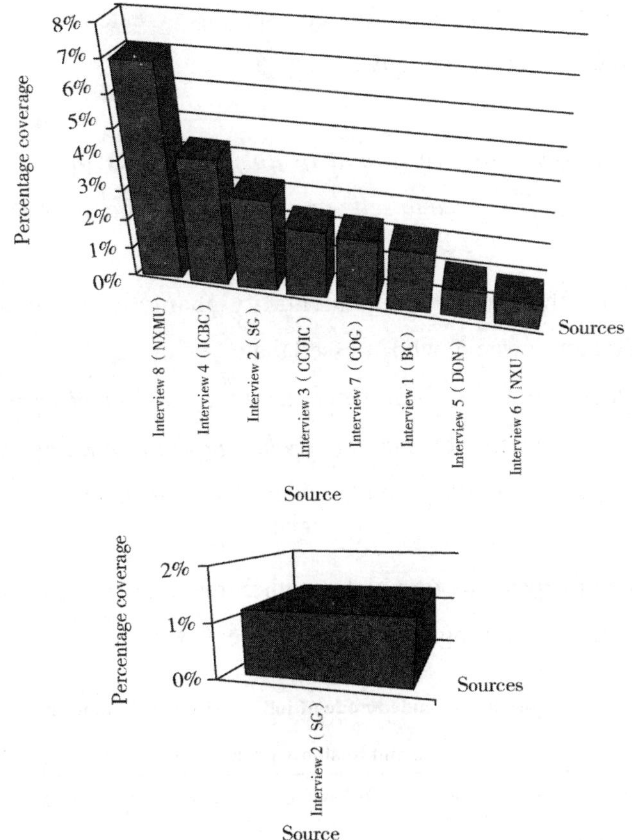

Figure 7–17 Productive skills and receptive skills needs

One of the themes, 'job development', can be generated from interviewee 2's comment from SG:

In general, foreign language training and specific language needs are only one part of the business of the company. In fact, foreign language training needs analysis is mainly based on the needs of an individual post and also aimed at the needs of businesses, as well as the efficiency of enterprises, which apparently should play a facilitating role to the business of the company.

Another theme, 'business promotion', was also created through coding the interview of interviewee 1; she stated:

Nowadays what we intend to do is to focus on local economic development and we need to sell our products and brands to the world.

Meanwhile, the third theme, 'mentality change', emerged during the interview with interviewee 5, who stressed that:

... in recent years, State Government has attached great importance to training of personnel, aiming to change their thinking, management philosophy, and mentality, broaden their views and so on.

These three themes thus formulate another tree node under the node of aims of implementing training programmes (see Table 7–38).

Table 7–38 Summary of coded node of job development, mentality change and business promotion

Tree node	Source	References	Words	Paragraphs	Percentages
Job development	5	15	192	12	6.57%
Mentality change	5	7	141	5	7.31%
Business promotion	3	4	41	4	1.37%

In addition, NVivo – as illustrated in Figures 7–18, 7–19 and 7–20 below – also codes the most used words from each interview source for these three themes, and these provide us with an overall perception of what each surveyed company and organisation actually needs in terms of foreign language training.

Meanwhile, the analysis of the ICBC interview transcription has also indicated that ICBC has decided to suspend its foreign language training programmes. This finding cannot be neglected because it can provide the researcher with the chance to find out the reasons underpinning the decision. In her interview, interviewee 4 mentioned that:

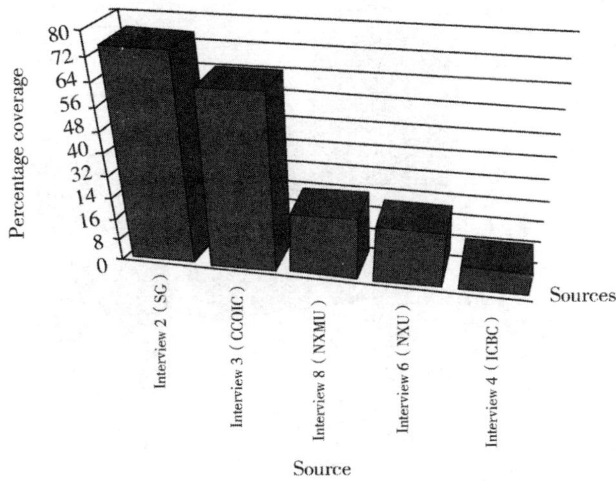

Figure 7–18 Job skills development

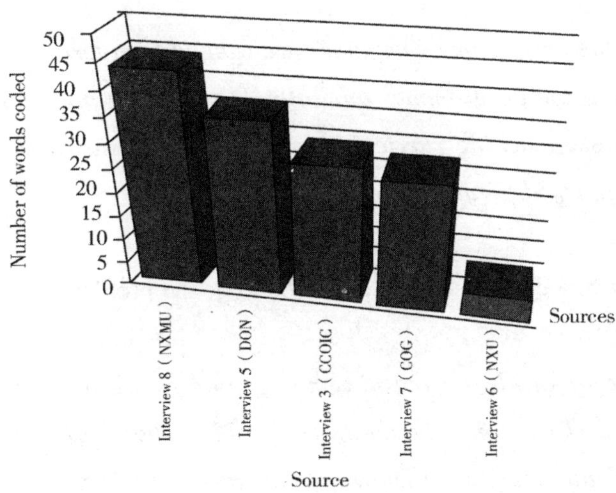

Figure 7–19 Mentality change

...the training for staff in our bank is not regular training. The last training we did was cooperating with Ningxia University for foreign language training for the staff. It was because of the request of the International Business Department who would like to improve their spoken English and business English. So we contacted Ningxia University to

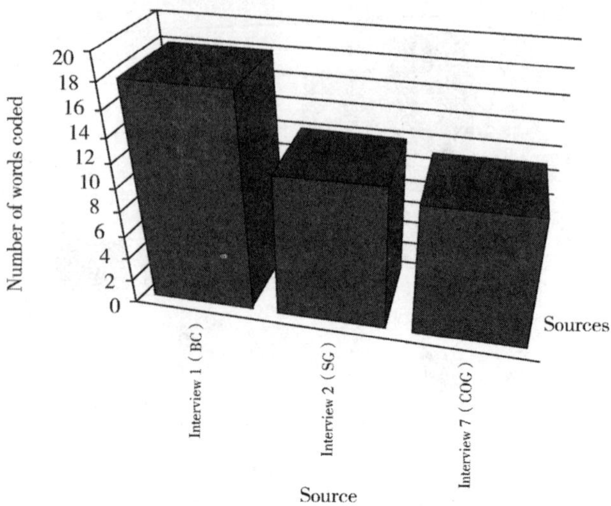

Figure 7–20 Business promotion

manage the programme. Originally we wanted long-term cooperation such as running the programmes annually, but as some problems emerged as to the messy teaching curriculum offered by Ningxia University after the training finished, we just cancelled it.

Interviewee 4 described what appeared to be the problem:

I don't think the training programmes we managed were ever successful. This is mainly due to the problem that staff learned little, and also basically they didn't know how to start and where to begin with their learning.

The problems that arose were a result of a lack of training objectives on both sides, which actually resulted in the trainer not offering the curriculum design to fit to the training needs, and little learning was achieved as a consequence.

7.4.4 Cultural awareness

The second dilemma that emerged after quantitative analysis which challenged the research is that both Chinese managers and staff reject the proposal of incorporating cultural awareness as a part of a training programme. The research continued to explore possible solutions for this through analysing the collected interview data. In order to confirm and validate the information collected in 2010, the manager interviewees were contacted again via email and telephone in an attempt to search for further reactions to the controversial interview responses.

In fact, very few responses were given concerning the concept of cultural awareness. However, after examining the transcriptions of interviews, a few relevant concepts emerged and were created as nodes for coding using NVivo. They include training pattern (short term or long term), individual project and the organisation's development strategy. A theme relating to the question could be identified and therefore, a tree node constructed as shown in Figure 7–21:

- Short-term or long-term of training pattern
- Individual learning project
- Company's development strategy

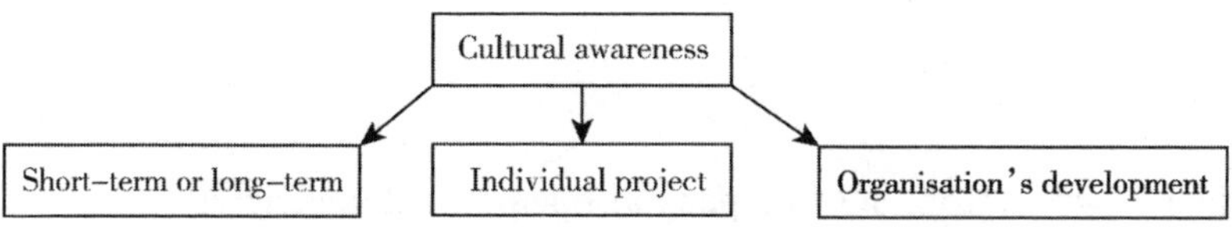

Figure 7–21 Tree nodes display

These three elements developed a thread, enabling the research to arrive at the answer to what actually happens when cultural awareness is rejected. These themes emerged from the analysis of managers' interviews which reflect their perception of cultural awareness. The NVivo analysis (as shown in Table 7–39 below) presents the results of three related coded nodes.

Table 7–39 **Node report for cultural awareness**

Tree node	Source	References	Words	Paragraphs	Percentages
Short-term	4	6	214	5	6.29%
Long-term	4	5	195	5	6.31%
Individual project	1	2	71	2	2.45%
Organisation's development	3	6	311	7	14.16%

From their interviews, it was clear that many managers believed that cultural awareness plays an important role in learning a foreign language, but that it also depends on what kind of training pattern their companies prefer because this will determine whether cultural awareness needs to be incorporated into training content. Interviewee 3 summarises:

From the personal work-related development, we should re-look at the goal of training programmes which is obviously to promote working skills. We are more inclined to run short courses. If you want to increase the possibility of achieving the learning target, or in other words, of improving its training effects, a training programme with about 2-3 months or 6 months concentrating on skills training will be more appropriate for us, but to increase cultural awareness needs a much longer time.

Interviewee 2 from SG Company also supported this view:

Because it is the need of specific posts, we generally will not spend money to help our employees to take long-term training courses. We might prefer short-term, because it is only for job requirements.

It is noted that the short-term training programme mainly focuses on developing participants' work-related skills only, so managers do not think it is necessary to incorporate cultural awareness into the programme. Some other managers, such as interviewee 3 and 1, however, did mention that there are times when cultural awareness should be included in the training programme content. Interviewee 3 continues:

> *On the other hand, we can't neglect the usefulness and benefit of long-term training in terms of backup talents for the company, or for some staff's personal career development. For long-term training, participants will have to get themselves more involved in the visiting cultures, and get in touch with the local culture to make sure that they would be more aware of the foreign cultures. It is more useful for increasing their cultural awareness than learning foreign languages.*

Meanwhile, interviewee 1 has his own view of long-term patterns of training:

> *...from the perspective of personal career development we will also consider the long-term, because we also require many outstanding talents to attend long-term training because it can bring long-term profits if considering sustainable development for our organisation.*

Evidently this comment related to the organisation's development strategy as to how to develop the available talent among the workforce for future use. It also indicates that cultural awareness usually takes some time to be adopted, which is not possible in a short – term course.

The chart in Figure 7–22 below shows to what extent nodes were coded in terms of cultural awareness based on the interview sources.

Obviously interview 8 (NXMU) has been coded much more regarding cultural awareness. Interviewee 8 frankly pointed out the key points when asked about the reason for rejecting incorporating cultural awareness into training programmes:

It was caused by the different mentality as many people still believe there is no need to get to know Western culture; or they even believe cultural exchange is not necessary for economic development. They may believe – arrogantly – that Chinese culture is the best culture in the world and Western culture could not be embedded into our culture.

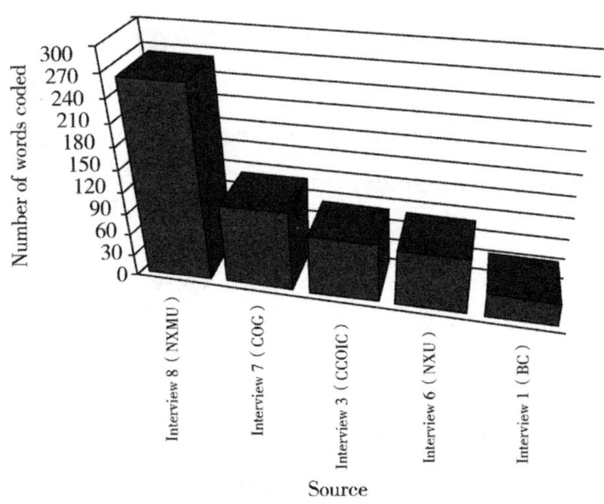

Figure 7–22 Culture awareness coded in the source

In the meantime, interviewee 7 from COG also expressed her worries in terms of cultural awareness in her interview, and she mentioned the mental conflict as well:

We won't deny the importance of cultural awareness when learning a foreign language but nowadays this term has become misleading so many people including our training participants believe this is a concept from Western culture. So they are so cautious in using this word. Apart from this, we spend money aiming to develop our staff's language skills, which might be used for the sake of our company's business development. We have to be aware that if too much Western culture is introduced into the training course this might result in negative problems, for instance, brain drain or uncertainty, which might be against our purposes for managing the foreign language training.

The extended interview conducted through email in relation to this has also shown the same concerns expressed by interviewee 3:

I think many participants have taken cultural awareness as a concept imported from Western culture. It might be playing a vital role in the context of Western society where companies and communities are mainly managed and grown by the obligation to the law and regulation. This can be evidenced by contract culture in Western countries. However, in China as a typical representative of Eastern culture, the concept of cultural awareness hasn't become deeply rooted in our own culture; on the contrary, family, kinship, network and social relationship, etc., and other benefit-based relationships have become criteria agreed with by Chinese people, so there must be lots of participants who don't think the Western concept of cultural awareness can have an effect on their language skills development. This is just because there is a gap in mentality in perceiving the concept.

7.4.5 Self-managed learning

Three themes emerge from the additional interviews based on the free nodes coded by NVivo analysis (see Figure 7–23). Table 7–40 below demonstrates the results of data analysis for the divergent perception of self-managed learning, and this gives the answer to the question that remained unresolved from quantitative analysis.

Table 7–40　　Free node report for self-managed learning

Free node	Source	References	Words	Paragraphs	Percentages
Confusion of concept	1	4	129	4	23.67%
Don't know how	1	2	65	2	11.23%
To be supervised	1	3	108	3	18.02%

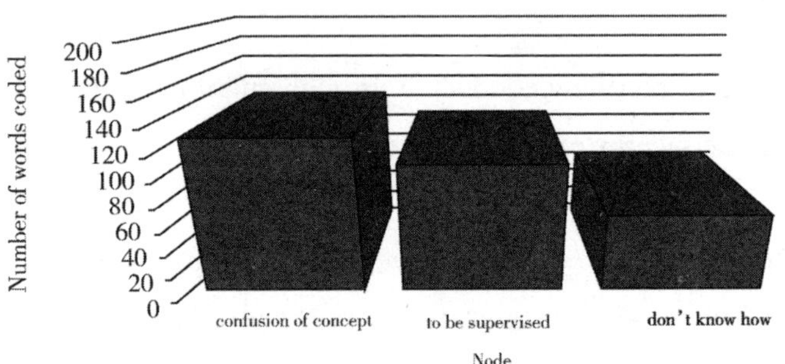

Figure 7–23　Themes coded by node

There are four references, four paragraphs and about 23.6% of total interview data coded in terms of 'confusion of concept'. These demonstrate that employers who chose not to use self-managed learning in training programmes did so mainly because of confusion over the concept of *self-managed learning,* a concept of Western-oriented learning style (Ip, 2000). Two references, two paragraphs and 11.23% were coded as a free node of '*don't know how*'; whilst three references, three paragraphs and 18.2% were coded under the free node of '*to be supervised*'.

Interviewee 9, an employee from the Bank of China (BC), when asked in the additional interviewthe reason why she disagreed with using self-managed learning, said "*Actually I have been confused with what is self-managed learning...*". Equally, three other respondents, interviewee 10 from Schaeffer, interviewee 11 from COG and interviewee 12 from DON expressed their confusion over their understanding of the concept. In the interviews, interviewee 9 further described it reasonably accurately although based on his personal understanding and actually she described, for example, a customised training programme that was entirely tutor-led:

In my understanding, I think self-managed learning should be used when I am interested in training content or training goals that are based on my own learning purposes.

As indicated, interviewee 12 was confused about how to explain the concept:

To update knowledge, increase knowledge and get in touch with new knowledge are the best ways to develop your ability. These can be considered as a way to motivate you to study.

Moreover, interviewee 11 continued to express his puzzlement:

To my understanding, self-managing learning can be labelled as what it is as long as I obtain some new information either from your friends, lecture rooms and the internet. I don't know whether it is correct or wrong and hope it is right... but honestly I am a bit confused with it.

In terms of how to conduct self-managed learning, interviewee 11 and 12 expressed their concerns about not knowing how to do this:

Interviewee 11: To be frank, if you just let me manage study by myself in terms of learning English, I really don't know where I shall start.

Interviewee 12: I prefer to be pushed and supervised to study foreign languages, so I don't know how to improve my English ability if you want me to learn by myself.

Therefore, interviewee 12 suggested training and supervision should take place first if using self-managed learning in teaching. She said:

I hope the organization would train us how to do it if they let us self-manage our foreign language study. I might do it if my company pushes me to take part in a training programme.

7.4.6 Regular report

Another question that needs to be explored further is about regular reports proposed for use in the evaluation of participants' learning progress. The results of the quantitative analysis revealed that staff respondents are reluctant to undertake regular reports but managers prefer with them for the evaluation. This sub-field of the research is closely related to the effectiveness of programme evaluation. In order to explore the answer in depth, extended interviews were conducted through email in an attempt to obtain clear answers from managers interviewed. Qualitative analysis of coding nodes themed 'regular report' using NVivo was also carried out (see Table 7–41 below).

Table 7–41 **Node report for regular reports**

Free node	Source	References	Words	Paragraphs	Percentages
Regular report	5	6	585	6	22.58%

There are six references, 585 words and representing 22.58% of the total interview text coded in the interview sources which demonstrate the deep concerns of the manager. The chart in Figure 7–24 below also gives us an idea just how deep these concerns relating to regular reporting are among the managers interviewed. Some, such as interviewee 1 and 3 mentioned that the participants' dislike of regular reports might be caused by the tightness of the training time because of the short-term programmes their companies are focusing on. They commented:

> *... and also we require the participants to write a period report to us including what they have done and what they have achieved, but it seems they don't want to do this as time is so tight. Anyway, it is a requirement from the company and they have to do it. And as far as I know they want to use some time to travel. But regular reporting I think is a good way to evaluate the learning process for participants and we will continue to enforce it as we use it as evidence to assess their learning objectives...*
>
> *We mainly manage short-term training programmes, a major form for adult learning in the society, and the time limitation has resulted in that participants don't want to communicate with each other and they don't want to be judged and assessed by a certain way of evaluation – say regular reports for instance.*

From their comments, a conflict between programme evaluation and personal preference can be noticed as there is a mismatch between the organisation's expectations and the participant's personal interests. The organisation is focusing on the results achieved at the end of programmes, and the managers who are in charge are committed to the goals set; however, the participants are reluctant to be cooperative in this respect.

Meanwhile, interviewee 3 expressed her concerns from another aspect:

> *...there is a variety of reasons for employees to attend a foreign language training programme. Many participants have to attend training without a choice because of the job requirements and they might be reluctant to do it. They might not be motivated to get themselves involved in the training and therefore mentally dislike regular reports ... they don't want to be judged and assessed by this way.*

Meanwhile, interviewee 2 from SG provided his unique perspective regarding this; he views regular reports as an incentive to increase participants' interest, and maintain their motivation in the process of training.

When the participants feel that their interest now is not the same as it was yesterday, the training manager will need to do something else. So we maybe have to manage a kind of regular assessment and ask participants to report what they are doing. In this way, they may maintain an interest in studying or generate motivation.

However, interviewee 5 (DON) and interviewee 8 (NXMU) considered regular reports as a way to ensure the effectiveness of the outcomes of foreign language training programmes. They both believed the money they spent on the course needs to be worthwhile, so the strict monitoring of the process of training was the best way to secure accurate evaluation. In addition, they expressed their appreciation of joint assessment with their partners. Interviewee 5 said,

To ensure effective assessment of the participants, they [the training providers] are required to report to us bimonthly, and at the same time, the top university administration will send us the general monitoring because we need to monitor their learning procedures as well. What's more, we will sign the contract with every individual participant before s/he goes to the training. It encompasses learning outcomes and punishments. If they are unable to get the degree or certificates by the end of the courses, they will be required to reimburse the fees for their studies during training to the government. For monitoring the learning of every individual participant, we are jointly doing this with the training provider Asia Centre in Illinois State University.

Similarly, interviewee 8 (NXMU) underpinned this idea by commenting:

Surely we want to do as it can be a better solution for how to monitor trainees' performance. We can adopt a variety of ways such as regular meetings, mid-term evaluation or other approaches. This is because we have invested to achieve a goal set before going for training and we need participants to hand in a report or summary either in English or Chinese telling us what they have learned and what skills they have developed. If this is done in practice, it will make more sense to me.

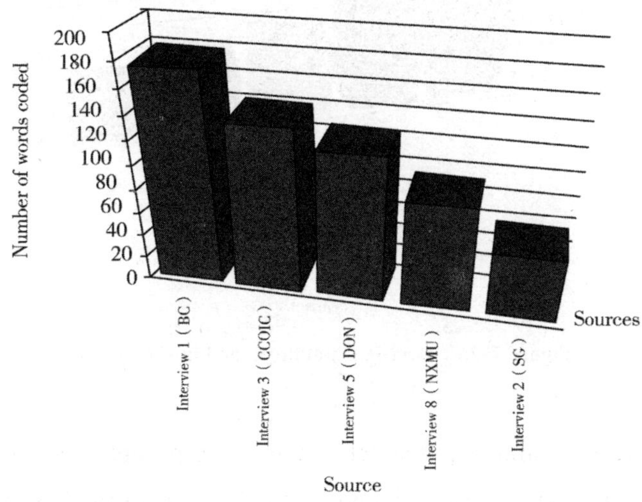

Figure 7–24 Regular report coded in the source

7.4.7 Decision making

The results of the quantitative analysis indicate a divergent perception relating to decision-making for a training programme, as two outliers, the respondent from the Organisation Department of Ningxia and the respondent from the Foreign Affairs Office of Ningxia Medical University, clearly stood out in the analysis (refer to Figure 7–14). To explore the possible answer in greater depth, extended interview were also conducted via email with two of the managers.

Table 7–42　　Node report for Decision making

Free node	Source	References	Words	Paragraphs	Percentages
Decision making	5	5	388	5	12.85%

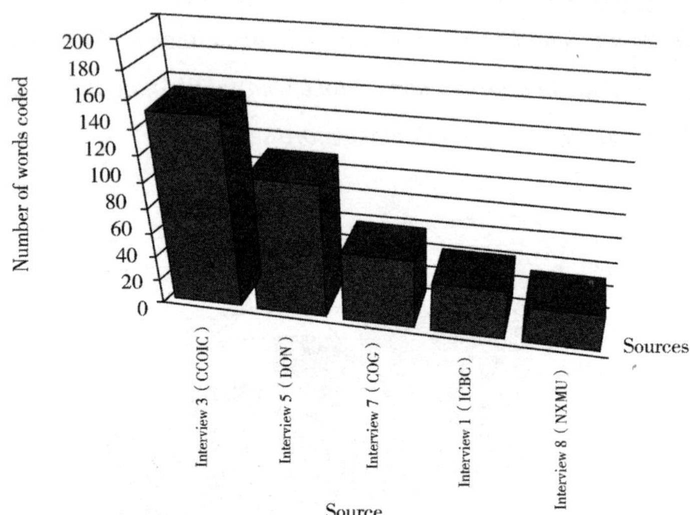

Figure 7–25　Decision-making coded in the source

There are five sources, five references, five paragraphs and 388 words coded in the interviews, which accounts for 12.85% in total (see Table 7–42 above).

A number of managers from five different companies and organisations gave their views on decision-making. The themes given by the managers interviewed are categorised as:

- Staff's individual training needs analysis
- Top leader's directive
- Size of training programmes provided
- Reputation of training providers

The first two themes are internally based, and the third and fourth are external. To be specific, in terms of decision-making, Interviewee 7 from COG describes how her company makes a decision to launch a foreign language training programme:

...it depends on the needs of both staff and practical work. Generally, the decisions that we take to run training programmes every year are proposed by us and decided by the factory. They generally respect our proposal. Of course, the proposals must be reasonable and the training model should also be reasonable, which can meet the demands of our factory...

However, interviewee 3 from CCOIC expresses an understanding of decision-making that looked into the background of the economic system and argues that if a decision is based on individual needs analysis only it will mean we have been following a market-oriented management system, which is obviously not the case so far. She continues:

...decision-making also has to depend on what our organisation needs, which means decisions must be made based on the objectives of the organisation as well...

In addition, she proposes using a mixed balanced method to arrive at a decision, in which a bottom-to-top orientation can be seen:

We are not running it in the same way that a real market-oriented economy does because we are not a real market economy but at least we are still on the way towards it, so a mixed balanced approach has been mainly used by engaging staff's contributions as well as the organisation's development strategy.

Meanwhile, the style of decision-making of top-down directive can be widely seen. This can be witnessed in the comments of interviewee 5 (DON), interviewee 8 (NXMU) and interviewee 1(ICBN):

Interviewee 8: Our department normally makes the decision to carry out training programme ourselves because, as you may be aware, the central government has laid much more emphasis on leaders' professional development training. Funding has been in place, so we just need to manage training programmes for another five years following the instruction from the top.

Interviewee 5: Decision-making also has to depend on the outcomes we might have achieved. We are working for the government and party so we are managing training programmes according to what we have planned. Once we have decided to run a training programme for this year then we start selecting the participants from cadres of different levels of organisations.

Interviewee 1: We haven't thought of managing the foreign language training programme through an international strategy because this decision should always have to go to headquarters.

It sounds as though one manager has become desperate about this situation:

Interviewee 8: Decisions are always made by people who have the right to speak their minds and what I can do is to make suggestions 0... so who knows what will happen next...

Besides, other external influential factors including the size and reputation of the training providers will also play a key role in helping companies to make their decisions. This is underpinned by interviewee 3's comment:

> *Also there are still lots of other components affecting our decision which include the size, reputation, and strength of the training providers, but usually the information relating to these is not available to us.*

Additionally, two attributes, age and years of service in the companies and organisations, are taken into account.

It should be noted that the demographic data collected show that the ages of the managers interviewed mostly fell into the range of 41-50, and years of serving in their companies and organisations is more than 20 years (see Figure 7–26 and 7–27). This finding is very significant as it helps to understand the Chinese managers' perceptions of foreign language training management from different generations (Ralston *et al.*, 1999b). This will be further discussed in the next chapter.

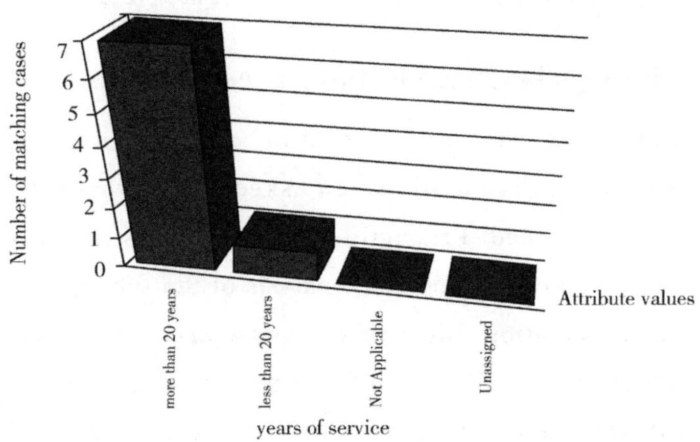

Figure 7–26 Interviewed managers' years of service

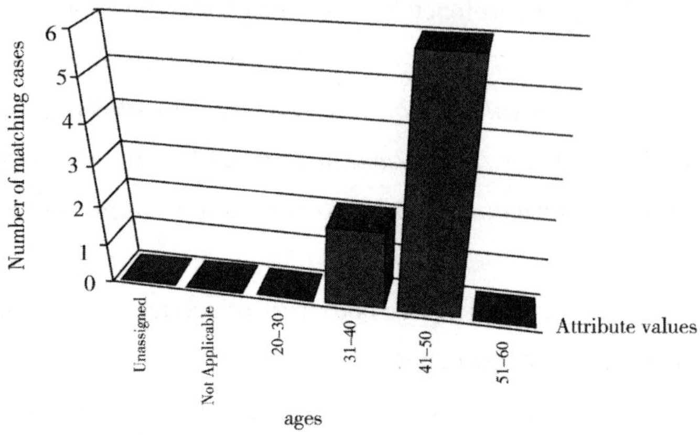

Figure 7–27 Interviewed managers' age ranges

7.5 Findings and summary

After analysing the qualitative data using NVivo's free and tree node techniques, a number of interesting themes emerged which can be reasonably taken as sensible answers to the questions arising from the quantitative data analysis. The findings that accompany these answers are presented below.

7.5.1 Foreign language training needs analysis

First of all, many companies seemed to have focused on their training objectives and productive skills when asked about what actual foreign language skills they need. Productive language skills in particular have been placed in an important position; analysis of the subsequent interviews offers a clear explanation. Most of the managers interviewed indicated that they expect their staff to be able to use their speaking and writing language abilities to promote their company's business and to be able to better communicate with international business partners after the training programme has ended. The findings support Turner's (1993) viewpoint that different language needs should be in accordance with individual organisations' development schemes.

It is, however, also assumed by many managers that staff participants in training programmes quite often take advantage of training as an opportunity to obtain more knowledge so that they would be likely to find a better job. Learning, or – to put it more precisely – gaining more knowledge, is culturally rooted in Chinese people's perceptions. For a long time Chinese people have lacked creativity, therefore, companies and organisations expect their staff to be more creative when using a foreign language in order to productively enhance communication with their business partners (Martinsons, 1996).

Secondly, the findings also show that there are numerous concerns in terms of whether content related to foreign language learning is targeted to support the development schemes of the training companies and organisations. Training outcomes such as job skills development, mentality change and business promotion are extensively emphasised, so the ultimate goal of foreign language learning is better directed at a more varied range of activities and could be accomplished more efficiently but indirectly without recourse to language learning only.

Thirdly, the specific actual training needs for different operators in the economy can be summarised on the basis of both main interviews and subsequent follow-up interviews. Higher education (NXU and NXMU), financial services (ICBC and BC) and manufacturing (SG and COG) prefer productive language skills, speaking and writing-based training, while only one company, the Schaeffler Group demands for listening and reading. At the same time, the manufacturing and financial services sectors such as SG, ICBC and BC heavily attach importance to job skills development and business promotion; while higher education and government organisations (NXU, NXMU, DON and CCOIC) draw attention to mentality change brought about in order to create a talent reserve. See details in the Table 7–43 below.

Table 7–43 **Findings for training needs analysis**

Economic Operation	Company /organisation	Needs Analysis
Manufacturing	SG, COG	Productive skills (speaking/writing), job skills development and business promotion
Financial Services	ICBC, BC	
Higher Education	NXU, NXMU	Productive skills and mentality change
Government organisation	DON, CCOIC	Mentality change

7.5.2 Cultural awareness

The analysis of the interviews has shown that the diverse perceptions of cultural awareness held by the Chinese managers and staff have resulted in the rejection of the proposal of incorporating it into learning content (see section 7.4.4). However, it has not been completely ignored by many managers (e.g. interviewees 1, 2 and 3) who candidly admit that cultural awareness would play an important role in learning a foreign language and believe this mainly depends on the training pattern, individual project design and overall organisational development scheme (see Figure 7–21 in section 7.4.4).

It is found that short-term training programmes usually do not tend to incorporate cultural awareness into their curriculum design because it is usually designed deliberately for achieving individual job development in a short period of time (e.g. interviewees 1, 2 and 3). Long-term programmes, though, are more likely to include this in the training scheme because Chinese companies and organisations want to develop their international mobility skills to ensure the reserve of talents for future development (e.g. interviewees 1, 7 and 8).

The findings have also shown that many believe cultural awareness is a Western concept which would not make a great deal of sense to both Chinese managers and staff. In order not to cause any uncertainty, possibly as a result of cultural awareness input, manager and staff respondents simply reject the concept. This result can be convincingly found within government organisations and higher education institutes (NXU, NXMU and DON).

7.5.3 Self-managed learning

The analysis of the additional follow-up interviews has given us an idea that the divergence in perceptions between staff and managers interviewed in terms of self-managed learning is caused by the confusion surrounding the concept, with staff affected in this way not knowing how to undertake self-managed learning. Therefore, the findings indicate that supervising and training themselves need to be arranged alongside the design of self-managed learning.

Conversely, however, the findings have shown no correlation between the different ownership of Chinese organisations and companies in terms of adopting self-managed learning as a pedagogical teaching style in training programmes.

7.5.4 Regular reports

The analysis has shown that a gap exists in managers' and staff's expectations of the regular report as a way of monitoring the learning process. Due to the short-term training pattern that many companies and organisations pursue, managers are much more committed to achieving the learning goals set prior to the implementation of the training course. Also, many even use it as a way to help participants maintain their interest and motivation; however, this has resulted in the misleading of participants who believe the managers who are engaged in the management of training courses might use their regular reports as a tool to judge their learning outcomes, something the participants dislike. At the same time, many managers are also concerned that the participants in training courses may make use of this chance not to concentrate fully on studying if there is no regular report required (e.g. interviewees 1, 2, 3, 5 and 8).

Meanwhile, the findings have demonstrated that higher education and government organisations are keen on using regular reports as a way to monitor the learning progress.

7.5.5 Decision-making

A wide range of relevant elements that influence decision-making emerged from the qualitative data analysis. These elements encompass individual needs analysis, top leader's directive, and size and reputation of training providers, which each has an impact on the decision-making process.

There are, however, two kinds of characteristics attributed to decision-making. One is bottom-up and the other top-down (see Figure 7–41). The former refers to decision-making which usually starts from collecting individual needs analyses from staff and responding to training demands from employees. The information collected, mainly from staff who hopes to develop their individual language skills will contribute enormously to helping companies and organisations to launch foreign language training programmes. Business or manufacturing companies, such as COG and SG, are representative of this 'bottom–up' approach. The latter approach, of 'top-down' favours the style of decision-making that largely depends on the top leaders' directives which is normally the case in government organisations such as DON and other financial organisations such as CCOIC and ICBC.

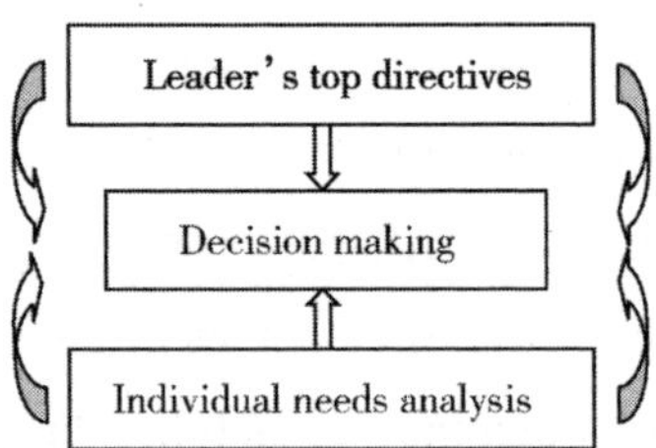

Figure 7–28 Model for decision making

7.6 Summary

To summarise, the analysis of the quantitative data collected from both staff and manager's attitudes towards the proposed modal was mainly undertaken in section 7.2 and 7.3. A range of statistics tests were used aiming at finding the answers to the addressed propositions. Staff and manager's data are respectively analysed before comparing the consistency between their attitudes.

The analysis of the interview data was mainly conducted in the section 4 using NVivo to undertake an in-depth exploration in order to address the five questions arising from the quantitative analysis. The findings have given the research a deeper understanding of how rejection took place in terms of answering questions about actual foreign language needs analysis, cultural awareness, self-managed learning, regular reports and decision-making. These results will help the research convincingly map out a comprehensive picture of the investigation.

Chapter 8 Discussion and Conclusions

8.1 Introduction

This part of the book discusses the findings from the analysis of the quantitative and qualitative research and establishes recommendations and implications so that new knowledge is established in the field. In addition, limitations and suggestions for future research will be indicated at the end of this chapter.

8.2 Discussion and implications

8.2.1 Creation of individual project

Initially, research propositions one and two are designed to address the proposal to create an individual project.

Research proposition one mainly relates to the individual task-based project. The results indicated that both managers and staff welcome the fact that a training programme may start with the creation of a project individually and independently because both groups of respondents believe it is important to define the individual's learning objectives. They also believe that individual project creation by Chinese trainees is a necessary and creative approach to meeting learning objectives.

Although the diversity of learning orientation among Chinese staff have been historically moulded at the era of opening up to the world (Douw *et al.*, 2001; Hu, 2005a; Ip, 2002), the unique Chinese Confucian culture still has had a major influence on Chinese learners learning styles (Li, 2010). For future globalisation development, China's foreign language education policy has fostered to adaptation and respond to both the Chinese developmental context and the global economy, to embrace as inclusively as possible all value systems within its culture, and to have an inclusive culture resulting from a creative transformation of the cultural legacy (Ip, 2009, MOE, 2001). By that, it is suggested that individuals' discourses of learning, learning expectations and learning requirements ought to be executed more by their educational learning concerns than by general demands of merely training efficiency (Evans, 2003). Therefore, in terms of responding to these changes, there is demand for a suitable foreign language training programme tailored to meet the diverging needs of staff and managers (Chee, 2002/2003; Qin *et al.*, 2010). These demands are strongly based on how organisations can meet the learning needs of their staff and managers by focusing on their development. It has become clear that the previous foreign language programmes such as the Online Chinese programme and task-based or content-based programmes were designed on the basis of the principle of goal-based scenarios (Schank, 1992) and anchored instruction, while the question of how to properly incentivise Chinese staff to engage in training has remained largely unaddressed. Many managers in the initial research complained that the current established training models are impractical because the design of the current training curricula goes beyond basic learning needs. They also expressed concern about the lack of approaches to enhance the creation of independent learning among the participants, and also expressed doubt over the effectiveness of the existing programmes. The outcomes of this research actually support the proposal integrated within the first-tier level of the model in which individual project creation is crucial to launching a training programme. At the meantime, time needs to be set aside to conduct a foreign language needs analysis among potential participants to establish whether a training programme is actually necessary.

Thus, the new contribution to the existing body of knowledge in the field may be added in this respect. Traditionally, to define the learning objectives for training programmes aiming at meeting either companies' and organisations' development strategy or the needs analysis of individuals, it is largely agreed that learning needs to be managed (Drucker, 1989; Kealey, 2009; Morgan, 1997; Nicholson, 2003; Pedlar,1991; Weightman , 2004). However, in the case of Chinese staff, who still tend to display an inverted learning style (Harshbarger, 1986; Littrell, 2005; Liu, 1997; Song, 1995), and generally believe that knowledge depends on the teachers' transmission rather than individual interpretations (Harshbarger, 1986), no needs analysis was usually ever required to be undertaken either by training providers or Chinese companies and organisations. To design an individual project prior to actual implementation is not onlyessential and innovative, it also promotes the quality of training for Chinese staff and managers. An individual project, particularly one that is established before actual practice, allows Chinese training participants greater freedom to display initiative and creativity, but it also requires full commitment and cooperation throughout training. In addition, individual project creation would avoid the ambiguity of learning targets and objectives, so therefore it is inevitably necessary in terms of the trainees' needs analysis before a training programme is implemented.

Proposition two is also designed to address the question of what individual foreign language needs participants have. The results indicate that the design of a foreign language training programme should focus on developing the trainees' work-related skills, professional skills and ability to solve problems relating to the requirements of the workplace. These proposals are perceived as reasonable and acceptable new ideas by both staff and managers, and ones which will guide and inform their future endeavours.

The review of the literature has shown that many foreign language students have been developed mainly by universities through a certain kind of rigid learning curriculum which is believed to go beyond the expectations for social or practical use (Chen 2004; Graddol, 2002). Chinese foreign language education is facing a dilemma over how to meet the increasing demand for practical foreign language use and how to change their teaching and learning orientation from that of a formal university, theory-based, learning to incorporating practical foreign language skills required in the workplace. In the meantime, feelings of wanting to be a part of the international business community and to increase their competitiveness within the international business community are also challenging many Chinese companies and organisations (Jiang, 2008; Littrell, 2005). The current situation that Chinese companies and organisations find themselves in has therefore placed higher education institutions at a crucial point where they may have to examine their developing orientation (Tang *et al.*, 2005).

Drucker (1989) and Morgan (1997) argue that deciding what skills to train individuals in, and develop, is equally important to direct the performance of people in companies and organisations. This has been conceptualised as management by objectives because it relates the organisational goals to the behaviour and performance of individuals by, for instance, setting individual learning targets and objectives (Nicholson, 2003). However, the argument is very ambigious and too general because the unique Chinese management culture has hampered the identification of the actual needs within Chinese companies; and it is usually difficult to ensure the consistency of perception of training needs between staff and the organisational goals (Chee, 2002/2003; Kealey, 2009). In the context of training programmes for Chinese staff, this clearly becomes much more significant as a gap between attitudes among Chinese staff and managers, which appear to have been established because of the influence of Chinese culture (Goodall *et al.*, 2004). Therefore, the attitudes of both groups must contribute to validating the training management. Reflecting on the investigation of where actual learning needs lie, the results from both managers and staff have provided evidence that the requirement for work-related foreign language skills is now being embraced, and proposition two is therefore supported.

Thus, the further knowledge of shifting to work-related skills training from general foreign language skills in a training programme has been established. The previous existing foreign language training programmes for Chinese staff and managers largely focus on developing the trainees' foreign language abilities in speaking, listening, writing and reading; but with increasing demands for the ability to cope with international business, the real needs of Chinese companies and organisations are gradually shifting to more exclusive, more practical, and more work-related foreign language training. This shift actually aims at enhancing the trainees' managerial capabilities in an effort to embrace international business practices (Jiang, 2008).

Furthermore, proposition three is also designed to examine in depth specific foreign language training needs. It mainly looks at attitudes towards professional skills and technical ability if these elements are incorporated into programme design. The findings have revealed that the Chinese companies and organisations have made increasing demands for these two learning objectives.

Initially many researchers (e.g. Kuo, 2005; Rogerson-Revell, 2007; Smith and Arkless, 1993) believed the foreign language training programme only focused on developing trainees' language ability. Many training providers from UK educational institutions and from other countries perceived language training programmes primarily as a way to improve learners' foreign language ability. In the meantime, Smith *et al.* (1993) also identified that the effectiveness of foreign language training is increasingly dependent on needs analysis, as discussed in the literature. Turner (1993) and other researchers (e.g. Anderson, 1987; Shared, 1986) pointed out that a training programme should be defined by specific learning objectives. More importantly, however, and also more difficult in this sense, is how to locate the training needs in the context of the Chinese organisations and companies which are presently striving to make their businesses internationally competitive. Solving the problem of language barriers can be done by managing a foreign language training progamme through channels of international communication. As reviewed in the literature, however, to import a foreign language training programme heavily featuring the Western autonomous learning style has challenged the educators (Wang, 2008). In addition, there are other major challenges to identifying specific learning needs, which requires a shift from institutional theory-based learning to professional and technical skills development. To be more specific, the purpose of sending staff and managers on training programmes at universities nowadays is no longer simply to develop their foreign language abilities. Instead, Chinese managers and staff need more abilities relating to their roles within the workplace. The findings of this proposition have explained the reasons why many Chinese managers in their interviews have shown little satisfaction with the current training programmes provided either locally or internationally.

Further, the findings also clarify the approach that can be applied to stimulate Chinese adults to engage in a foreign language training programme, and this evidently justifies the statement by Wang (2008), that an outstanding learning characteristic of Chinese adult learners is that they often aim to develop their understanding within their academic discipline which allows them to participate actively in productive activity. So aiming at integrating professional skills and technical abilities into foreign language training courses might be one of the alternative approaches which not only draws the attention of training managers but also increases the scale of engagement by Chinese trainees. If learning content is more linked to the participant's workplace, and engages them in developing their professional and technical skills, the learning experience is thus contextualised by the requirements of the work activity as part of a process that trainees are compelled to follow in order to understand the standards and values associated with the practice of work (Billett, 2002). The answers from managers and staff are evidently in agreement in supporting the proposal.

In addition, the positive attitudes towards integrating the development of the characteristics of professionalism into the foreign language training content also emphasise the contribution of work experience to the development of competence and occupational identity. With culture shock likely to hamper their study progress in a completely new environment, participants will use their current knowledge and innate ability offered by their work experience to participate in the relevant learning activities (Guile and Griffiths, 2001). This on the one hand will primarily help them to rapidly integrate in the workplace provided by the training provider within a learning context in which they normally need a period of time to adapt themselves before full engagement. On the other hand, it has offered an inspiration to the educational sectors on how to narrow the gap between training curriculum design and actual needs and demands, in particular for Chinese staff and managers.

8.2.2 Implementation of training

Propositions four, five, six and seven are designed to identify the attitudes of Chinese managers and staff towards how to successfully design and implement a foreign language programme. The propositions included exploring communication ability, cultural awareness, on-going evaluation and specific foreign language needs analysis from each interviewed company and organisation, as well as envisaging the pedagogical approach for Chinese trainees.

8.2.2.1 Learning content

The findings raised a great deal of uncertainty in these respects. In terms of learning content as regards language communication ability, cultural awareness and specific foreign language skills, on the one hand, the analysis of staff data signified that the participants who want to develop their communicative ability are also willing to develop cultural awareness when undertaking training abroad. At the same time, the findings also suggest that developing either the ability to communicate in a foreign language or cultural awareness as part of a foreign language training programme will positively impact on the organisation's operational success. Thus, this is consistent with research proposition four in respect of developing communicative ability and cultural awareness. However, the findings also showed that training staff are reluctant to incorporate communicative abilities and cultural awareness into their needs analysis for individual projects because the respondents have expressed negative attitudes, although they agree that developing foreign language skills is positively associated with communicative ability development and cultural awareness.

On the other hand, the findings from the analysis of the managers' data highlighted the positive attitudes of this group towards incorporating the improvement of communicative abilities such as listening, speaking, writing and reading into the learning content; however, the managers rejected the need to enhance cultural awareness among learners. The attitudes of staff and managers towards cultural awareness appeared inconsistent and controversial, and a clear divergence emerged. This result has been collaborated by the later comparative analysis between managers' and staff's data, which ascertained divergent perceptions about incorporating cultural awareness into learning content. This as a result triggered the researcher's curiosity into exploring the answers through interviewing Chinese managers.

The findings of the qualitative analysis using NVivo have clearly denoted that including cultural awareness in foreign language training programmes for Chinese companies and organisations depends greatly on training patterns – short term or long term. Short-term training programmes mainly focus on training participants' work-related skills, including professional and technical abilities which may have been outlined and set up in their individual projects. Cultural awareness will normally be set as a goal for Chinese training providers; however, it will generally feature as a characteristic of long-term training because its training objective is to cultivate the backup talents for the future development of companies and organisations.

These findings have given us a picture of how the strategy for future development of Chinese companies and organisations has been constructed. Those organisations which are essentially overseen by local government with more power for self-management, such as NXMU, CCOIC and NXU, prefer to have cultural awareness included in their training programmes; whilst those companies which are mainly international manufacturing businesses such as SG and COG will embrace the short-term training which focuses on work-related foreign language skills. As indicated in the literature review, many companies and organisations are engaged in increasing their competitive strength within the international business arena, and they have stratified their development strategy into two categories: short-term training for renewing trainees' work-related skills and professional and technical ability; and long-term training for developing talents with knowledge of international regulations, laws, and international business as well as foreign language proficiency. These trainees will be potentially nominated to play a leadership role in future development. Thus, cultural awareness as a key factor for improving trainees' comprehensive abilities could be included in training content in order to meet the long-term training expectations of the Chinese people (Graddol, 2002).

Training providers have to remain alert when involving cultural awareness in training programmes, because the findings from the analysis of the interviews conducted in this study imply that there are misleading perceptions of cultural awareness because of its Western origins. As a result, culture would be viewed with suspicion by Chinese managers and staff as it appears to be related to politics, at a time when China is transforming from a central-planning economy to a freer market-oriented economy. Instead, the data from the interview have demonstrated that many managers are proud of their home culture and have actually requested increasing awareness of Chinese students' learning culture and respect for Chinese culture in relation to learning style.

So, the results show that one needs to be clear what forms of training are intended – short-term or long-term – before designing a foreign language programme for Chinese companies and organisations, before deciding if cultural awareness will be incorporated into the programme. Otherwise, the controversial attitudes towards cultural awareness may emerge and raise suspicion from

Chinese participants.

In addition, the awareness of ownership of training partners adds credit to programme design because organisations with different ownership will focus differently on the forms of training. For those government-owned organisations, cultural awareness needs to be included because they are interested in long-term training programmes; whilst in those privately-owned business-oriented companies and organisations, cultural awareness isn't necessarily a feature of teaching and learning, as a short-term programme for the purpose of developing skills is mainly needed.

8.2.2.2 Pedagogy

Proposition six was designed to address pedagogical style, and intended to look at what approaches applied in training that relied on international channel of communication would be effective. The findings partly support the hypothesis that integrating formal instruction into teaching practice is warmly welcomed by training participants, which is consistent with the discussion in the literature. As indicated in the literature review, due to a shortage of facilities and learning resources, and the historic belief that English language teaching and learning was predominantly teacher-centred, formal instruction dominated foreign language classes, focusing on teaching foreign language knowledge, with little freedom given to students for autonomous learning (Chen, 2004). The majority of staff and managers who have been the backbone of their employers' organisations and who are most likely to be selected for further training by the companies and organisations surveyed are greatly affected by this typical teaching approach. They learned the foreign language at schools over the years when China was still struggling with foreign language education reform and was heavily affected by the traditional teaching approach. In spite of this, because of the influence of Confucian culture, which develops Chinese learners' introverted learning style (Littrell, 2005; Peacock, 2001), many Chinese staff believe knowledge can only be transferred through lectures and have become accustomed to formal instruction (Anderson, 1993; Peacock, 2001). In their experience, formal instruction is necessary for them to obtain knowledge of a foreign language as well as to ensure skills development. They are therefore reluctant to interpret and extend what they have learned through their own independent investigation (Harshbarger, 1986). They still retain the traditional teaching and learning style for the sake of their own comfort. However, along with the educational reform which was introduced following awareness of the negative impact of the introverted learning style, China has openly announced 'quality-oriented' teaching and learning which has largely imported Western learning perceptions with the characteristic of self-managed learning or antonomous learning. The import of Western perceptions of learning and teaching to China has shifted the roots of Chinese foreign language education, and has inspired Chinese foreign language teachers on how to develop Chinese language ability effectively (Zhou, 2004).

The findings from the analysis of the qualitative data show that self-managed learning still remains a new or less familiar concept to Chinese adult learners. This approach is about individuals managing their own learning and includes people taking responsibility for decisions about what, how, when and where they learn (Cunningham *et al.*, 2000). Many participants in the survey expressed confusion over the definition, and stated their willingness to be supervised if self-managed study is designed. Although – as indicated in the analysis – self-managed learning is not a new concept to many managers, it may still mislead staff participants.

The idea of combining traditional Chinese teaching methods and the mark of the Western learning style has no doubt been widely adopted as a logical development (Liu, 2006, Jiang, 2008), but as far as self-managed learning is concerned, proper supervision should be in place in order to guarantee what participants will be able to learn, because Chinese participants might be more than usually confused by the concept of self-managed learning. These findings can be considered as further knowledge to be added to the pedagogic innovation contributing to a successful foreign language training programme through international collaboration.

In addition, the discovery may also inspire researchers in the field in the sense that Chinese adults prefer using two kinds of learning styles stimultaneously to acquire knowledge in training because they usually like to take time thinking, analysing and judging logically before arriving at a conclusion (Anderson 1993; Nelson, 1995). Thinking-oriented rather than feeling-oriented learning is applied, so therefore using both Western and Chinese teaching and learning styles is a better way to accommodate Chinese learners through an international communication strategy (Peacock, 2001).

8.2.2.3 Problem-solving ability

What abilities Chinese employees need to develop are another important factor involved in the implementation of a foreign language training programme. Individual project creation is a way to help employees identify the scope of learning so as to engage fully with a commitment to their learning (Turner, 1993). Project-based foreign language teaching and learning programmes have contributed to improving learners' foreign language skills, real-life skills, sustained motivation, and engagement (Beckett, 1999). The review of relevant literature in this respect has commonly reported these attributes, in particular regarding the improvement of foreign language abilities, because much of the literature only consists of reports of how language teachers make use of project creation for the purpose of English language learning in a general sense (Gu, 2002). However, most previous programmes have ignored Morries' (1979) point of view; he advocated that to undertake a project based on training needs requires that the conduct is viewed as a way to manage a 'problem-solving cycle'; and he viewed foreign language project management as a channel which helps the individual participant to develop the ability to solve the problems. The results and findings of this study have added further understanding of project-based foreign language training in the sense of what the ultimate objectives are for a language training programme in this era of Chinese economic readjustment. The attitudes of employees towards the proposed problem-solving ability have given us an indication that the improvement of foreign language skills is not the only trigger for Chinese companies to launch a training programme. What they actually need from the management of a foreign language programme is to develop employees' abilities to solve work-related problems when they are involved in international business. This requires advanced qualifications not only in foreign language proficiency but in the use of foreign language to solve real problems related to the workplace. These demands are expected to be met and developed through the implementation of the programme, which aims to meet individual learning needs based on trainees' individual projects. It is also believed, as revealed in the findings, that the ultimate goal for developing employees' problem-solving ability is to update the level of development of the company after solving any existing problems which challenge the company's development. Thus, developing employees' ability to solve problems has become increasingly crucial to Chinese companies and organisations.

In addition, through a comparison of the managers' and staff's data, the findings have interestingly suggested that managers have higher expectations in terms of developing problem-solving abilities than the staff themselves, although they expressed their positive attitudes towards this as well. In the meantime, two extreme pieces of negative data emerged in the analysis (see Figure 7–9). Some divergence between the perceptions of staff and managers can be seen at this point. This result could be understandable because it is the manager who usually maintains his stance and believes that developing problem-solving ability is a part of the integrated endeavours required for the benefit of companies and organisations. However, staff may not look that far ahead; instead considering attending training programmes as a chance to develop their own foreign language abilities only. Managers usually have more forward-looking views in terms of overall development of the company (Hofstede, 2001), but staff may view a training opportunity as a springboard for future career development, as expressed by managers in the interviews (e.g. interviewee 3 from CCOIC). The findings are also supported by Turner (1993) who stresses that productivity measures linked to a particular project may mean different things to different people in different contexts.

The preference for involving the development of trainees' problem-solving ability is also in accordance with Tierney *et al.* (1999; 2011) and Proctor (2010) who advocate that the role of the employee, as well as improving their ability to solve work-related problems, and the expectations of the managers for them to develop creative ability is associated with an enhanced sense of employees' capacity for creative work.

In sum, further knowledge of the subject can be recognised with respect to project-based foreign language learning. The common benefits from such learning and teaching are learners' involvement, enhanced foreign language skills, and increased work-related content knowledge, as well as improved self-esteem and confidence; but along with the recognition of developing problem-solving ability, this kind of learning and teaching may be more sensible and significant as it not only makes knowledge transfer possible, but transfers knowledge into practical ability.

8.2.3 Individual project evaluation

Evaluation is always a sensitive topic when assessing a training programme (Lingham, 2006). This is because the effectiveness lies in the connotations of the term itself, which is hard to define against input of efforts and outcomes of production (Kerzner, 1984).

8.2.3.1 Joint evaluation

Joint evaluation is conceptulised as part of the very model. As indicated in the literature review (section 5.5), it is important to understand organisational and participants' training objectives when an evaluation is conducted (Lingham *et al.*, 2006). This study has suggested an innovative method for evaluating an international collaboration foreign language programme by hypothesising that training providers and trainee partners could be invited to jointly engage in the evaluation either at the stage of generating individual learning projects or at the end stage of the programme evaluation. Findings have indicated positive attitudes towards this proposal and have shown evidence that a training programme run through an international communication strategy can be creatively evaluated by a joint panel rather than a one-sided evaluation previously carried out by the client only, or even without evaluation at all.

The findings of the investigation provide us with the solution to resolve the dilemma in the area of the evaluation for foreign language international training programme. It will help the training programme to be undertaken with quality and effectiveness. Over the years managers, when interviewed, have expressed deep concerns over the effectiveness of a foreign language training programme as they have doubted the extent to which trainees are able to apply the knowledge, skills and attitudes they obtained in the training – suggesting the importance of the applicability and effectiveness of training programmes (Lingham *et al.*, 2006). It is especially important in a programme managed through international collaboration. The findings obtained from both initial research and later interviews with Chinese managers have clearly indicated that setting up a system which assists in the redesign and adjustment of the programmes based on Chinese companies and organisational and participant perspectives and needs is increasingly urgent. Yet, the phase of evaluation for international training programme has been among the most overlooked aspects in training (McClelland, 1994; Carter, 2002; Lingham *et al.*, 2006). This drawback can clearly be seen in the literature regarding the theoretical framework of project-based foreign language learning. McClelland (1994) also mentions that budgetary and other constraints have caused many trainers to employ standardised, commercially available evaluation instruments that have many disadvantages. However, many trainers have ignored the necessity of evaluating motivation, outcomes, and in-progress evaluation, as well as whether the training is aligned with the companies' organisational goals and visions, and if these requirements are closely covered by individual learning projects.

Horowitz (1989) and Lingham *et al.* (2006) highlight the concern that standard evaluation of training programmes have not considered actual instruments and measures to capture knowledge gained and retained in training programmes, examine whether the training result was targeted to the objectives, as well as how to improve later training programmes, which suggests the importance of innovation in programme evaluation. The result of the investigation, therefore, gives comfort to those who hold these views and suggest solutions for many of these problems.

In the meantime, it is said that Chinese people pay more attention to relationships, which can determine whether a business relationship is accepted or rejected; after all, according to Hofstede's (1980) cultural dimensions, China is a high-context country, in which choice of communicative style plays an important role, and word choice becomes very important. Suspicion of the quality of training course delivery often emerges if negotiation, dialogue, compromise and mutual respect have not been properly established (Luo, 2000; Warner, 2004). In addition, as Cast *et al.* (2002) pointed out, allowing continuity in structural arrangments and continued interaction establishes confidence and maintains self-esteem among the training partners. This aspect of the study's findings also support the importance of enhancing mutual collaboration in assessment so as to build up a relationship which features collaborative spirit and harmonious relations. Considering the nature of Chinese harmony inherited from Confucian culture, it is not difficult to establish that to maintain businesses harmoniously requires the establishment of sustained ways for maintaining mutual respect and self-esteem (Hegan, 2005; Wong, 2007). Inevitably, the Confucian feature of harmony has become embedded in managerial behaviours of Chinese companies and should not be ignored (Child and Warner, 2003; Warner, 2004).

Therefore, it could be inferred that the need to invite Chinese partners and trainers to be involved in evaluating the outcomes and effectiveness of the programme is a new attempt to ensure the effectiveness of an international training programme.

8.2.3.2 Assessment of regular reports

Regular reporting as a way to assess progress of an ongoing programme has been positively accepted by Chinese staff and managers. The result has clearly indicated that self-report data can and should be utilised by companies and organisations to measure participants' training performance. However, as Prodsakoff *et al.* (2003) indicate, regular self-reporting is a complex issue as it may bias these reports. Existing research suggests that trainees have the potential to prejudge their responses more in an upwards direction than they should be, based on higher expectations from companies and organisations and self-enhancement effects (Chiaburu, 2010). In various situations, employees may be more likely to inflate how they evaluate themselves to appear more competent or capable to their employers (e.g. Pfeffer and Fong, 2005). In the context of Chinese culture, however, the results of quantitative analysis have shown that Chinese staff are unwilling to undertake regular self-reporting to home training companies because, as explained by Manager Xu from CCOIC in the follow-up interview, participants are more likely to inflate their performance than to be misjudged by their managersas having less commitment in engaging with their training programmes. So instead of reporting to their managers regularly, which requires more commitment, they prefer self-managed study with more freedom.

Interestingly, a divergent expectation in this respect clearly appears after the comparison between the attitudes of managers and staff. The reasons for this dilemma rest on the different points of views on the role of regular reports. In the literature review, Turner *et al.* (1993) stated that self-reporting needs to be made against set individual targets. This is true for Chinese managers who usually use the regular report as a way of examining the results possibly achieved at the end of the programme, and they usually compare the ongoing progress of staff against the expected goals which may benefit their organisations. So they mentioned in the interviews that involving regular reporting in the assessment just makes training something that maintains their motivation and monitors their learning progress. In spite of this, due to the heritage of the Confucian tradition of paternalism, many supervisors who expect favourable outcomes from the programme (Warr *et al.*, 1995) still consider the evaluation of staff performance as a power tool, whereby punishment will be meted out to those who may fail to meet their learning objectives, or fail the company's expectations. Thus, on the contrary, training staff may have a different perspective on this as they are worried that regular reporting is something that may provide their supervisors with information to make judgements which may be misused and therefore may cause negative performance feedback. The findings add further support to Chiaburu's (2010) arguments that trainees will overgeneralise their self-reported training transfer by reporting positive performance only. Conversely, Chinese staff are reluctant to undertake regular ongoing reports, rather than bias their performance cheatingly upwards, because they are suspicious of being misjudged, which they fear may have a negative impact on their careers.

Megginson (1995) suggested that a friendly monitoring tool needs to be established by drawing a closer relationship between the programme deliverers and the programme recipients. This friendly control in a sense needs to establish closer relationships or harmony, as explained previously. This is precisely in line with the Chinese Confucian philosophy of managerial strategy which looks at business management as a channel to establish harmonious relationships. To address the controversy surrounding ongoing assessment (referred to as 'regular reports' in this study), a joint evaluation approach such as timely negotiation, communication and keeping both sides informed can be the best answer for achieving a friendly and harmonious bilateral collaboration. The results of the positive attitudes on joint evaluation by getting training partners (such as supervisors from training organisations) engaged in evaluations have clearly demonstrated that within a carefully desgined framework, both staff and managers are willing to access 'primary and real data' representing trainees' performances so as to erase the suspicions of both staff and managers.

The findings also appear to indicate that those Chinese organisations operating in the business and manufacturing fields such as SG, COG, BC and

CCIOC favour the use of self-reporting, while other sectors such as the state-governed DON, NXU and NXMU have adopted a firm stance to enforce regular reports.

8.2.3.3 Flexible approaches to decision-making

To identify the essence of decision-making within Chinese companies and organisations is inevitably difficult. China has shown a distinctive prevailing decision-making style that reflects differences in cultural values and the relative needs for achievement and information (Martinsons and Davison, 2007; Child & Warner, 2003). As discussed in the literature review, style of leadership and Confucian paternalism still maintain their effect on Chinese managerial behaviours and decision-making processes (Child *et al.*, 2003). The findings of this study have partly embraced the arguments (as demonstrated in section 7.2.9.3, 7.4.5 and 7.5.5) of the qualitative analysis that many managers, particularly those from government-dominated sectors, DON for instance, adhere strictly to an obedience hierarchy and believe senior leaders will act like fathers (Ip, 2000). So top-down directives feature in all decision-making. Ip (1996), though, points out that authoritarian paternalism actually suppresses autonomy and freedom. Overall, though, the results of this study in terms of decision-making have challenged the arguments in the literature. Evidence of flexible approaches used to make a decision on the basis of staff individual needs analysis, scope of training provided, and the reputation of the training providers, has been identified through analysis of the interview data. These data seem to confirm the perception that a balanced method involving bottom-up, as well as top-down, orientation is gradually being constructed. Besides, the factors influencing decision-making largely include whether staff's individual needs analyses fall within the company's or organisational development schemes, and also depend on training providers' current training scale and reputation. That is, Chinese companies and organisations, such as COG, CCOIC and SG, will make their decisions to run a foreign language training programme after looking at their staff and managers' individual needs analysis, and searching for availability of a training provider by specifically considering the provider's current training scale and reputation (Hashim, 2001). The emerging style of decision- making has released more freedom to decision-makers in companies and organisations which are mainly operating in the business and manufacturing sectors in China; this suggests that a fundamental change in the management of Chinese state enterprises is taking place.

A further finding suggests the idea of using Ralston *et al.*'s (1999b) 'New and Current Generation' definition for Chinese managers. The current generation of Chinese managers is aged from 41 to 50 years old; they are more flexible in accepting autonomy in decision-making. The new, emerging managers are aged between 31 and 40, and they are less committed to Confucian philosophy (Child *et al.*, 2000), which might indicate the trends of future change.

In terms of looking for availability of training providers, two components can be extracted from the qualitative data analysis, namely size and reputation of foreign language training organisations. The implications for foreign language training providers and managers is that information on current training scale and reputation needs to be properly reported when advertising and marketing courses.

8.2.4 Two-tier novel model

The research has sought to evaluate a proposed novel model by testing eight extracted propositions. The findings mostly lend support to the assertions in terms of creating individual projects, the relevant elements impacting on the effectiveness of implementation and the quality of programme design and evaluation. However, awareness needs to be maintained when implementing a training programme as the answers to propositions four and seven, arguably, conflict, as explained in the previous sections (section 7.2.9.3, 7.4.4 and 7.4.6).

The literature suggests that to design a strategic project, a foreign language training programme in the context of this research needs to properly define the project so as to ensure that is is planned, transferable, and sustainable, with clear vision, clear values and strong culture (Capon, 2008; Johnson, 2005; Lynch, 2006; Mintzberg ,1987). The purpose, the scope and the objectives need to be well defined (George, 1988; Turner, 1987). Meanwhile, monitoring, control and evaluation are required for the sake of effective control of programme outcomes (Meighan, 1991; Turner, 1999). Inspired by Kolb's Learning Model (Weightman, 2004) and enlightened by Turner's (1993) model of project management, together with a deep awareness of Chinese adult learning style, influence of Chinese culture and foreign language educational background (Hu, 2002b; Ip, 2000; Jin and Cortazzi, 2003), the researcher has proposed a new model with two-tier levels to manage a foreign language training programme for Chinese learners. The justification for the proposed model may help to assuage the doubts that many in the field have voiced whether Western methods of management education can be successfully applied to Chinese education (Wang, 1999; Warner, 1991).

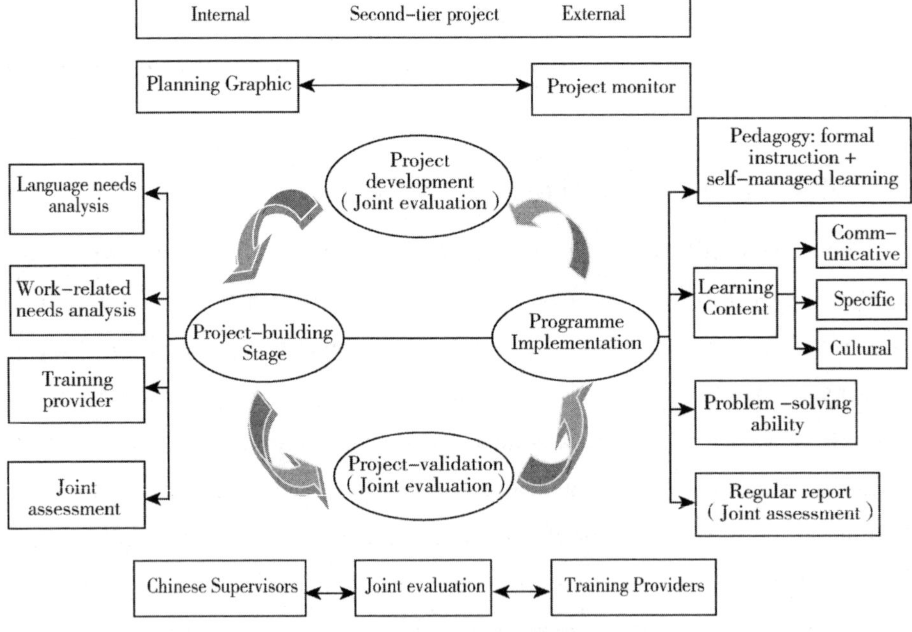

Figure 8–1 The updated project model

To implement the model, however, based on the findings, it is necessary to ensure the following components are already in place prior to commencing training (see Figure 8–1 above):

- Specific work-related individual needs analysis needs to be undertaken and time needs to be set aside to conduct this.
- Specific foreign language skills used for workplace skills development need to be assessed.
- Curriculum design blending formal instruction and self-managed study is taken into account.
- Curriculum designed to develop trainees' ability to solve problems within the workplace is considered.
- Joint evaluation, collaboratively undertaken by both training provider and demander needs to be considered.
- Identification of different perceptions of training orientation and aims of evaluation between staff and managers is essential.
- Identification of the operation of Chinese companies and organisations needs to be addressed.

All the above elements will add credits to the success and effectiveness of running a project-based foreign language programme for Chinese learners.

8.3 Contribution to knowledge

8.3.1 A novel model

The research has demonstrated the value of a proposed novel model based on two-tier levels of management which allows for an educational organisation to develop a meaningful foreign language training programme for Chinese companies and organisations, namely by creating individual projects prior to the implementation of training programme. To date, limited research has been devoted to examining and testing the key aspects critical to creating successful training and development initiatives in terms of training Chinese employees. The proposed model, however, takes into account relevant factors that are important to Chinese companies and organisations and meaningful to the employees and managers by conducting an ongoing process of individual project creation, validation, evaluation and redesign throughout the life of the foreign language training programme. In creating an individual project with the key purposes of either helping participants to develop positive change initiatives in their workplace, or training, providers should be aware that having specific learning objectives for each trainee will increase the meaningfulness of the programme, since they are able to influence their learning interests, maintain their motivation, keep learning targeted and demonstrate their potential success to their supervisors and managers (see confirmed P1 and P2 in section 7.2.7, 7.2.8 and 7.2.9.1). The specific learning objectives also help to establish harmonious relationships and respect for traditional Chinese culture and managerial culture in order to monitor the effectiveness of the training and maintain sustainable collaboration. It is expected that the outcomes of this research will be widely applied within the practice of foreign language training programmes managed by an increasing number of Chinese organisations and companies, from the northwest region of China in particular. It is also hoped that the findings will help meet demand for an effective and appropriate foreign language training approach from Chinese companies who have established business relationships with international partners.

8.3.2 The updated knowledge added to project-based foreign language learning

The justification for the new model has refined the model of project-based foreign language learning and teaching proposed by Beckett (2006). Originally, project-based foreign language teaching and learning focused solely on English language learning with the aim of developing learners' foreign language ability only, emphasising practising and teaching listening, speaking, writing and reading abilities and as a content-based approach (Eyring, 1989; Fried-Booth, 2002; Stoller, 1997). However, with the demand for work-related skills and improved workplace problem-solving abilities among modern Chinese companies and organisations, the research found that Chinese companies and organisations need more than foreign language skills in order to enhance their international competitive ability (see confirmed P3 and P6 in section 7.2.7, 7.2.8 and 7.2.9). Many existing foreign language training programmes are no longer able to meet the real needs and demands of Chinese learners because the training design cannot meet their companies' and organisations' needs, which essentially seek to invest in developing work-related and technical skills in their workforce rather than just focusing on foreign language skills (see confirmed P3 in section 7.2.7, 7.2.8 and 7.2.9). The need to develop a combination of foreign language skills and work-related and technical skills appears to be urgent. In fact, in response to this, this study has posited the value of project-based foreign language learning and teaching into organisational training management by blending a project-based foreign language learning pedagogy into Chinese adult training management (see confirmed P5 in section 7.2.7, 7.2.8, 7.2.9 and 7.4.5); and has therefore opened up a new field of knowledge. Along with the consideration of Chinese culture of management and adults' learning style, it is hoped this updated project-based foreign language learning model will help to fill the gap in learning requirements for Chinese trainees.

8.3.3 An international collaborative project

The study has developed an international collaborative programme model starting with individual project needs and implementing the programme with respect to training provider and Chinese trainees' culture, and concluded with suggestions that joint evaluations are carried out by inviting both sides involved to take part in the assessments. This training programme is the first to focus on respecting the unique Chinese culture and understanding Chinese managers' perceptions in terms of self-esteem in particular. Besides, the study suggests a model which can address the disconnection in terms of training content, managerial strategy, pedagogy and evaluation, particularly cultural awareness, between the training designer and the Chinese training partner (see the section 7.2.9 and 7.4.4 in relation to P4). In addition, the research suggests that Western educators need to actively adapt their managerial strategy and orientation in order to fit themselves into Chinese contexts and promote collaboration between Chinese partners, training providers, participants and evaluators.

8.3.4 Customised evaluation

Another significant contribution of the research is to develop customised measures that capture the participants' engagement and bring the involved members onto the same management board. While the training provider imposes most of the control in evaluation and assessment, this has been justified as a meaningful method to satisify training customers. Training customers believe (as mentioned in Chapter Five) that client partners view themselves as the owner and the investing country where recipient's supervisors and managers are from expect more responsibility to evaluate the progressiveness of training (Tuner, 1993; 1999). Numerous studies have highlighted the importance of evaluation; however, few have focused their attention on whether such an evaluation yields useful information for the organisation or company and the members concerned (Lingham *et al.*, 2006). The customised measures of evaluation achieved by bringing together training provider, training partner and trainee appeared attractive to Chinese companies and organisations involved in the research. Both staff and manager-nominated participants have seen their value in terms of both individual project learning (foreign language skills improvement and work-related skills development) and their applicability (also see confirmed P1 and P2 in section 7.2.7, 7.2.8 and 7.2.9). As discussed above, effective training supports employees' learning and development by providing new knowledge and opportunities to put this knowledge into practice (Lingham *et al.*, 2006; Prahalad, 2000; Turner, 1999). The research proposes that evaluation should be in line with participants' individual learning projects and based on participants' own regular reports to monitor its applicability, which will in turn highlight its importance and meaningfulness to either the organisations or those organisational members involved. In this study, collaborative evaluation makes knowledge transfer possible, which may benefit both the organisational objectives and participants' career development, as well as securing the effectiveness and quality of training (see the confirmed P8 in section 7.2.9).

8.3.5 Educational management

The research also found that there are divergent perceptions between Chinese managers and training staff in terms of cultural awareness, self-managed learning, regular reports and decision-making. These may pose a dilemma for foreign training providers in managing a training programme for Chinese companies and organisations. In the meantime, however, it advocates use of a distinctive new management style which enables resolution of the dilemma. The analysis has provided evidence that this divergence mainly rests upon different perceived attitudes towards the purpose of foreign language training and the ultimate development goals of organisations.

In relation to cultural awareness, the study has made a further original contribution in that training staff differ in this respect; they tend to perceive it as a purely Western concept unrelated to language training, whilst managers differ in that they take it as a value which needs to be embraced within a long-term training programme, and think it could be designed into the learning content for the sole purpose of training the future leadership of the company or organisation. This is related to Chinese companies' and organisations' development ambitions (see the findings in section 7.4.4 and 7.5).

For the evaluation measure of regular reporting, further contributions have been made in highlighting the importance of understanding the failure of communication between Chinese trainees and supervisors. The divergence mainly lies in the participants' weakness in defending their performance because supervisors from training partners will impose a penalty on trainees if their training performance does not meet the training requirements (see section 7.4.6 and 7.5).

In relation to decision-making, the major contribution to knowledge is that, contrary to what we used to believe, a rather flexible method of both 'top-down' and 'bottom-up' styles is slowly being adopted by Chinese managers. A decision actually depends on the quality of the individual project as well as the structure and operation of Chinese companies and organisations, but the trigger for decision-making in the end still needs to come from the development goals of the organisation (see section 7.2.9.3 and 7.4.7).

In addition, the converged attitutes in favour of work-related and professional and technical skills foreign language training suggest that foreign language training management needs to alter its foucs from general business-oriented training to work-related or professional and technical skills orientation.

To summarise, these findings have made new knowledge available to the field of international educational management. Because Chinese organisational culture is one important aspect of the context (Bush, 2003), the results of the research will provide an immediate framework and necessary information for international educational managers when making decisions. Walker *et al.* (2002) refer to issues of context and stress the need to avoid decontextualised paradigms when researching and analysing the educational market. This implies that management strategies should encourage Chinese training companies' and organisations' participation and give full rein to trainees' initiatives. The role of people concerned should be active and developmental; the partners' relationship needs to be open and co-operative, grounded in mutual commitment and respect (Cheng, 2009; Turner,1999; Stephen, 1998).

8.4 Implications

This is a foreign language programme designed by merging Chinese learning style and teaching approach and Western learning methods at a crucial point where China is at the stage of transforming its educational system to one that is more Western-oriented, and one which will provide a better fit with the learning needs and training objectives of Chinese trainees. Meanwhile, attitudes towards a combination of China's learning style and that of the West may inspire Western educators to adjust their teaching styles and facilitate the process of knowledge transfer for Chinese companies and organisations. It is hoped that the findings from this research will inspire Western educators to open up their classrooms to companies and organisations in a timely fashion, in an effort to cooperate within the real workplace. This will be helpful to build up and increase educational institutions' knowledge resources. This will hopefully ensure the delivery of appropriate programmes to Chinese companies and organisations in order to meet increasing demands for work-related skills training.

In the meantime, identifying the actual needs of Chinese companies and organisations under the current situation where China's economy has rapidly developed and increased its influence on the world's economy becomes increasingly important. Either the short-term impact or long-term impact needs to be viewed by international educational institutions. The research in this sense has provided detailed information and acknowledged how Chinese organisations blueprint their development schemes by making use of foreign language training programmes. For the time being, as indicated in this research, the role of foreign language training has been changed. International education institutions should not simply consider a foreign language training programme, as it is often referred to by Chinese educational management, as an opportunity for foreign language skills development. They should know that this preceived role of training programmes may only have a short-term impact on the development of

Chinese companies and organisations rather than a channel to establish a long-term impact on the Chinese educational market. To provide Chinese learners with work-related skills and technical skills while maintaining an awareness of the need to respect Chinese culture is essential.

The new knowledge of the contradictory attitudes in relation to cultural awareness will remind training providers in the field of international educational management that it is important to keep in mind that the goal of the foreign language training programme run through international collaboration is not cultural assimilation. Rather, it is to develop bicultural individuals who have a sensitivity to and an appreciation of cultural diversity (Lu *et al.*, 2003). It will further remind them that it is advisable to involve learning content about culture *per se*, both target and home culture, to ensure that participants retain their home culture identity out of a sense of respect.

It is hoped that the findings in this study will convince foreign language training managers that, apart from the need to provide training aligned with organisational goals and visions, foreign language training focused on career development should also be tailored and customised to the career needs of individuals – based on individual, needs-tailored projects within a specific period of time, and based on applicability. Meanwhile, short-term and long-term patterns of training will be taken into account as Chinese companies and organisations have different training goals and associated strategies.

Inevitably, a shift from the 'top-down' to 'bottom-up' in terms of managerial behaviour within Chinese companies and organisations indicates that, during this transitional stage in China's economic development, managerial behaviour is becoming flexible and less rigid. Confucian influence is slowly losing its power within China's education management. The study demonstrates to foreign language training institutes that the focus on how to trigger a training programme needs to be altered in accordance with the situation change.

The customised evaluation through joint efforts from programme providers, participants and training partners has created a communication channel which provides a feedback system to redesign and adjust further iterations of the programme based on organisational and participant perspectives and needs. The implications of this point are that there is no automatic system in place to facilitate the continuous improvement of the training programme. The new feedback system is to help training institutes identify the gap between the present programme and upcoming ones. It is legitimate to take the view that the collaborative evaluation is therefore crucial for the quality and effectiveness. Lingham *et al.* (2006) also support this point of view in their research.

8.5 Conclusions

8.5.1 Achieving research objectives

The objectives of this research have all been achieved and findings of the research are discussed in section 8.2. In section 8.3 and 8.4, the contributions and implications of the research are summarised. The findings of expanding training content by developing Chinese trainee's work-related and professional skills along with foreign language abilities have answered to objective one. Ineffectiveness and lack of communication of existing programmes have seen the shortcomings in current practices implemented by programme providers. The objective two has thus been accomplished. The evaluation of the significance of the novel model as the objective three has been completed with updated knowledge based on the findings (see section 8.2). The overall findings of the research have provided information to foreign language training suppliers to develop an effective management strategy for project-based training for Chinese organisations; thus achieving objective four.

8.5.2 Synthesising literature, methodology and data

This research develops and tests a novel model with two-tier levels of project-based foreign language training programme for Chinese organisations.

The literature cited and the initial research has seen the rationale for the designed methodologies – pragmatism – a mixed method to be used to collect evidence for the novel model. Questionnaire, interview as well as follow-up interviews were the methodologies used in this research with the effort to collect data. Data analysis was rigorously undertaken and it was clearly reported (see Chapter 7). The data and literature were also synthesised with efforts to identify gaps in the knowledge, and therefore generate the new knowledge with an original perspective (see Chapter 8).

8.5.3 Benefits and limitations

Anybody who pretends to have reached perfection or even shows himself satisfied degrades himself and his work (May, 2001; Sutton *et al*, 2011). There is no single all-embracing theory of educational management. This study not only elicits benefits but also suffers a number of limitations that can be addressed through further research. It is admitted that research on foreign language training for Chinese organisations is still in its infancy. Benefits and limitation of the research can be highlighted as follows (see Table 8–1).

8.5.4 Opportunities for future research

Based on this study's proposal of a model for use in international training collaboration, further research needs to investigate several case studies in order to address the model's feasibility. As such, future research will need to:

- Explore attitudes of training provider managers in order to find out their perceptions in terms of the aspects of learning content, teaching strategy and evaluation – by doing this, a comparison of perceptions in the field between international training providers and Chinese training partners may be made.
- To further explore the time, scope and learning specifications required for creating individual projects and possible meetings among the partners needs to be investigated. Inevitably these elements are vague in the current research.

Table 8–1 **Benefits and limitations**

Benefits	Limitations
• Generating an original model which can be used to train Chinese organisations.	• Single researcher with limited resources.
• Developing the ability of international educational practitioners to establish a management strategy for two-tier level of project-based training involving international educational communication.	• Only one voice from training sending organisations producing original qualitative data.
• Based on innovative methodology using vigorous quantitative and qualitative techniques.	• Not been possible to vigorously test the model, particularly testing the model in other Asian countries and regions.
• Adding the new knowledge to the theory of Beckett's project-based foreign language learning.	
• Advocating an innovative evaluation system for international education practitioners.	

Source: Author's research

- Include a wider range of relevant components affecting collaborative programmes. This is because of the complexity and diversity of tasks in most 'real-life' domains, meaning there is greater evidence of content relevance and representativeness required to support and predict the outcome especially considering is it extremely difficult to provide.
- Finally, more specific uniquely designed evaluation measures regarding how to attract potential providers and users and what criteria to follow need to be explicitly addressed in order to ensure validity and reliability of the joint evaluation.

Additionally, the same study should also be replicated in other Asian countries and regions. This would enable benchmarking of the relative importance of the cultural variables.

8.5.5 Personal learning

Conducting a PhD project independently has benefited the researcher and it has substantially and significantly distinguished the researcher from the past. Over the years, the researcher has successfully transformed himself from a Chinese *national* researcher into an *international* researcher. Conducting the PhD project has given the researcher considerable experiences, with individual responsibility for the PhD project and commitment to comply with structured procedures and regulations, for example, international research perspectives, intellectual property and the ethics policies. In spite of coping with the challenges of undertaking independent research, in an international context, the researcher has not only gained the knowledge in his prime area of foreign language teaching and learning, but also expertise in the other related fields such as international education management, staff development and cross-culture communication. In addition to these, the researcher has been qualified to use advanced updated research software, NVivo 8, SPSS and others, which are popular to international researchers when conducting research either qualitatively or quantitatively. Hence, doing a doctorate has been a valuable experience in learning.

Reference

Adamson, B. & Morris, P. (1997). "The English Curriculum in the People's Republic of China". *Comparative Education Review* 41: 3-36.

Alan, B. & Stoller, F. L. (2005). "Maximizing the Benefits of Project Work in Foreign Language Classroom". *English Teaching Forum* 43 (2): 10-21.

Allen, L. Q. (2004). "Implementing a Culture Portfolio Project within a Constructivist Paradigm". *Foreign Language Annals* 37: 232-239.

Alliger, G. M. & Janak, E. A. (1989). "Kirkpatrick's Levels of Training Criteria: Thirty Years Later". *Personnel Psychology* 42 (2): 331-331.

Alon, I. & Mclntyre, R. J. (2005). *Business and Management Education in China: Transition, Pedagogy and Training*. Singapore, World Scientific Publishing Co. Pte. Ltd.

Andersen, E. G. (1987). *Goal Directed Project Management*. Kogan Page.

Anderson, J. (1993). "Is a Communicative Approach Practical for Teaching English in China? Pros and Cons". *System* 21 (4): 471-480.

Andreu, R. & Sieber, S. (1999). "Knowledge and Problem Solving: A Proposal for a Model of Individual and Collective Learning". Working Paper, Spain: IESE Publishing, 1/99, Barcelona.

Anon. (1986). 《教育改革重要文献选编》 [*Selected important Documents on Educational Reform*]. Beijing, People's Education Press.

Anon. (2002). "Languages for All: Languages for life, A Strategy for England". Retrieved 10, January, 2011, from www. dfes. gov. uk/eydcp.

Anon. (2006). *Business: English Beginning to Be Spoken Here: The Language*

Business in China. London, The Economist.

Anon. (2006). "Learning Objectives, Essential Thematic Areas, Time Allocation, with an Example of Cross-curricular Approach". Retrieved 25 April, 2011, from http: //www. ibe. unesco. org/fileadmin/user_upload/HIV_and_AIDS/publications/Tool_5_Dec06_FINAL. pdf.

Anon. (2011). "Alacra Store: Premium Business Information Source". Retrieved 23 August, 2011, from http: //www. alacrastore. com/storecontent/Thomson_M&A/FAG_Kugelfischer_Georg_Schaefe_acquires_remaining_interest_in_Ningxia_FAG_Xibei_Railway_from_Ina_Holding_Schaeffler_Group-1628724040.

Argyris, C. & Schon, D. (1978). *Organisational Learning: A theory in action perspective*. New York, Addison-Wesley.

Atkinson, R. (2002). *Introduction to Psychology (11th edition)*. Fort Worth TX, Harcourt Brace Jovanovich.

Atkinson, R. L., Atkinson, R. C., Smith, E. E. & Bem, D. J. (1993). *Introduction to Psychology (11th edition)*. Fort Worth TX, Harcourt Brace Jovanovich.

Atkinson, J. (2001). *Developing Teams through Project Based Learning*. Gower, Aldershot.

Au, W. (2007). "High Stakes Testing and Curricular Control: A Qualitative Meta Synthesis". *Educational Researcher* 36: 258-267.

Authors, J., Peter, P. & Churchill, Gilbert A. (1984). *The Relationships among Research Design Choices and Psychometric Properties of Rating Scales: a Meta-analysis. Volumes 8-13 of Wisconsin Working paper.* Wisconsin, Publisher Graduate School of Business, University of Wisconsin-Madison.

Babanoury, C. (2005). "Real World Business Language Tasks in Action". *Journal of Language for International Business* 16 (2): 13-23.

Babanoury, C. (2006). "Collaborative Company Research Projects: A Blueprint for Language, Context, and Culture Learning". *The Journal of Language for International Business* 17 (1): 15.

Baizhu, Chen & Yi, F. (Spring 2000). "Determinants of Economic Growth in

China: Private enterprise, Education, and Openness". *China Economic Review* 11 (1): 1-15.

Baker, T. L. (1994). *Doing Social Research (2nd Ed.)*. New York, McGraw-Hill Inc.

Bandevelde, H. (2001). When a Language Is Good Business. *Sunday Times*. London.

Bargiela-Chiappini & Harris, S. (1997). *The Languages of Business: an International Perspective*. Edinburgh, Edinburgh University Press.

Baron, A. & Walters, M. (1994). *The Culture Factor, Corporate and International Perspectives*. London, Institute of Personnel Development (IPD).

Barron, B. J. S. (1998). "Doing with Understanding: Lessons from Research on Problem and Project-based learning". *Journal of the Learning Sciences* 7: 271-311.

Bartel, A. P. (1989). "Where Do the New United States Immigrants Live?" *Journal of Labour Economics* 7 (October): 371-391.

Bartel, A. P. (1994). "Productivity Gains from the Implementation of Employee Training Programs". *Industrial Relations* 33 (4): 411-425.

Bash, L. (2003). *Adult Learners in the Academy*. Bolton, MA: Anker Publishing.

Basuki, W. (2010). *Gender Factors in Strategic Managerial Behaviour in Small Medium-sized Enterprises (SMEs)*. PhD Thesis. Southampton, Southampton Solent University.

Bates, A. W. (1997). "The Impact of Technological Change on Open and Distance Learning". *Distance Education* 18 (1): 93-109.

Bazeley, P. (2004). "Issues in Mixing Qualitative and Quantitative Approaches to Research". *Applying qualitative methods to marketing management research*. J. G. R. Buber, & L. Richards Basingstoke, UK, Palgrave Macmillan: 141-156.

Bazeley, P. (2007). *Qualitative Data Analysis with NVivo*. London, SAGE Publications.

Beckett, G. H. (1999). "Project-based Instruction in a Canadian Secondary School's ESL Classes: Goals and Evaluations". *Unpublished doctoral dissertation*. Vancouver, University of British Columbia.

Beckett, G. H. (2005). "Academic Language and Literacy Socialization through Project Based Instruction: ESL Student Perspectives and Issues". *Journal of Asian Pacific Communication* 15: 191-206.

Beckett, G. H. & Slater, T. (2005). "The Project Framework: A Tool for Language and Content Integration". *English Language Teaching Journal* 59: 108-116.

Beckett, G. H., Ed. (2006). *Project-based Second and Foreign Language Education: Past, Present, and Future*. A volume in research in second language learning. Greenwich, Connecticut, Information Age Publishing.

Bee, F. (1994). *Training Needs Analysis and Evaluation*. London, Institute of Personnel and Development.

Beretta, A. & Davies, A. (1985). "Evaluation of the Bangalore Project". *ELT Journal Volume* 39 (2 April): 121-127.

Berger, J. B. & Milem, J. F. (2000). "Organisational Behaviour in Higher Education and Student Outcomes". *Higher Education: Handbook of Theory and Research (Vo. 15)*. J. Smart. New York, Agathon.

Berk, L. E. & Winsler, A. (1995). *Scaffolding Children's Learning: Vygotsky and Early Childhood Education*. Washington National Association for the Education of Young Children.

Bernardi, R. A. (2006). "Associations between Hofstede's Cultural Constructs and Social Desirability Response Bias". *Journal of Business Ethics* 65: 45-53.

Berrel, M., Wrathall, J. & Wright, P. (2001). "A Model for Chinese Management Education: Adapting the Case Study Method to Transfer Management Knowledge". *Cross Cultural Management* 8 (1): 28-43.

Beyer, J. M. & Trice, H. (1979). "A Re-examination of the Relations between Size and Various Components of Organisational Complexity".

Administrative Science Quarterly 24: 48-64.

Biggs, J. (1999). *Teaching for Quality Learning at University: What the Student does*. Buckingham. The Society for Research into Higher Education and Open University Press.

Biggs, J. & Tang, C. (2007). *Teaching for Quality Learning at University (3rd ed)*. Buckingham, SRHE and Open University Press.

Billett, S. (2002). "Critiquing Workplace Learning Discourses: Participation and Continuity at Work". *Studies in the Education of Adults* 43 (1): 56-67.

Black, T. R. (1999). *Doing Quantitative Research in the Social Sciences: An Integrated Approach to Research Design, Measurement and Statistics*. London, SAGE Publications.

Blaikie, N. (2000). *Designingsocial Research*, Cambridge: Polity.

Blumenfeld, P. C., Soloway, E., Max, R. W., Krajcik, J., Guzdial, M. & Palincsar, A. (2001). "Motivating Project-based Learning: Sustaining the Doing, Supporting the Learning". *Educational Psychologist* 26: 369-398.

Bowden, V. (1997). "The Career States System Model: a New Approach t Analysing Careers". *British Journal of Guidance and Counselling* 25 (4): 474-490.

Bradburn, N. M., Sudman, S. & Wansink, B. (2004). *Asking Questions: the Definitive Guide to Questionnaire Design-for Market Research, Political polls, and Social and Health Questionnaires*. San Francisco, CA Jossey-Bass.

Braun, W. H. & Warner, M. (2002). "Strategic Human Resource Management in Western Multinationals in China: The Differentiation of Practices across Different Ownership Forms". *Personnel Review* 31 (5): 553-579.

Bredget, S. (2006). *Action Research: a Methodology for Change and Development*. Maidenhead, Berkshire, Open University Press.

Brookfield, S. D. (2006). *The Skilful Teacher: on Techniques, Trust, and Responsiveness in the Classroom*. San Francisco, Jossey-Bass.

Brown, H. (1994). *Principles of Languages Learning and Teaching*. Englewood

Cliffs, NJ, Prentice Hall Regents.

Brown, J. C. (1989). "Situated Cognition and the Culture of Learning". *Educational Researcher* 18 (1): 32-42.

Bruce, S., Hawkins, P., Sharp, M. & Keller, A. (2009). "Experience Based Suggestions for Achieving a High Survey Response Rate". Retrieved 12 April, 2010, http: //www. virginia. edu/case/education/documents/surveyresponseratesummarypaper-final. pdf.

Brumfit, C. (2004). "The Challenge of the 21st-Century Agenda for Foreign Language Learning in England's Universities". *Arts and Humanities in Higher Education* June 2004 (3): 175-193.

Brumfit, C. J. (1984b). "The Bangalore Procedural Syllabus". *ELT Journal* 38 (4): 233-241.

Bryman, A. & Cramer, D. (2001). *Quantitative Data Analysis with SPSS Release 10 for Windows: a Guide for Social Scientists*. Philadelphia, Routledge.

Bryman, A. (2004). *Social Research Methods (2nd ed.).* Open University Press.

Bryman, A. (2008). *Social Research Methods (3rd ed.).* Oxford, Oxford University Press.

Bush, T. (2003). *Theories of Educational Management.* London, SAGE Publications.

Canagarajah, A. (2002). "Globalization, Methods and Practice in Periphery Classrooms". *Globalization and Language Teaching* D. Block, & Cameron, D. (Eds.). London, Routledge: 134-150.

Cao, X. (2007). "On the Translation of English and Chinese Proverbs Based on the Relevance Translation Theory". *Journal of Xihua University: Philosophy and Social Sciences* 2007 (03).

Capon, C. (2008). *Understanding Strategic Management.* Essex, Pearson Education Limited.

Carnoy, M. D. (1993). *The New Global Economy in the Information Age: Reflections on Our Changing World.* Pennsylvania, The Pennsylvanian State University Press.

Carter, G. & Thomas, H. (1986). "Dear Brown Eyes: Experiential learning in a project-orientated approach". *English Language Teaching Journal* 40: 196-204.

Carter, S. D. (2002). "Matching Training Methods and Factors of Cognitive Ability: A Means to Improve Training Outcomes". *Human Resource Development Quarterly* 13 (1): 71-87.

Cast, A. D. & Burke, P. J. (2002). "A Theory of Self-Esteem". *Social Forces* 80 (3): 1041-1068.

Chan, A. (2001). *China's Workers under Assault: The Exploitation of Labour in a Globalising World*. Armonk NY, M. E. Sharpe.

Chan, W. T. (1963). *Source Book in Chinese Philosophy*. Princeton, NJ, Princeton University Press.

Charles, M. & Marschan-Piekkari, R. (2002). "Language Training for Enhanced Horizontal Communication: A Challenge for MNCs". *Business Communication Quarterly* June, 2002 (65): 9-29.

Chee, H. (2002/2003). "Exporting Management to China". *The Ashridge Journal* Winter 2002/2003: 14-19.

Chen, J. F., Warden, C. A. & Chang, H. T. (2006). "Is English a Brand: The Impact of English Language Learning on Product Evaluation". *The Journal of Language for International Business* 17 (1): 29.

Chen, M. (1995). *Asian Management Systems*. London, Routledge.

Chen, M. J. & Miller, D. (2011). "The Relational Perspective as a Business Mind-set: Managerial Implications for East and West". *The Academy of Management Perspectives (formerly The Academy of Management Executive) (AMP)* 25 (3): 6-18

Chen, M. J. (2001). *Inside Chinese Business: A Guide for Managers Worldwide*. Boston, Harvard Business School Press.

Chen, T. (2003). "Reticence in Class and Online: Two ESL Students' Experiences with Communicative Language Teaching". *System* 31 (259-281).

Chen, Y. (2004). "China's Mass Higher Education: Problem, Analysis, and

Solutions". *Asia Pacific Education Review* 5 (1): 23-33.

Cheng, Y. C. (2009). "Hong Kong Educational Reforms in the Last Decade: Reform Syndrome and New Developments". *International Journal of Educational Management* 23 (1): 7.

Chiaburu, D. S., Sawyer, K. B. & Thoroughgood, C. N. (2010). "Transferring More Than Learned in Training: Employees and Managers (over) Generalisation of Skills". *International Journal of Selection and Assessment* 18 (4): 380-393.

Child, J. & Warner, M. (2003). Culture and Management in China. *Culture and Management in Asia*. M. Warner. London, Routledge Curzon.

ChinaGate. (2011). "Study Overseas - 10000 Chinese officers Trained Abroad". Retrieved 9 September, 2011, from http: //www. wenxuecity. com/news/ 2011/09/17/1473540/print.

Chong, T. A. & Duance C. T. (2003). "Cognitivism, constructivism, and work performance". *Academic Exchange*: 274-278.

CILT (2003). *East of England Language Skills Capacity Skills Audit*. London, CILT.

Clarke, W. M. (1999). "An Assessment of Foreign Language Training for English-speaking Exporters". *Journal of European Industrial Training* 23 (1): 9-15.

Claxton, C. S. & Ralston, Y. (1978). *Learning Styles: Their Impact on Teaching and Administration ASHE-ERIC, Higher Education Research Report, No. 10*. Washington, DC, Association for the Study of Higher Education.

Cleland, D. I. (1983). *Systems Analysis and Project Management*, McGraw-Hill.

Clenton, J. (2010). Learning Styles and the Japanese. Retrieved 10 April, 2010, from www. sussex. ac. uk.

Coffield, F., Moseley, D., Hall, E. & Ecclestone, K. (2004). "Learning Styles and Pedagogy in Post-16 Learning: A Systematic and Critical Review". Retrieved January 15, 2008, from http: //www. lsda. org. uk/files/PDF/1543. pdf

Cohen, J. (1988). *Statistical Power Analysis for the Behavioural Sciences (2nd ed)*. Hillsdale, N. J, Lawrence Erlbaum Associates.

Coleman, J. A. (1992). "Project-based Learning, Transferable Skills, Information Technology and Video". *Language Learning Journal* 5: 35-37.

Collier, P. M. & Agyei-Ampomah, S. (2009). *Performance Strategy: Strategic level, Performance Pillar*. Oxford, CIMA.

Collins, A. (1988). "The Computer as A Tool of Learning Through Reflection". *Learning Issues for Intelligent Tutoring Systems*. H. M. Lesgold. New York, Springer-Verlag: 1-18.

Collins, A., Brown, J. S. & Holum, A. (1991). "Cognitive Apprenticeship: Making Thinking Visible". *American Educator* 6 (11): 38-46.

Collins A., John, B. & Ann H. (1991). *Cognitive Apprenticeship: Making Thinking Visible*, American Education

Collis, J. & Hussey, R. (2003). *Business Research Methods for Undergraduate and Postgraduate Students*. Basingstoke, Palgrave McMillan.

Coolican, H. (1999). *Research Methods and Statistics*. London, Hadder and Stoughton.

Cooper, D. R. & Schindler, P. S. (2008). *Business Research Methods (10th edition)*. New York, N. Y., McGraw Hill.

Cranton, P. (2000). *Planning Instruction for Adult Learners (Second Edition)*. Toronto Wall & Emerson, Inc.

Creswell, J. W. (1999). "Mixed-method Research: Introduction and Application". *Handbook of educational policy* G. J. Cizek. San Diego, CA, Academic Press: 455-472.

Creswell, J. W., Clark, P., Gutmann, V. L. & Hanson, W. (2003). "Advanced Mixed Methods Research Design". *Handbook of Mixed Methods in Social & Behavioural Research*. A. T. C. Teddlie. Thousand Oaks, CA, SAGE Publications.

Creswell, J. W. (2007). *Designing and Conducting Mixed Methods Research*. London, SAGE Publications.

Creswell, J. W. (2009). *Research Design: Qualitative, Quantitative, and Mixed*

Methods Approaches, SAGE Publications.

Cronbach, L. J. & Richard J. S. (2004). "My Current Thoughts on Coefficient Alpha and Successor Procedures". *Educational and Psychological Measurement,* 64 (03): 391-418.

Crystal, D. (2006). *Language and the Internet.* Shanghai, Shanghai Scientific and Technological Education Publishing House.

Csikszentmihalyi, M. (1988). *Optimal Experience: Psychological Studies of Flow in Consciousness*. New York, Cambridge University Press.

Csikszentmihalyi, M. (1990). *Flow: the Psychology of Optional Experience*. New York, Harper & Row.

Csikszentmihalyi, M. (1993). *The Evolving Source: A Psychology for the Third Millennium*. New York, Harper Collins.

Cunningham, I., Bennett, B. & Dawes, G. (2000). *Self-managed Learning in Action*, Gower Publishing.

Dalton, G. R. (2008). "Training China's Business Elite". *The China Business Review* 46 (3): 17.

Davies, B. M. (2007). *Doing a Successful Research Project*. New York, Palgrave Macmillan.

Davies, N. F. (1976). "Receptive Versus Productive Skills in Foreign Language Learning". *The Modern Language Journal* 60 (8): 440-443.

De La Fuente & Ciccone, A. (2002). *Human Capital and Growth in a Global and Knowledge-based Economy: Report for the European Commission.*

De Vaus, D. A. (2002). *Surveys in Social Research*. Leonards, Australia, Routledge.

Deal, T. E. & Kennedy, A. A. (1982). *Corporate cultures: the Rites and Rituals of Corporate Life*. Reading, MA, Addison-Wesley.

DeKeyser, R. M. (1998). "Beyond focus on form: cognitive perspectives on learning and practicing second language grammar". *Focus on Form in Classroom Second Language Acquisition*. C. Doughty & William, J. (Eds). Cambridge, Cambridge University Press: 42-63.

Denzin, K. (2009). *The Research Act: a Theoretical Introduction to Sociological Methods*. Publisher, Transaction Publishers.

Dickey, D. A. & Fuller, W. A. (1981). “Likelihood Ratio Statistics for Autoregressive Time Series with a Unit Root”. *Journal of the American Statistical Association* 74: 427-431.

Dillon, R., Madden & Firtle (1994). *Marketing Research and Marketing Environment*. IRWIN.

Dinmore, I. (1997). “Interdisciplinary and Integrative Learning: An Imperative for Adult Education”. Retrieved 25 May, 2011, from http: //www. questia. com/googleScholar. qst?docId=5000442034.

Doughty, C. & Williams, J. (1998). “Issues and Terminology”. *Focus on Form in Classroom Second Language Acquisition*. C. Doughty & Williams, J. (Eds). Cambridge, Cambridge University Press: 1-11.

Douw, L., Huang, C & Ip, D. F-K (2001). *Rethink Chinese Transnational Enterprises: Cultural Affinity and Business Strategies*. Routledge.

Drucker, P. (1989). *The Practice of Management*. London, Heinemann Professional.

Du, J. X., Havard, B., Adams, J. & Li, Heng. (2005). “A Project-based learning approach: online group collaborative learning”. *International Journal of Information and Communication Technology Education* 1 (4): 13-24.

Easterby-Smith, M., Thorpe, R. and Lowe, A. (1991). *Management Research: An Introduction*. London, SAGE Publications.

Easterby-Smith, M., Thorpe, R. and Lowe, A. (1996). *Management Research: An Introduction*. London, SAGE Publications.

Edvinsson, L. & Malone, M. (1997). *Intellectual Capital*. Cambridge, MA, Harvard Business School Press.

Egbert, J. (2003). “A Study of Flow Theory in the Foreign Language Classroom”. *The Modern Language Journal* 87 (499-518).

Egri, C. (2004). “Generation cohorts and Personal Values: A Comparison of China and the United States”. *Organisation Science* 15 (2): 210-230.

Elias, J. L. (2005). *Philosophical Foundations of Adult Education*. Malabar: FL, Krieger Publishing Company.

El-Kot, G. A. H. (2001). *Team Player Styles, Team Design Variables and Team Work Effectiveness in Egypt.*A thesis submitted to the University of Plymouth in partial fulfilment for the degree of doctor of philosophy, Human resources studies group. University of Plymouth Business School.

Ellis, R. (1985). *Understanding Second Language Acquisition*. Walton Street, Oxford, Oxford University Press.

Ellis, R. (1994). *Classroom Second Language Acquisition: The Study of Second Language Acquisition.* Oxford, Oxford University Press.

Evans, R. (2003). *Language Barriers and Learning (Mis)chances 'Intercultural' or 'Xenophobic' Communication, Organisational 'Intercultural' and Discourses of Learning in a Business Context. EDUCATION-LINE.*

Eyring, J. L. (1989). Teacher Experience and Student Responses in ESL Project Work Instruction: A Case Study. Unpublished doctoral dissertation. Los Angeles, University of California.

Eyring, J. L. (2001). "Experiential and Negotiated Language Learning". In M. CelceMuricia (Ed.), *Teaching English as a Second or Foreign Language (3rd ed)*. Boston, Heinle & Heinle.

Fan, P. & Zhang, Z. G. (2004). "Cross-cultural Challenges When Doing Business in China". *Singapore Management Review* 26 (1).

Fang, X. & Warschauer, M. (2004). "Technology and Curriculum Reform in China: A Case Study". *TESOL Quarterly* 38: 301-323.

Farh, J. L., Tsui, A. S., Xin, K. R. & Cheng (1998). "The Influence of Relational Demography and *Guanxi*: The Chinese Case". *Organization Science* 9 (2): 1-18.

Ferragatti, M. L. & Carminati, E. (1984). "Airport: An Italian Version". *Modern English Teacher* 2 (4): 15-17.

Field, A. (2009). *Discovering Statistics Using SPSS*. SAGE Publications.

Firth, A. (1995). *The language of negotiation*. Berlin, Mouton de Gruyter.

Fisher, C. (2004). *Researching and Writing a Dissertation for Business Students*. London, Prentice Hall.

Fisher, R. A. (1966). *The Design of Experiments*. Edinburgh, Hafner.

Flick, U. (2006). *An Introduction to Qualitative Research*. London, SAGE Publications.

Flick, U. (2009). *An Introduction to Qualitative Research*. London, SAGE Publications.

Footitt, H. (2005). The national languages strategy in higher education. *Research Report 625*, DfES.

Fosnot, C. T. (1996). *Constructivism: Theory, Perspectives, and Practice*. New York, Teachers' College Press, Columbia University.

Fragoulis, I. (2009). "Project-based Learning in the Teaching of English as a foreign Language in Greek Primary Schools: From Theory to Practice". *English Language Teaching* 2 (3): 113-119.

Fried-Booth, D. L. (1982). "Project Work with Advanced Classes". *English Language Teaching Journal* 36: 98-103.

Fried-Booth, D. L. (1986). *Project Work*. New York, Oxford University Press.

Fried-Booth, D. L. (2002). *Project Work (2nd ed.)*. New York, Oxford University Press.

Fung, Y. L. (1966). *History of Chinese Philosophy (Volume II): The Period of Classical Learning*. Princeton First Princeton Paperback Printing.

Gagne, R. (1975). *Essentials of Learning for Instruction*. New York, Holt Reinehart & Winston.

Gardner, D. (1995). "Student Produced Video Documentary Provides a Real". *Language Learning Journal* 12: 54-56.

Gareis, R. (1990). *The Handbook of Management by Project*. Manz.

Gareis, R. (2005). *Happy Projects*. Vienna, Manz.

Garson, G. D. (2007). "Testing of Assumptions, Key Concepts and Terms". Retrieved 15 September, 2007, from http: //www2. class. ncsu. edu/garson/ pa765/statnote. htm.

George, D. J. (1988). *A Guide to Capital Cost Estimating*. Institution of chemical engineering.

Gibbon, R. & Waldman, M. (2004). "Task-specific Human Capital". *The American Economic Review* 94 (2): 203-204.

Gillespie, D. F. & Mileti, S. (1981). "Heterogeneous Samples in Organisational Research". *Sociological Methods & Research* 9: 375-388.

Goldberg, M. F. (2002). *15 School Questions and Discussion: From Class Size, Standards, and School Safety to Leadership and More*. Lanham, MD, Scarecrow Press.

Goldstein, I. L. & Ford,J. K. (2002). *Training in Organizations: Needs Assessment, Development and Evaluation (3rd ed.)*. Pacific Grove, CA Brooks Cole.

Gomm, R. (2004). *Social Research Methodology: a Critical Introduction*. Basingstoke, Palgrave Macmillan.

Gomm, R. (2009). *Key Concepts in Social Research Methods*. Basingstoke Palgrave Macmillan.

Goodall, K., Warner, M. & Lang, V. (2004). "HRD in the People's Republic: The MBA 'with Chinese Characteristics'?" *Journal of World Business* 39 (4): 311-323.

Graddol, D. (2002). *The future of English*. London, The British Council.

Gross, A. & McDonald, T. (1998). "Meeting Diverse Staffing Needs in China". *GROing Connexions* 3 (2).

Gruber, T. R. (1993). "A Translation Approach to Portable Ontologies". *Knowledge Acquisition* 5 (2): 199-220.

Gu, P. (2001). Multimedia English Teaching in China: Theory and Practice.

Gu, P. (2002). "Effects of Project-based CALL on Chinese EFL Learners". *Asian Journal of English Language Teaching* 12: 195-210.

Gu, P. (2004). "Tech View: Leaving the Bathtub to Make Waves". *Essential Teacher* 1: 32-35.

Guile, D. & Griffiths, T. (2001). "Learning through Work Experience". *Journal of Education and Work* 14 (1): 113-131.

Gul, E. O. & Sarah, E. R. (2006). "A Project-based Approach to Entrepreneurial Leadership Education". *Technovation* 26 (2): 195.

Gundling, E. (2003). *Working Globe Smart, 12 People Skills for Doing Business across Borders*. Mountain View, CA, Davies-Black Publishing.

Guo, Y. (2007). "Project-based ESL Education: Promoting Language and Content Learning". Retrieved 15 March, 2011, from http: //www. atesl. ca/cmsms/home/newsletters/december-2007/project-based-esl-education/.

Guo. Z. & Huang. (2002). "Hybridized Discourse: Social Openness and Functions of English Media in Post-Mao China". *World Englishes* 21 (2): 217-230.

Hagen, S. (1999). *Business Communication across Borders*. London, Languages National Training Organization in Association with Centre for Information on Language Teaching and Research.

Hagen, S. (2005). *Language and Culture in British Business: Communication, Needs and Strategies*. London, CILT, the National Centre for languages.

Hagen, T. (2000). *Teaching and Learning in the Language Classroom*. Oxford, Oxford University Press.

Haines, S. (1989). *Projects for the EFL classroom: Resource Material for Teachers*. Walton-on-Thames, UK, Nelson.

Hale, R. (2000). "To Match or Mis-match? The Dynamics of Mentoring as a Route to Personal and Organisational Learning". *Career Development International* 5 (4/5): 223-234.

Hall, R. (1968). "Professionalization and Bureaucratization". *American Sociological Review* 33: 92-104.

Hall, R. E. (2005). "Euro Centrism in Social Work Education: From Race to Identity across the Lifespan as Biracial Alternative". *Journal of Social Work* (101-114).

Hampden-Turner, C. (1990). *Corporate Culture.* London, Hutchinson Business Books.

Harmer, J. (2001). "The Practice of English Language Teaching". Retrieved 04 July, 2011, from http: //203. 72. 145. 166/ELT/files/57-4-12. pdf.

Harris, K. C. (1996). "Collaboration within a Multicultural Society Issues for Consideration". *Remedial and Special Education* 17 (6): 355-362.

Harris, L. (2005). "UK Public Sector Reform and the 'Performance Agenda' in UK Local Government: HRM challenges and dilemmas". *Personnel Review* 34 (6): 681-696.

Harshbarger, B. T. (1986). "Dealing with Multiple Learning Styles in the ESL Classroom". Retrieved 16 September, 2010, from http: //www. cat. ilstu. edu/teaching_tips/handouts/support. shtml.

Harzing, A. W. K. (1996). "How to Survive International Mail Surveys: an Inside Story". *Innovation and International Business, Proceedings of the 22nd EIBA Conference* 1: 313-339.

Hashim, J. (2001). "Training Evaluation: Clients' Roles". *Journal of European Industrial Training* 25 (6/7): 374-374-379.

Hayes, N. (2000). *Doing Psychological Research*. Buckingham. Open University.

He, A. E. (2011). "Educational Decentralization: a Review of Popular Discourse on Chinese-English Bilingual Education". *Asia Pacific Journal of Education* 31 (1): 91-105.

Hedge, T. (1993). "Project Work". *English Language Teaching Journal* 47 (3): 276-277.

Hedge, T. (2000). *Teaching and Learning in the Language Classroom*. Oxford, Oxford University Press.

Held, D. & Thompson, J. (1999). "Global Transformations". Retrieved 20 November, 2010, from www. polity. co. uk/global/executive. htm.

Henry, J. (1994). *Teaching through Projects*. London, Kogan Page.

Hilton-Jones, U. (1988). *Project-based Learning for Foreign Students in an English-speaking Environment.* (ERIC Document Reproduction Service No. ED 301054).

Ho, R. (2003). *Project Approach: Teaching (2nd ed.).* (ERIC Document Reproduction Service No. ED 478224).

Hofstede, G., Bond, M. Hi. & Luk, C. L. (1993). "Individual Perceptions of Organizational Cultures". *Organization Studies* 14: 483-485-483.

Hofstede, G. (1994). "The Business of International Business Is Culture". *International Business Review* 3 (1): 1-14.

Hofstede, G. (1996). *Cultures and Organisations: Software of the Mind.* London, McGraw-Hill.

Hofstede, G. (2001). *Culture's Consequences': Comparing Values, Behaviours, Institutions, and Organizations across Nations (2nd ed.).* Thousand Oaks, CA, SAGE Publications.

Hofstede, G. (2001). *Culture's Consequences: Comparing Values, Behaviours, Institutions, and Organisations across Nations (Second edition).* Beverly Hills, SAGE Publications.

Hofstede, G. (2003). *Culture's Consequences: Comparing Values, Behaviours, Institutions and Organisations across Nations.* Newbury Park, CA: SAGE Publications.

Holt, M. (1994). "Dewey and the Cult of Efficiency: Competing Ideologies in Collaborative Pedagogies of the 1920s". *Journal of Advanced Composition* 14 (1): 73-92.

Honey, P. (1992). *A Manual of Learning Styles.* Maidenhead, Honey.

Howitt, D. & Cramer, D. (2008). *Introduction to Statistics in Psychology.* Harlow, Prentice Hall Pearson.

Hu, G. (2002a). "Recent Important Developments in Secondary English-language Teaching in the People's Republic of China". *Language, Culture and Curriculum* 15: 30-49.

Hu, G. (2002b). "English Language Teaching in the People's Republic of China". *English Language Education in China, Japan, and Singapore. R. E. Silver,* Hu, Guangwei. & Lino, Masakazu (Ed). Singapore, National Institute of Education: 1-77.

Hu, G. (2005a). "English Language Education in China: Policies, Progress, and Problems". *Language Policy* 4: 5-24.

Hu, G. (2005b). "China English, at Home and in the World". *English Today* 21 (3): 27-38.

Huang, Y. S. (1996). *Inflation and Investment Controls in China: The Political Economy of Central-local Relations during the Reform Era*. Cambridge, UK, Cambridge University Press.

Hussey, J. & Hussey, R. (1997). *Business Research: a Practical Guide for Undergraduate and Postgraduate Students*. New York, Palgrave.

Hutchinson, T. & Waters, A. (1987). *English for Specific Purposes: a Learning-centred Approach.* Cambridge, Cambridge University Press.

Ip, P. (2002). *Constructing a Social Contract for Corporations*. Zhong He, Legein Publication.

Ip, P. (2008). "Corporate Social Responsibility and Crony Capitalism in Taiwan". *Journal of Business Ethics* 79: 167-177.

Ip, P. (2009). "Is Confucianism Good for Business Ethics in China?" *Journal of Business Ethics* 88 (3): 463.

Ip, P. K. (1996). "Confucian Familial Collectivism and the Underdevelopment of the Civic Person". *Research and Endeavours in Moral and Civic Education*. N. K. Man. Hong Kong, The Chinese University Press: 39-58.

Ip, P. K. (2000). "Developing Virtuous Corporation with Chinese Characteristics for the Twenty-First Century". *The Dragon Millennium: Chinese Business in the Coming World Economy*. F. J. Richter. Westport, Connecticut, Quorum Books: 183-206.

Ireland, J. (1991). "Finding the right management approach". *The China Business Review* 18 (1).

Jackson, K. F. (2010). "Ethical Considerations in Social Work Research with Multiracial Individuals". *Journal of Social Work Values and Ethics* 7 (1): 1-10.

Jaramillo, J. A. (1996). "Vygotsky's Sociocultural Theory and Contributions to the Development of Constructivist Curricula". *Education* v117 (n1): (138).

James, W. (2000). "What Pragmatism Means". *Pragmatism and the Classical American Philosophy: Essential Readings and Interpretive Essays (2nd ed.)*. J. J. Stuhr. New York, Oxford University Press: 193-202.

Jessen, S. A. (1988). "Some Reflections on Project Performance in Developing Countries". *Proceedings of the 9th World Congress on Project Management*. D. Gower, (Ed), INTERNET.

Jiang, Z. (2008). "Developing Chinese Managers-reasons for Enrolling on a Postgraduate Management Programme in the UK". *Asian Social Science* 4 (5): 88-92.

Jiangang, M. (2000). "Relevance: Criterion and Interpretation in Translation". *Foreign Language and Their Teaching* 2000 (3).

Jin, L. & Cortazzi, M. (2003). "English Language Teaching in China: A Bridge to the Future". *English Language Teaching in East Asia Today*. W. K. Ho. Singapore, Times Academic Press: 131-145.

Johnson, G. S. (2005). *Exploring Corporate Strategy*. London, Financial Times/ Prentice Hall.

Johnson, K. (2008). *An Introduction to Foreign Language Learning and Teaching*. Pearson Education.

Jonassen, D. H. (1999). "Designing Constructivist Learning Environments". *Instructional-design Theories and Models: A New Paradigm of Instructional Theory* C. M. Reigeluth. (Ed). NJ, Lawrence Erlbaum.

Kapetanios, G. (2005). "Unit-root Testing against the Alternative Hypothesis of up to *m* Structural Breaks". *Journal of Time Series Analysis* 26: 123-133.

Karen, E. B. -S., Lowe, P., Miles, J. & Swender, E. (2000). "ACTFL Proficiency Guidelines-speaking Revised 1999". *Foreign Language Analysis* 33 (13-18).

Kay, J. (1993). *Foundations of Corporate Success: How Business Strategies Add Value*. Oxford, Oxford University Press.

Kealey, J. (2009). "Meeting China's Training Needs". *China-Britain Business Review* February 22-23.

Keefe, J. W. (1979). *Learning Style: An Overview. NASSP's Student Learning Styles: Diagnosing and Proscribing Programs*. Reston, VA, National Association of Secondary School Principals.

Keller, G. F. & Kronstedt, C. R. (2005). "Connecting Confucianism, Communism, and the Chinese Culture of Commerce". *The Journal of Language for International Business* 16 (1): 60-75.

Kenneth, D. B. (1994). *Methods of Social Research*. New York, The Free Press.

Kenny, B. (1993). "Investigative research: How it Changes Learner Status". *TESOL Quarterly* 27: 217-231.

Kerzner, H. (1984). *Project Management*. New York, John Wiley & Sons, Inc.

King, B. M. & Minium, E. M. (2003). *Statistical Reasoning in Psychology and Education (4th ed.)*. New Jersey, John Wiley & Sons, Inc.

Kinnear, P. R. & Gray, Co. D. (2010). *PASW Statistics 17 Made Simple*. New York, Psychology Press.

Kiresuk, T. J., Smith, A. & Cardillo, J. E. (1994). *Goal Attainment Scaling: Applications, Theory and Measurement*. New Jersey, Lawrance Erlbaum Associates, Inc.

Kirk, J. & Miller, M. L. (1986). *Reliability and Validity in Qualitative Research. Publisher,* SAGE Publications.

Knowles, D., Mughan, T. & Lloyd-Reason, L. (2006). "Foreign Language Use among Decision-makers of Successfully Internationalised SMEs: Questioning the Language-training Paradigm". *Journal of Small Business and Enterprise Development* 13 (4): 620-641.

Kohonen, V. (2001). "Towards Experiential Foreign Language Education". In V. Kohonen, R. Jaatinen, P. kaikkonen& J. Lehtovaara (Eds.), Experiential Learning in foreign language education. Harlow, UK, Pearson Education.

Kolb, D., Rubin, IM. & J, Osland. (1991). *Organisational Behaviour: An Experiential Approach (5th ed.)*. London, Prentice Hall.

Kolb, D., R. I. (1974). *Organisational Psychology: An Experiential Approach*. London, Prentice Hall.

Kong, Haiyan. & Cheung, C. (2009). "Hotel Development in China: a Review of the English Language Literature". *International Journal of Contemporary Hospitality Management* 21 (3): 341-355.

Krashen, S. (1981). *Second Language Acquisition and Second Language Learning*. Oxford, Pergamon Press.

Kumar, S., Siddique, S. & Wong, Y. (2005). *Mind the Gaps: Singapore Business in China*. Singapore, Institute of Southeast Asian Studies.

Kuo, W. W. (2005). "Survival Skills in Foreign Languages for Business Practitioners: the Development of an Online Chinese Project". *The Journal of Language for International Business* 16 (1): 1-17.

Lam, S. S. (1998). "Organisational Performance and Learning Styles in Hong Kong". *The Journal of Social Psychology* 138 (3): 401-402.

Larkin, J. (1989). *What Kind of Knowledge Transfers*. HIllsdale, NJ, Erlbaum Associates Publishers.

Larson-Freeman, D. (2002). The Grammar of Choice. *New Perspective in Grammar Teaching in Second Language Classrooms*. E. Kinkel& Sandra, F. (Eds). Mahwah, NJ, Lawrence Erlbaum: 103-118.

Lee, M. M. T., Li, B. K. W. & Lee, I. K. B. (1999). *Project Work: Practical Guidelines*. Hong Kong, Hong Kong Institute of Education.

Leeuw., E. D. (2009). "Surveynet". Retrieved 24 August, 2011, from www. surveynet. ac. uk/sqb/about/qbworkshop100408/deleeuw. ppt.

Legutke, M. & Thomas, H. (1991). *Process and Experience in the Language Classroom*. Harlow, UK, Longman.

Levinshon, K. R. (2007). "Cultural Differences and Learning Styles of Chinese and European Trades Students". *Institute for Learning Styles Journal* 1: 12-22.

Levinsohn, K. R. (2007). "Cultural Difference and Learning Styles of Chinese and European Trades Students". *Institute for Learning Styles Journal* 1 (Fall 2007): 12-22.

Levis, J. M. & Levis, G. M. (2003). "A Project-based Approach to Teaching

Research Writing to Non-native Writers". *IEEE Transactions on Professional Communication* 46: 210-221.

Levy, M. (1997). *Project-based Learning for Language Teachers: Reflecting on the Process.* In R. Debski, J. Gassin, & M. Smith (Eds.), *Language Learning through Social Computing.* Melbourne, Applied Linguistic Association of Australia and Harwood Language Centre.

Li, J. (2003). "Strategic Human Resource Management and MNEs' performance in China". *The International Journal of Human Resource Management* 14 (2): 157-173.

Li, J. (2010). Learning to Self-Perfect: Chinese Beliefs about Learning Revisiting the Chinese Learner. C. K. K. Chan and N. Rao (Ed.), Springer Netherlands. 25: 35-69.

Lin, L. (2002). "English Education in Present-day China". *ABD* 33 (2): 8-10.

Lingham, T., Richley, B. & Rezania, D. (2006). "An Evaluation System for Training programmes: a Case Study Using a Four-phrase Approach". *Career Development International* 11 (4): 284-300.

Little, R. (1999). *The Confucian Renaissance.* Sydney, The Federation Press.

Littlewood, W. (2006). *Foreign and Second Language Learning.* Cambridge, Cambridge University Press.

Littrell, F. F. (2005). *Business and Management Education in China: Transition, Pedagogy, Training and Collaboration*, ME Sharpe.

Littrell, R. F. (2002). "Desirable Leadership Behaviours of Multi-cultural Managers in China". *The Journal of Management Development* 21 (01): 5-74.

Littrell, R. F. (2005). "Teaching students from Confucian cultures". *Business management education in China: Transition, Pedagogy and Training.* Alon, I. & Mclntyre, R. J. Singapore, World Scientific Publishing Co. Pte. Ltd: 115-139.

Liu, M. H. & Jackson, J. (2009). "Reticence in Chinese EFL Students at Varied Proficiency Levels". *TESL Canada Journal* 26 (2): 65-81.

Liu, N. F. (1997). "Why do Many Students Appear Reluctant to Participate in Classroom Learning Discourse?" *System* 25 (3): 371-384.

Liu, S. (2001). *Towards an Integrated Approach to Organisational Learning in International Joint Ventures*.PhD thesis, University of Glamorgan, Pontypridd.

Liu, S. (2006). "Developing China's Future Managers: Learning from the West?" *Education and Training* 48 (1): 6-14.

Liu, S. H. (1998). *Understanding Confucian Philosophy: Classical and Sung-ming*. West Port, Connecticut and London, Greenwood Press.

Lockett, M. (1988). "Chinese Culture and the Problems of Chinese Management". *Organization Studies* 9 (4): 475-496.

Lok, P., Rhodes, J. & Cheng, V. (2009). "A Framework for Strategic Decision Making and Performance among Chinese Managers". Retrieved 21 Oct., 2011, from http: //itls2. econ. usyd. edu. au/_data/assets/pdf_file/0013/30460/itls-wp-09-17. pdf.

Long, M. H. & Robinson, P. (1998). "Focus on Form: Theory, Research, and Practice". *Focus on Form in Classroom Second Language Acquisition*. C. Doughty & J. Williams. (Eds). Cambridge, Cambridge university press.

Lu, L. & Alon, I. (2003). *Influences of Confucianism on the market economy of China*. Westport: CT, Preager.

Lu, Q. (2000). *China's Leap into the Information Age: Innovation and Organisation in the Industry*. Oxford, Oxford University Press.

Luo, Y. (2000). *Guanxi and Business*. Singapore, World Scientific.

Lynch, R. (2006). *Corporate Strategy (4th edition)*. London, Financial times: Prentice Hall.

Madeline, E. & Rebecca, O. (1990). "Adult Language Learning Styles and Strategies in an Intensive Training Setting". *The Modern Language Journal* 74 (3, Autumn): 311-327.

Manolova, T. S. & Manev, I. M. (2004). "Internationalisation and the Performance of the Small Firm: a Review of the Empirical Literature between 1996 and 2001". *Emerging Paradigms in International Entrepreneurship*. M. V. Jones & Dimitratos, P. (Eds) (2001). Edward Elgar, Cheltenham: 37-63.

Manthner, M., *et al.* (2002). *Ethics in Qualitative Research*. London, SAGE Publications.

Marchington, M. (1996). *Core Personnel and Development*. London, Chartered Institute of Personnel and Development.

Martinsonsa, Maris G. & Davisonb, R. M. (2007). "Strategic Decision Making and Support Systems: Comparing American, Japanese and Chinese Management". *Decision Support Systems* 43 (1): 284-300.

Marquand, M. (1994). *The Global Learning Organisation*. London, Inwin.

Martinsons, M. G. & Martinsons, A. B., (1996). "Conquering Cultural Constraints to Cultivate Chinese Management Creativity and Innovation". *The Journal of Management Development* 15 (9): 18-18+.

Martinsons, M. G. & Davison, R. M. (2007). "SDM and Support Systems: Comparing American, Japanese and Chinese Management". *Decision Support Systems* 43: 284-300.

Matheson, J. L. (2007). "The Voice Transcription Technique: Use of Voice Recognition Software to Transcribe Digital Interview Data in Qualitative Research". *The Qualitative Report* 12 (4): 547-560.

Matthews, W. (2003). "Constructivism in the Classroom: Epistemology, History, and Empirical Evidence". *Teacher Education Quarterly* 30 (3): 51-64.

May, T. (2001). *Social Research: Issues, Methods and Process*, Open University.

McClelland, S. (1994). "A Model for Designing Objective-oriented Training Evaluations". *Industrial and Commercial Training* 26 (1): 3-9.

McDaniel, C. & Gates, R. (2001). *Marketing Research Essentials (3rd ed.)*. Cincinnati, OH, South-Western Publishing.

Mckeen, J. D. & Guimaraes, T. (1997). "Successful Strategies for User Participation in Systems Development". *Journal of Management Information Systems* 14 (2): 133-150.

Mckeinley, R. K., *et al.* (1997). "Reliability and Validity of a New Measure of Patient Satisfaction with Out of Hours Primary Medical Care in the United Kingdom: Development of a Patient Questionnaire". *British Medical Journal* 314: 193-198.

Megginson, D. (1995). *Mentoring in Action: a Practical Guide for Managers*. London, Kogan Page.

Meighan, M. (1991). *How to Design and Deliver Induction Training Programmes*. London, Kogan Page.

Melvin, S. (2008). "Training the Troops". *The China Business Review* 22 (6).

Meng, J. G. (2000). "Relevance: Criterion and Interpretation in Translation". *Foreign Languages and Their Teaching* 08.

Miller, G. A. (1987). "Meta-analysis and the Culture free Hypothesis". *Organisation Studies* 8: 309-326.

Mincer, J. & Polachek, S. (1974). "Family Investment in Human Capital: earnings of Women". *Journal of Political Economy, University of Chicago Press* 82 (2): S76-S108.

Mintzberg, H. (1987). "The Strategy Concept II: Another Look at Why Organizations need Strategies". *California Management Review* 30: 25-32.

Mintzberg, H. (1988). "Opening up the Definition of Strategy". *The Strategy Process*. J. M. Quinn. New Jersey, Prentice Hall.

Mintzberg, H. (1994). *The Rise and Fall of Strategic Planning*. New York, Free Press.

MOE. (2001). "Development of Development and Planning, 2000 nian zhongguo jiaoyu shiye fazhan tongji jiankuang. [Statistics on China's educational development in 2000]". Retrieved 03 June, 2008, from http: // www. edu. cn/20011219/3014655.

Mohan, B. & Beckett, G. H. (2001). "A Functional Approach to Research on Content-based Language Learning: Recasts in Causal Explanations". *Canadian Modern Language Review* 58: 133-155.

Morgan, G. (1986). *Images of Organisation*. Newbury Park, SAGE Publications.

Morgan, G. (1997). *Images of Organisation*. Beverly Hills, Calif: Sage.

Morris, P. W. (1979). "Interface Management: an Organisational Theory Approach to Project Management". *Project Management Quarterly* 10 (2).

Morse, J. M. (1991). "Approaches to Qualitative-quantitative Methodological triangulation". *Nursing Research* 40: 120-123.

Mughan, T. (1993). "Culture and Management Crossing the Linguistic Rubicon". *Language and Intercultural Training* 13 (1).

Mullen, M. R. (1995). "Diagnosing Measurement Equivalence in Cross-national Research". *Journal of International Business Studies* 26 (3): 573-596.

Nadler, L. N., Z. (1994). *Designing Training Programs: the Critical Events model*. Houston, Gulf Publication Co.

Nelson, G. (1995). "Cultural differences in learning styles". *Learning Styles in the ESL/EFL Classroom*. J. Reid. Boston, MA, Heinle & Heinle: 3-18.

Newman, F. & Holzman, L. (1997). *The End of Knowing: a New Developmental Way of Learning*. Routledge.

Newman, I. & Ridenour, C. R. (2008). *Mixed Methods Research: Exploring the Interactive continuum*. Illinois, Southern Illinois University.

Nicholson, N. (2003). "Motivating Problem People". *Harvard Business Review*: 57-65.

Nordhaug, O. (2003). *International Management: Cross-boundary Challenges.* Malden, MA Blackwell

Norton, A. (2007). *CIMA's Official Learning System: Managerial Level Paper P5: Integrated Management*. London, Elsevier.

Norton, B. & Toohey, K. (2001). "Changing Perspectives on Good Language Learners". *TESOL Quarterly* 35[2 (summer, 2001)]: 307-322.

Nunan, D. (2002). "The Impact of English as a Global Language: Policy and Planning in Greater China". *Hong Kong Journal of Applied Linguistics* 7 (1): 1-15.

Nunnally, I. C. (1978). *Psychometric theory*. New York, McGraw-Hill.

Nyaw, M. K. & Henley, J. S. (1986). "Introducing Market Forces into

Managerial Decision Making in Chinese Industrial Enterprises". *Journal of Management Studies* 23 (6): 635-656.

Ogden, S. (1993, Winter). "Educational and Modernisation: The Chinese Experience". *Pacific Affairs*: 572.

Oliver, K. (2010). "Cognitive Constructivism & Social Constructivism: Anchored Instruction". Retrieved 10 May, 2010, from http: //viking. coe. uh. edu/~ichen/ebook/et-it/ai. htm.

Oliver, R. & Omari, A. (1999). "Using Online Technologies to Support Problem Based Learning: Learners Responses and Perceptions". *Australian Journal of Educational Technology* 15: 158-179.

Orr, T. (2002). The Nature of English for Specific Purposes. *English for Specific Purpose*. T. Orr. Alexandria, Virginia, Teachers of English to Speakers of Other Languages: 1-3.

Ou, R., Yong Shi,& Xu, X. (1996). *Business in the South and North: the Different Regional Styles and Business Cultures of Chinese Businessmen*. Hainan, International News Press.

Oxford, R. (1990). *Language Learning Strategies*. New York, Newbury House.

Oxford, R. S., Burry (1995). "Assessing the Use of Language Learning Strategies Worldwide with ESL/EFL Version of the Strategy Inventory for Language Learning". *System*: 153-175.

Padgett, G. S. (1994). "An Experiential Approach: Field Trips, Book Publication, Video Production". *TESOL Journal* 3 (3): 8-11.

Pallant, J. (2005). *SPSS Survival Manual: A Step by Step Guide to Data Analysis Using SPSS Version 12 (2nd ed.)*. Maidenhead, Open University Press.

Pansiri, J. (2005). "Pragmatism: A Methodological Approach to Researching Strategic Alliances in Tourism". *Tourism and Hospitality Planning & Development* 2 (3): 191-206.

Papandreou, A. P. (1994). "An Application of the Projects Approach to EFL". *English Teaching Forum* 32 (2): 41-42.

Patton, M. Q. (1990). *Qualitative Evaluation and Research Methods (2nd ed.)*.

Newbury Park, CA, SAGE Publications.

Peacock, M. (2001). "Match or Mismatch? Learning Styles and Teaching Styles in EFL". *International Journal of Applied Linguistics* 11 (1): 1-20.

Pedlar, M. (1991). *The Learning Company: A Strategy for Sustained Development*. London, McGraw-Hill.

Pfeffer, J. & Fong, C. T. (2005). "Building Organisation Theory from First Principles: The Self-enhancement Motive and Understanding Power and Influence". *Organisation Science* 16: 372-388.

Phillips, D., Burwood, S. & Dunford, H. (1999). *Projects with Young Learners*. Oxford, Oxford University Press.

Phillips, L. W. (1981). "Assessing Measurement Error in key Informant reports: a Methodological Note on Organisational Analysis in Marketing". *Journal of Marketing Research* 18: 395-415.

Piaget, J. (2000). "Commentary on Vygotsky". *New Ideas in Psychology* 18: 241-259.

Podsakoff, P., Mackenzie, M. & Podsakoff, N. P. (2003). "Common Method Biases in Behavioural Research: A Critical Review of the Literature and Recommended Remedies". *Journal of Applied Psychology* 88: 879-903.

Poland, B. D. (1995). "Transcription Quality as an Aspect of Rigor in Qualitative Research". *Qualitative Inquiry September* 1 (3): 290-310.

Polit, D. F., Beck, C. T. & Hungler, B. P. (2001). *Essentials of Nursing Research: Methods, Appraisal and Utilization.* Philadelphia, Lippincott William & Wilkins.

Powell, T. C. (2001). "Competitive Advantage: Logical and Philosophical Considerations". *Strategic Management Journal* 22 (9): 875-888.

Prahalad, C. (2000). *Managing Discontinuities: the Emerging Challenges (Vol. Organisational Development and Transformation: Managing Effective Change)*. Singapore, McGraw-Hill.

Prefume, Y. (2007). "Constructivism in Foreign Language Learning". *Academic Quarterly* Spring, 2007: 5-9

Proctor, T. (2010). *Creative Problem Solving for Managers: Developing Skills for Decision Making and Innovation.* London, Routledge

Pugh, D. S. & Hickson, D. J. (1976). *Organisation Structure in Context: the Astopn Programme I.* Farnborough UK, Saxon House.

Qin, C. Y. & Baruch, Y. (2010). "The Impact of Cross-cultural Training for Expatriates in a Chinese Firm". *Career Development International* 15 (3): 296-318.

Ralston, D. A., Egri, C. P., Stewart, S., Terpstra, R. H. & Xu Kaicheng (1999b). "Doing Business in the 21st Century with the New Generation of Chinese Managers: a Study of Generational Shifts in Work Values in China". *Journal of International Business Studies* 30 (2): 415-428.

Reagan, T. (1999). "Constructivist Epistemology and Second/foreign Language pedagogy". *Foreign Language Annals* 32 (4): 413-425.

Reid, J. (1987). "The Learning Style Preferences of ESL Students". *TESOL Quarterly* 21 (1): 87-111.

Reid, J. (1998). *Understanding Learning Styles in the Second Language Classroom*. NJ, Pearson Education.

Reid, M. & Barrington, H. A (1999). *Training Interventions*. London, Institute of Personnel and Development.

Richards, L. (1999). *Using NVivo in Qualitative Research.* London, SAGE Publications.

Ridenour, C. S. & Newman, I. (2008). *Mixed Methods Research: Exploring the Interactive Continuum.* Illinois, USA, SIU Press.

Robson, C. (1993). *Real World Research: A Resource for Social Scientists and Practitioners-researchers*. Oxford, Blackwell Publishers.

Rogerson-Revell, P. (2007). "Using English for international business: a European case study". *English for Specific Purposes* 26 (2007): 103-120.

Sanchez, A. (2004). "The Task-based Approach in Language Teaching". *International Journal of English Studies* 4 (1): 39-71.

Sarantakos, S. (1993). *Social Research*. Melbourne, Macmillan Education

Australia.

Sato, C. (1982). "Ethnic Styles in Classroom Discourse". *On TESOL*. R. W. E. Mary. Washington, DC, Teachers of English to Speakers of Other Languages.

Saunders, M., Lewis, P. & Thornhill, A. (2000). *Research Methods for Business Students*, Prentice Hall: Harlow.

Saunders, M. & Lewis, P. (2003). *Research Methods for Business Students*. Harlow, England; London, England, Prentice Hall.

Savignon, S. J. & Wang, C. C. (2003). "Communicative Language Teaching in EFL Contexts: Learner Attitudes and Perceptions". *International Review of Applied Linguistics in Language Teaching* 41 (3): 223-249.

Savoie, J. M. & Hughes, A. S. (1994). "Problem-based Learning as Classroom Solution". *Educational Leadership* 52 (3): 54-57.

Schank, R. C. (1992). "Goal-based Scenarios". Retrieved 3 March, 2011, from http: //cogprints. org/624/1/V11ANSEK. html.

Schlevogt, K. A. (2000a). "Doing Business in China, Part I: the Business Environment in China-getting to Know the Next Century's Superpower". *Thunderbird International Business Review* 42 (1): 85-111.

Schlevogt, K. A. (2000i). "China's Western Campaign". *Far Eastern Economic Review* 163 (33): 29.

Schlevogt, K. A. (2002). *The Art of Chinese Management: Theory, Evidence, and Applications*. Oxford, Oxford University Press.

Segars, A. H. (1997). "Assessing the Unidimensionality of Measurement: A Paradigm and Illustration within the Context of Information System research". *Omega* 25 (107-121).

Sethi, V. & William R. King (Dec. 1994). "Development of Measures to Assess the Extent to Which an Information Technology Application Provides Competitive Advantage". *Management Science* 40 (12): 1601-1627

Shanahan, D. (1997). "Articulating the Relationship between Language, Literature, and Culture: Toward a New Agenda for Foreign Language

Teaching and Research". *The Modern Language Journal* 81 (2): 164-174.

Shared, D. (1986). "Management by Projects: an Ideological Breakthrough". *Project Management Journal* 17 (1): 61-63.

Sheppard, K. & Stoller, F. L. (1995). "Guidelines for the Integration of Student Projects in ESP classrooms". *English Teaching Forum* 33 (2): 10-15.

Silverman, A. D. (2001). *Interpreting Qualitative Data: Methods for Analysing Talk, Text and Interaction (2nd edition)*. SAGE Publications.

Silverman, D. (2004). *Qualitative Research: Theory, Method and Practice.* London, SAGE Publications.

Simpson. (1997). *An Agenda for Adult Education Research in China: a Cross-cultural Comparison.* SCUTREA 1997 Conference Proceedings.

Skehan, P. (1998). *A Cognitive Approach to Language Learning.* Oxford, Oxford University Press.

Smith, B. (1985). *Project Concepts: in Effective Project Administration.* Institution of Mechanical Engineers.

Smith, B. & Bond, M. H. (1998). *Social Psychology across Cultures: Analysis and Perspectives (second edition)*. London, Allyn & Bacon.

Smith, J. & Arkless, C. (1993). "Guidelines on Good Practice in Foreign Language Training". *Journal of European Industrial Training* 17 (7): 14-18.

Smith, P. B. (1992). "Organizational Behaviour and National Cultures". *British Journal of Management* 3: 39-51.

Smith, P. B., Peterson, M. F. & Wang, Z. M. (1996). "The Manager as Mediator of Alternative Meanings: A Pilot Study from China, the USA and U. K. ". *Journal of International Business Studies* 27 (1): 115-137.

Snow, M. A., Met, M. & Genesee, F. (1989). "A Conceptual Framework for the Integration of Language and Content in Second/foreign Language Instruction". *TESOL Quarterly* 23: 201-219.

Song, B. (1995). "What does Reading Mean for East Asian Students?" *College ESL* 5 (2): 35-48.

Stephen, F. & Sergeant, A. (1998). "Managing People in China: Perceptions of Expatriate Managers". *Journal of World Business* 33 (1): 17.

Stoller, F. L. (1997). "Project Work: A Means to Promote Language and Content". *English Teaching Forum* 35 (4): 2-9, 37.

Stoller, F. L. (2004). "Content-based Instruction: Perception on Curriculum Planning". *In M. McGroarty (Ed.), Annual Review of Applied Linguistics.* New York, Cambridge University Press.

Stryker, S. B. & Leaver, B. L. (1997). *Content-based Instruction in Foreign Language Education: Models and Methods.* Washington, D. C., Georgetown University Press

Stufflebeam, D. L. & Shinkfield, A. J. (2007). *Evaluation theory, models & applications.* San Francisco, Jossey-Bass.

Sutton, C. D. & David, M. (2011). *Social Research: An Introduction.* London, SAGE Publications.

Svinicki, M. (1998). "A Theoretical Foundation for Discovery Learning". *The American Journal in Psychology* 275 (6): 54-57.

Tang, F. L. & Shen, J. L. (2005). "Thoughts about Problem-Based Learning and the Educational Reality of China". *Comparative Education Review* 2005, 1.

Tang, J. (2005). *Managers and Mandarins in Contemporary China: the Building of an International Business Alliance.* Abingdon, Oxon, Routledge.

Tang, Y. J. (1991). *Confucianism, Buddhism, Daoism, Christianity.* Washington, D. C., The council for research in values and philosophy.

Tashakkori, A. & Teddlie, C. (1998). *Mixed Methodology: Combining Qualitative and Quantitative.* Thousand Oaks, CA, SAGE Publications.

Tashakkori, A. & Teddlie, C. (2003a). *Handbook of Mixed Methods in Social and Behavioural Research.* Thousand Oaks, CA, SAGE Publications.

Taylor, M. (2006). "Is China Ready to Welcome the World in English?" *China Staff* 12 (10): 18.

Taylor, R. *et al.* (Jun, 2001). "Development and Validation of a Questionnaire to Evaluate the Effectiveness of Evidence-based Practice Teaching". *Medical*

Education 35 (6): 544-547.

Teijlingen, E. R. V. & Hundley, V. (2011). "The Importance of Pilot studies". Retrieved 23 September, 2011, from http: //eprints. bournemouth. ac. uk/10149/1/SRU35_pilot_studies. pdf.

The Cognition and Technology Group at Vanderbilt (CTGV). (1990). "Anchored Instruction and Its Relationship to Situated Cognition". *Educational Researcher* 19 (6): 2-10.

Tierney, P., Farmer, S. M. & Graen, C. B. (1999). "An Examination of Leadership and Employee Creativity: The Relevance of Traits and Relationships". *Personnel Psychology* (52): 591-620.

Tierney, P. & Farmer, S. M. (2011). "Creative Self-efficacy Development and creative performance over time". *Journal of Applied Psychology* 96 (2): 277-293.

Toloken, S. (2007). "China's Pool of Managerial Talent Growing but Still Lags Business Need". *Business Insurance* 41 (13): 2.

Trompenaars, F. (1993). *Riding the Waves of Culture*. London, The Economist Books.

Tse, D. (1999). "New ownership forms in Transitional Economies: Emergence, Characteristics and Performance of China's Joint Stock Companies". *Chinese Management Centre*: 23-45.

Turner, J. R. (1993). *The Handbook of Project-based Management.* Berkshire, McGraw-Hill Book Company Europe.

Turner, J. R. (1999). *The Handbook of Project-based Management: Improving the Process for Achieving Strategic Objectives*. McGraw-Hill, Maidenhead.

Van Lier, L. (2005). "The Bellman's Map: Avoiding the 'Perfect and Absolute Blank' in Language Learning". In R. Jourdenais & S. Springer (Eds.), Content, Tasks, and Projects in the Language Classroom: 2004 Conference Proceedings. Monterey, CA, Monterey Institute of International Studies.

Vieira, W. E. (2004). "Reflections". *Consulting to Management* 15 (1): 27-31.

Walker, A. & Dimmock, C. (2002). *School Leadership and Administration:*

Adopting a Cultural Perspective. London, Routledge Falmer.

Wallace, B. & Oxford, R. L. (1992). "Disparity in Learning Styles and Teaching Styles in the ESL Classroom: Does This Mean War?" *AMTESOL (Alabama-Mississippi Teachers of English to Speakers of Other Languages Journal)* 1: 45-68.

Walliman, N. S. (2001). *Your Research Project: a Step-by-step Guide for the First-time Researcher*. London, SAGE Publication.

Wallraff, B. (2000). "Beijing multilingual". Retrieved 9 November, 2000, from http: //www. theatlantic. com/issues/2000/11/wallraff-graddol. htm.

Walsh, P. J. & Wang, E. (1999). "Same Bed, Different Dreams: Working Relationships in Sino-American Joint Ventures". *Journal of World Business* 34 (1): 69-93.

Wang, Q. & Dong, J. (2006). "A Strategic Consideration about the Information Resources Management (IRM) Talent Construction in Shandong Province" *Sci-Tech Information Development & Economy* 12 (12).

Wang, V. C. (2009). "Effective Teaching with Technology in Adult Education". *International Journal of Web-based Learning and Teaching Technologies* 4 (4): 17-31.

Wang, X. (2002). "The Post-communist Personality: the Spectre of China's Capitalist Market Reforms". *The China Journal* 47: 1-17.

Wang, Y. (2008). "A Review of Studies on Learner Beliefs". *Journal of Hainan Normal University (Social Sciences)* 2008 (5).

Wang, Y. P. (2004). "Cross-Cultural Influence on Strategic International Human Resource Control of Taiwanese High-Tech Subsidiaries in USA". Retrieved 08 August, 2011, from http: //jgxy. usx. edu. cn/DAOM/032_ChristinaWang. pdf.

Wang, Z. X. (2007). 《对企业人员外语培训工作的思考》 [An investigation on company staff's foreign language training]. 《现代企业教育》 *(Modern Enterprises Education)* 2 (2): 139-140.

Warner, M. (1991). "Management Education and Training Strategies in the

People's Republic of China: An Overview". Unpublished paper No. 1991/8, Management Studies Group, Department of Engineering, Cambridge University, Cambridge.

Warner, M. (2004). "Human Resource Management in China Revisited: Introduction". *The International Journal of Human Resource Management* 15 (4): 617-634.

Warr, P. & Bunce, D. (1995). "Trainee Characteristics and the Outcomes of Open Learning". *Personnel Psychology* 48 (347-375).

Warschauer, M. (2000). "The Changing Global Economy and the Future of English Teaching". Retrieved 11 November, 2010, from http: //www. gse. uci. edu/markw/global.

Weightman, J. (2004). *Managing People*. London, Chartered Institute of Personnel and Development, CIPD House.

Weiss, A. (2003). "Avoiding the Tribalisation of Consulting". *Consulting to Management* 14 (1): 13-15.

Westwood, R. (1997). "Harmony and Patriarchy: The Cultural Basis for 'Paternalistic Headship' among the Overseas Chinese". *Organization Studies* 18 (3): 445-480.

Whiddett, H. S. (2002). "How to Nurture Motivation". *People Management* July 11: 52-53.

White, C. (2004). *Strategic Management*. Basingstoke, Palgrave.

Whittington, R. (2001). *What is Strategy-and does it Matter?* TJ International, Padstow, Cornwall.

Wilkinson, I. & Young, L. (2002). "On Cooperating: Firms, Relations and Networks". *Journal of Business Research* 55 (2): 123-132.

Willemse, I. (2004). *Statistical Methods for Business and Basic Calculations*. Lansdowne, South Africa, Juta & Co.

Williams, J. & Chaston, I. (2004). "Links between the Linguistic Ability an International Experience of Export Managers and Their Export Marketing Intelligence Behaviour". *International Small Business Journal* 22 (5):

463-486.

Wong, M. (2007). " *Guanxi* and its Role in Business". *Chinese Management Studies* 1 (4): 257-276.

Wood, A. & Head, M. (2004). "Just What the Doctor Ordered: The Application of Problem-based Learning to EAP". *English for Specific Purposes* 23: 3-17.

Worthey, K. M. (1987). Learning Style Factors of Field Dependence/independence and Problem-solving Strategies of Hmong Refugee Students. Unpublished master's thesis, University of Wisconsin, Stout, WI.

Wortzel, L. H. (1979). "New Life-style Determinants of Women's Food Shopping Behaviour". *Journal of Marketing* 43 (3): 28-39.

Woziniak, L. (2003). "Companies in China Struggle to Train, Retain Qualified Managers; Leadership Style, Language Differ even among Recruits from Hong Kong, Taiwan". *The Wall Street Journal* A (8).

Wright, C. & Wright, S. (1994). "Do Languages Really Matter? the Relationship between International Business Success and a Commitment to Foreign Language Use". *Journal of Industrial Affairs* 3 (1): 3-14.

Wu, B. D. (2001). "Enhance the Construction of Party to Build the First-class Socialist University". *Research and Practice of Higher Education* 2: 1-4.

Wu, Y. A. (2001). "English Language Teaching in China: Trends and Challenges". *TESOL Quarterly* 35 (1): 191-194.

Xie, A. P., Rau, P. L., Tseng, Y., Su, H. & Zhao, C. (2008). "Cross-cultural Influence on Communication Effectiveness and User Interface design". *International Journal of Intercultural Relations* September: 10.

Xinhua. (2010). "More than 8000 Chinese Managers and Cadres Sent to Train in Singapore". Retrieved 06 May, 2010, from http: //news. sina. com. cn/c/2010-05-06/084320215060. shtml.

Xinhua. (2010).《中国干部集体留学新加坡受训者已达 8000 余人》[Over 8000 Chinese Cadres Receiving Training in Singapore]. Retrieved 6 May, 2010, from http: //news. sina. com. cn/c/2010-05-06/084320215060. shtml.

Yelon, S. & Berge, Z. L. (1988). "The Secret of Instructional Design". *Performance and Instruction* January: 11-13.

Yu, L. (1999). *The Analects of Confucius (English & Chinese)*. Beijing, Foreign Languages Press.

Zhai, F. & Shantong, Li. (2000). The Implications of Accession to WTO on China's Economy. *Third Annual Conference for Global Economic Analysis*. Melbourne, Australia: 2-16.

Zhang, H. Y. (2003). "Internationalisation of Talents and the Training for Internationalised Talents". *Journal of Fujian Agriculture and Forestry University (Philosophy and Social Science)* 6 (4): 81-83.

Zhao, B. H. (2010). "How to Enhance Cross-cultural Awareness in TEFL". *Cross-Cultural Communication* 6 (2): 100-104.

Zhao, L. (2001). *In Search of a Future of Life-long Learning in China: a Review of Cross-cultural Issues in Local Managers' Training in International Joint Ventures in the People's Republic of China*. London, SCUTREA.

Zhou, Z. (2004). 《复合型外语人才培养模式理论与实践研究——对专业定位的思考》 [Exploration of the Theories and Practice for Training Foreign Language Talents with Inter-disciplinary Abilities: Reflecting on English major's Identification.] 《宁夏大学学板》(人文社会科学版) [*Journal of Ningxia University (Humanity and Social science)*] 2004 (3): 11-16.

Zhu, H. (2003). "Globalization and New ELT Challenges in China". *English Today* 19 (4): 36-41.

Zhu, H. M. (2003). "Globalization and New ELT Challenges in China". *English Today* 19 (4): 36-41.